OTHER BOOKS BY MELINDA RIBNER

*Everyday Kabbalah: A Practical Guide for
Jewish Meditation, Healing, and Personal Growth*

New Age Judaism: Ancient Wisdom for the Modern World

A Gift of a New Beginning

Kabbalah
Month by Month

TAMMUZ
AV
SIVAN
ELUL
IYAR
TISHREI
NISSAN
CHESHVAN
ADAR
KISLEV
SHEVAT
TEVET

CANCER
LEO
GEMINI
VIRGO
TAURUS
LIBRA
ARIES
SCORPIO
PISCES
SAGITTARIUS
AQUARIUS
CAPRICORN

SEEING
HEARING
SUBCONSCIOUS
ACTION
THINKING
SEX
SPEECH
SMELL
LAUGHTER
SLEEP
EATING
ANGER

RUEVEN
SHIMON
ZEVULUN
GAD
ISSACHAR
EPHRAIM
YEHUDAH
MENASHAH
NAFTALI
BENJAMIN
ASHER
DAN

Kabbalah Month by Month

A Year of Spiritual Practice and Personal Transformation

MELINDA RIBNER

JOSSEY-BASS
A Wiley Company
www.josseybass.com

Published by

JOSSEY-BASS
A Wiley Company
www.josseybass.com

Jossey-Bass books and products are available through most bookstores. To contact Jossey-Bass directly, call (888) 378-2537, fax to (800) 605-2665, or visit our website at www.josseybass.com.

Substantial discounts on bulk quantities of Jossey-Bass books are available to corporations, professional associations, and other organizations. For details and discount information, contact the special sales department at Jossey-Bass.

We at Jossey-Bass strive to use the most environmentally sensitive paper stocks available to us. Our publications are printed on acid-free recycled stock whenever possible, and our paper always meets or exceeds minimum GPO and EPA requirements.

All Bible quotations are from *The Living Torah,* Aryeh Kaplan (New York: Maznaim Publishing Corp., © 1981) and *Tanach: The Torah, Prophets, Writings,* edited by Nosson Scherman (Brooklyn, N.Y.: Mesorah Publications, © 1996).

Text Design by Paula Goldstein.

Library of Congress Cataloging-in-Publication Data
Ribner, Melinda.
Kabbalah month by month: a year of spiritual practice and
personal transformation / Melinda Ribner.
   p. cm.
ISBN 0–7879–6152–3 (alk. paper)
1. Spiritual life—Judaism. 2. Cabala. 3. Self-actualization
(Psychology)—Religious aspects—Judaism. 4. Jewish devotional
calendars. I. Title.
BM723 .R525 2002
296.1'6—dc21

FIRST EDITION
HB Printing 10 9 8 7 6 5 4 3 2 1

Contents

I dedicate this book to four loving, giving, holy men.

*To my father of blessed memory, Yitzchok ben Avraham; to
Isaac Ribner, who died twenty-one years ago; to my uncle of blessed memory,
Yerachmiel ben Avraham; and to Dr. Richard Ribner, the older brother
of my father who died the year I was writing this book. My uncle's death
was a great loss for me. My uncle was not only my uncle, he was a father
to me after my father died. He was also my rebbe, for he always lifted
my consciousness to the highest spiritual vision. He was a best friend,
a soul companion. We had adventures together, and he was so much
fun to be with. I miss him terribly. May the souls of these wonderful
men be elevated by the love and blessings of this book.*

*I also dedicate this book to my brother, Stephen Ribner.
What an awesome brother I have. May he and his family and my
mother, Corinne, be blessed with good health, deepening faith, and joy.*

*And finally I dedicate this book to my soul mate.
Where are you?*

Introduction

Thousands of years ago, the Jewish mystical tradition also known as kabbalah revealed a very profound and powerful system for healing and transformation. Though the knowledge remains relatively obscure, it has influenced many current forms of healing. According to kabbalah, the Jewish calendar as a whole is a road map for personal transformation. It is the original twelve-step program.

Kabbalah Month by Month provides guidelines, meditations, and strategies to promote personal growth each month. Knowing when the auspicious and inauspicious times for starting new projects, making business partnerships, or celebrating weddings according to kabbalah is important. The information in this book provides a framework for understanding the flow of events in one's life. Although I am familiar with this knowledge and have allowed it to guide me and my work with clients and students for many years, I continue to be amazed at how much people's lives actually mirror the monthly energies.

It has been a joy to write this book. It has been fascinating to see the connections between all the elements that compose and reflect the energy of each month. Though I have added a modern psycho-spiritual dimension to this material to make it accessible, I have not changed the basic components for each month as prescribed by ancient kabbalistic texts such as *Sefer Yetzirah*. As you study and work with this material, keep in mind that kabbalah is a heavenly transmission; it is not rational or the product of the human mind. It is my prayer that your study of this material will help you to see how awesome and holy kabbalah is. And from this, may you be blessed with a glimpse of how holy God is, and how holy you are.

In the secular calendar, a new month begins in the middle of the moon's cycle. In the Jewish calendar, a new month begins with the new moon. The Hebrew word for "month" is *chodesh,* which also means "newness." Each of the twelve months brings in new energies and offers unique opportunities to realize one's personal potential and overcome the limitations hindering the true expression of one's essence. It is no coincidence that there are twelve months, twelve astrological signs, twelve tribes in Israel, and twelve permutations of the tetragrammaton, the letters of the Divine Name, YHVH.

There are also twelve kabbalistic prescriptions for healing, one for each month. For example, according to kabbalah, the Hebrew month of Tevet (December-January) is an optimal time to work on transforming one's anger. The month of Kislev (November-December) is for healing through sleep and paying attention to one's dreams. The month of Shevat (January-February) is the time to conceive of new projects. At the beginning of each chapter and throughout the book, I share stories from my therapy practice and my personal life to demonstrate the healing energies of each month. Of course, clients' names have been changed, but the stories are true.

The energy forecasted for each month reflects the various components associated with the month. According to kabbalah, each month has a Hebrew letter, a Hebrew tribe, an astrological sign, a holiday or holidays, and a permutation of the tetragrammaton associated with it. Each monthly chapter includes a review of the Torah portions read during that month. Each Torah portion has a hidden message relevant to the events occurring in one's life if one understands the code. It is for this reason that the Torah is called a Tree of Life and why the Alter Rebbe, Rabbi Shneur Zalman, the founder of the Lubavitch Chassidic sect, said that the Jew lives with the times; he was referring to the Torah portions of the week.

The holidays of each month encapsulate the energy and spiritual opportunity of the month. With one exception, every Jewish month has a holiday in it. This empty month (October–November) is reserved for a future holiday that will take place during messianic times. Many Jewish holidays are not widely known. According to kabbalah, a Jewish holiday is not just a celebration of a particular historical event; rather, it is a spiritual transmission of cyclical energies occurring at the time of holiday that are actually sourced in the particular permutation of the Divine Name for that month. As you study this material, your knowledge and appreciation of the holidays will be heightened and you will understand why the holidays occur when they do. For example, it becomes clear that the Torah could only be received in the month of Sivan (May–June). Passover could only occur in Nissan (March–April). Each month is uniquely suited to hold its particular holiday.

Like astrology, which reveals trends for each month according to the movement of planets, kabbalah derives its knowledge of the energies and trends of the month from the various permutations of the letters of the Divine Name. The mysteries of the Divine Name and its permutations cannot be fully explained without a kabbalistic interpretation of creation and an in-depth presentation of the kabbalistic map of reality, which may be found in my book *New Age Judaism*. For now suffice it to say that it is the position, sound, and shape of the letter in the permutation that makes the difference in the energy for each month.

Much like a computer program, each permutation regulates and directs the flow of energy for that month. Each month corresponds to a particular permutation that is a unique conductor or grid for the flow of Divine Light for that month. Understanding each permutation is illuminating and complex. Everything that occurs in each month and everything that has occurred historically in that month are only revelations of spiritual light vibrating at different frequencies as it flows through the various spiritual worlds through the sounding of the permutation of the Divine Name.

This knowledge is hinted at in the book of Genesis. The Bible simply tells us that creation occurred through divine speech, "God spoke . . . and it was so." Though this is only a metaphor, for God doesn't speak as we do, it is a very important and meaningful metaphor with increasing relevance today. Science now also understands what kabbalah proclaimed thousands of years ago, that all physical matter is concentrated energy pulsating at different sound vibrations.

To the uninitiated, this material may seem mystical or superstitious, but that doesn't mean it isn't true. Many things exist that are beyond our powers of conception or reasoning. Just as there are various seasons and fluctuations in our weather, there are also fluctuations in the spiritual energies available. Those who are attuned to these energies are very aware of such changes and know how to use this knowledge for their personal growth and success. Rather than promoting fatalism, this knowledge actually increases our capacity to make meaningful and effective choices for our highest good. It is my sincere intention and hope that you will be empowered by this material.

During the writing of this book, my knowledge and respect for astrology increased as I learned to appreciate the connections between astrology and kabbalah. Astrology has been a controversial subject in the Jewish world, for people fear that it undermines free will and self-determinism. I believe now that this is a misunderstanding. Even though it is generally said that the Jew is above the influence of the stars, this does not mean Judaism does not believe in the power of astrology. Quite the contrary. The Bible, the Talmud, the *Zohar* ("The Book of Splendor"), and many other kabbalistic books give credence to and reference on numerous occasions a belief in astrology.

It is my hope that you will not only read this material each month, but reread it and reflect upon it many times throughout the month. Like a good friend, this book is there to guide and inspire you to grow in the ways that you most want for yourself.

Keep the goals and practical recommendations for each month in mind, practice the meditations, and use this book as a companion guide.

After reading the General Guidelines and Goals section of each chapter, you might want to write out your personal spiritual, emotional, and physical goals for the month and the strategies and activities you see yourself using to implement those goals. Then at the end of the month review your progress. Also at the end of the month, highlight the major events and themes of the month, how they affected you personally, and what soul qualities you were able to develop and express through them. And the Practical Recommendations: In what ways were you able to put any or all of them into practice?

Though each month, according to kabbalah, has its unique energy and its own holidays and it is best to study and meditate upon the chapter of the current month, don't be rigid about this. Allow yourself to be guided to read any section of the book at any time. You may need to feel a little more joy in your life, no matter what the month, so you might want to read the chapter on Adar, the month of joy and laughter. If you need to feel more adventurous, read about Kislev, rekindling dreams. If you feel emotionally stuck, with a lot of anger, review Tevet, the month devoted to the transformation of anger.

Though holidays occur at specific times, we need to tap into the energy and grace of all of the holidays on a daily basis to be fully human. Every day we need a little taste of Rosh Hashanah to open to the newness available each moment of our lives. We need a little Yom Kippur to feel forgiveness for ourselves and others. We need a little Chanukah to be empowered to take risks and go for what we want. And we need a little Passover to receive divine grace to take us beyond our limitations. Let your higher wisdom guide you.

Keep this book by your bed or on your desk so it's easily accessible when you feel the urge to consult it. The monthly charting of the map of time in this book will support your personal growth in the most gentle, continuous, and practical way. You will need a Jewish or astrological calendar, readily available at Jewish bookstores or establishments, to know the current Hebrew month. Those who study the material in this book, keep it close to their hearts, practice the meditations, and seek to live from its teachings will be transformed in the ways that they really want. The more you open and work with the energy of each month, the deeper your experience and the greater your receptivity for the following month. Each month builds upon the preceding ones.

In conclusion, I thank my students for requesting that I write this book. It has been their enthusiasm for this material that encouraged me to do it. We have all benefited from this knowledge, and we want to share it with others. I thank my editor, Alan Rinzler, for selecting this book and having a vision of how to make it helpful and beautiful for readers. Finally, I extend my love and blessings to you, my reader, for a wonderful year, a year of blessings. May this book guide you, strengthen you, and open you to the goodness and joy that spiritual growth offers. May we be blessed to meet each other in the near future.

Kabbalah
Month by Month

Tishrei

MONTH: *September-October*

ENERGY: *Opening to Newness*

AREA OF HEALING: *Sex*

ASTROLOGICAL SIGN: *Libra*

HEBREW LETTER: *Lamed*

HEBREW TRIBE: *Ephraim*

DIVINE NAME PERMUTATION: *VHYH*

HOLIDAYS: *Rosh Hashanah, Yom Kippur, Succot, Shemini Atzeret, Simchat Torah* s the first Jewish month, Tishrei is a time for clarifying priorities and setting directions for the upcoming year. At the time of the writing of this book, Tishrei began just one week after the attack on the World Trade Center on September 11, 2001. Because of the attack, that Tishrei was a particularly intense time of reassessment and clarification of life priorities and direction for many people.

Like most people in New York City, I was grief-stricken and anxious after September 11. With the bridges and tunnels closed, it was not possible to leave Manhattan during the days immediately following the attack. There was no exit, nowhere to turn except to God and friends and family.

I was glued to the television those first days. It almost felt like a religious obligation for me to see and hear the accounts of the people who died. I did not know anyone who had died in the catastrophe; nevertheless, I was emotionally devastated and cried for the dead as if they were close friends. It was as if a veil had been lifted, and I could now see so clearly how connected we all are to each other, and how artificial and unnecessary are all the walls that we construct to separate us from one another. I thought of those who died, prayed for them, and included them in the kaddish I said daily for my uncle. To me they were holy martyrs. Though a somewhat nauseating stench pervaded the air, there was also a great feeling of love in New York. New Yorkers have always shared an unspoken bond, but now we felt connected to each other in a much deeper way than ever before. We smiled at each other on the streets.

When, a few days before the beginning of this Tishrei, it was finally possible to leave the city, I confess I fled as soon as I could. Frightened and emotionally drained, I went to spend the Rosh Hashanah holiday in the country with friends. Feeling somewhat like a homeless war refugee, I entered into the holiday depressed and uncertain about what the new year would bring. It was a heartbreaking holiday, and I cried several times. I knew that my life would change, but it was not clear in what way. I prayed for personal clarity and guidance about the next steps I would have to take to fulfill my life purpose as well as for the strength and the courage to follow through. On Rosh Hashanah, I intuited that I would leave New York, but I did not want to leave out of fear or abandon my friends or students. Actually I had wanted to leave New York for many years, and I prayed that I now would be able to do so.

Returning to the City for Yom Kippur several days later was actually uplifting. At the request of some of my students, I decided to do an alternative meditative and creative service for Yom Kippur and open it to the general community. The grapevine worked surprisingly well, and about seventy-five people attended the gathering, many of whom I did not know. The service was quite extraordinary, and we experienced a tremendous blessing of love, intimacy, and holiness that day. I felt empowered to be giving and sharing in this way and found meaning and strength in doing what I could to help other people on a spiritual level. I considered staying in New York to be of service to others.

The Succot holiday that followed was cozy and intimate, but in the middle of it, as this country formally entered war, it became clear that I could not run away from the guidance that I should leave New York. Once I decided to leave, however, everything flowed. I didn't know exactly where I was going, but I was going and that felt good. It did not feel as if I was running away; rather, I felt centered and joyful. I felt I was finally willing to open up to newness, and I was going forward to claim what and who I am in a deeper and more powerful way than ever before.

As soon as the holidays were over, I rented a car and began to explore the beautiful country in upper New York state and the Berkshires. Because I had not really driven in over twenty years, I was amazed to experience myself driving on highways, over bridges, and in New York City traffic. I had never really done that before, even when I used to drive, but the time was right and I felt new doors were opening for me. I bought a laptop computer so I could continue working on this book.

As I began to travel in this new year, I remembered the story of Abraham, who was told by God, "Leave your family, country, and birthplace and go to a land I will show you." Like Abraham, I do not know exactly where I am going, but I am fine with that and confident that clarity of direction will soon come. I am happy to feel new movement in my life and anticipate a year of newness and adventure.

Energy: Opening to Newness

Tishrei is a time of rebirth and renewal. The energy of this month is generative and transforming. It signals the beginning of a new year, a time of letting go of the past, of emptying oneself of old concepts. Its hallmarks are the willingness to be vulnerable, to be not knowing but becoming, to be open to new possibilities. This energy can create a new order for you personally that will transform your life this year and in years to come. This month is the most powerful time to expand your spiritual awareness and transform your life in the ways you have always wanted, but it also requires a great deal of personal inner work. There must always be a balance between the personal effort and grace.

In Tishrei, this balance is reflected in nature. The autumnal equinox approaches; the days and nights are now of equal length. The weather is also generally balanced, not too hot and not too cold in most parts of the world. The rainy season has not yet begun. This balance in Tishrei is represented by the astrological symbol of the scales of Libra.

As the first month of the year, Tishrei teaches us that everything begins from a place of balance. To begin anew, we must first find this place of balance within ourselves.

In Judaism, Tishrei is considered both the seventh month as well as the first. Certain sections of the Torah call Tishrei the seventh month because they begin the year with Nissan (March–April), yet Tishrei is widely known and celebrated as the first month of the Jewish calendar, and is considered so according to Jewish law.

The name Tishrei contains the same Hebrew letters as the word *bereshit,* which means "beginning" and is, interestingly, the first word in the Torah. Tishrei begins with the holiday of Rosh Hashanah, which in Hebrew means "head of the year." Tishrei is the beginning of the year, and Rosh Hashanah celebrates the creation of the human being.

The numbers one and seven are considered the most beloved in kabbalah. As the seventh month, the midpoint of the year, and as the first month, the beginning of an entirely new year, Tishrei is the time of harvesting and the time of beginning of new projects. Schools reopen and people return to work after the summer holidays. No other month has as many holidays as Tishrei does, some of them among the most important Jewish holidays. As the first month of the year, Tishrei sets the tone for what will happen during the upcoming year.

It is no coincidence that there are so many Jewish holidays this month. As the seasons change in many places throughout the world, people feel particularly vulnerable at this time. The holidays were given to us to bathe, shelter, protect, and fortify ourselves during this time of vulnerability and transition. During this month, practicing Jews live in a spiritual bubble—they are either celebrating a holiday or, in the interim days, preparing for the next one. After the September 11 tragedy, the gift of the abundance of holidays was appreciated more than ever. Tishrei may be likened to a spiritual shopping center where we have the opportunity to fill our baskets with blessings for the next year. The various holidays are each particular stores where we receive different spiritual gifts. In olden times, the granaries were stocked up at this time to sustain people through the cold winters. So, similarly, during Tishrei we stock up on blessings of Godliness to sustain us for the year ahead.

At this time there is natural turning inward and reaching upward in our consciousness. There is a more intense search for personal meaning, for clarity of one's life purpose. Through these efforts and the heavenly grace available at this time, people do gain clarity about their life mission and do initiate important transformational and life-enhancing changes to support their new vision.

For example, Donna began to feel that Israel was being misrepresented in the media after the September 11 tragedy and felt called upon to do something. A shy, quiet, petite woman, Donna became in this one month a public spokeswoman for Israel. She appeared at many different synagogues and gatherings distributing important materials she had prepared. She rose to meet the need and brought forth the hidden potential within herself to become a leader and make a most important contribution.

Another example was Donald. He had recently started dating Jill a few months earlier. On Rosh Hashanah, it became clear to him that he wanted to marry her. When there is clarity, one doesn't doubt or procrastinate. He did not wait. He proposed right after Rosh Hashanah, and she accepted.

Sometimes changes come from clear vision, and other times there is just more spiritual energy available this month to help people find themselves more open to new possibilities. Stephen, for example, had been hibernating in grief most of the year after the death of his mother. Much to his surprise, he began dating again during Tishrei. The energy of newness is flowing in Tishrei for those who are ready to receive it. Being open to new ideas, new experiences, new people, a new place to live, new work, or anything new brings joy. Tishrei is a joyous month. If we want to begin thinking and acting differently in the coming year, Tishrei is an amazing and unique spiritual opportunity to open to newness and take leaps forward in our lives.

During this month, our appreciation of the bonds with family and friends is heightened. All the holidays bring people together. The energy of this month supports the establishment and deepening of relationships with others.

This month is considered an excellent time for sexual healing. In Judaism, sex is acknowledged as important, essential, and even holy. It is the foundation of life. According to kabbalah, the genitals correspond to the *sephira,* the divine emanation, of *yesod,* which means "foundation." Because Tishrei is the foundation for the rest of the year, similarly sex is the beginning of life and the foundation of all relationships, whether they are sexual in nature or not. It is sexual energy that is the source of all creativity as well as actual physical life.

It is no accident that life begins through the sexual act. Sex is God's gift to us, and it is a way that we can draw close to Him as well as to another person. God could have chosen to perpetuate the species in another way, but instead chose to involve us as His partners in this most intimate and deep way. Sex brings unity with another person on the spiritual, emotional, and physical levels and, through unity with this person, unity with all of creation.

According to the Ramban (Nachmanides), sex brings blessings of spiritual healing not only to the people who are engaging in the act, but also to the world. Performed

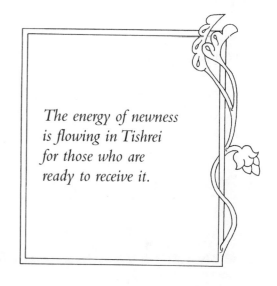

The energy of newness is flowing in Tishrei for those who are ready to receive it.

with the proper intentions in the appropriate manner, sex becomes a vehicle for experiencing Godliness. As such, sex is the most pleasurable human experience.

It is for this reason that our appreciation of sex needs to be elevated in general, and particularly during this month. It is a shame that God's gift to the human race is not fully honored and appreciated. Too often, people experience sex in a negative or limited way and feel guilty, anxious, or ashamed about it. As a therapist, I often deal with sexuality issues. Rather than experiencing sex as a source of pleasure or holiness, many people find sex a source of anxiety, shame, or obligation. Sexual dysfunction issues between partners should be addressed, particularly this month.

General Guidelines and Goals

The following guidelines and goals enable us to direct our energies in the ways that are optimal for our growth and transformation in accordance with the energy of this month. It is recommended that you read and meditate upon them often in the course of the month. Reflect on their applicability to you, and allow them to direct and inspire you often this month.

1. SET A VISION FOR THE NEW YEAR.

As the first month of a new year, Tishrei is an opportunity for a new beginning. Every year brings with it new blessings, with new opportunities and possibilities. What we open to during this month sets the course for the entire year.

Because we have been endowed with free will, we are not bound to the past and have no need to carry its baggage. If we keep doing what we have done in the past, it is likely we will get the results we have in the past. The energy of this month proclaims that we can change. We can be the people we want to be and have lives that reflect who we really are. This is the time to let go of the old excuses to justify not having what you want in your life now and open to a new you.

During the days of this month, particularly when you engage in the celebration of the holidays, take time to envision what you want for yourself. Ask yourself, "Am I living a life worthy of who I am?" For example, are you living where you want to live? Do you do the kind of work you love and get paid what you want? Do you have the kinds of relationships you want in your life? Do you support your physical well-being with nourishing, healthy foods and exercise? Do you have outlets for creative expression? Do you have times for recreation and play? Do you have a vibrant prayer or meditative practice? If the answer is no or not entirely to any of these questions, you need to open to newness.

Reflect on what you want, visualize yourself living the life you want, and pray for God's blessing. When you can accept that you are blessed in the way you want, begin to formulate your goals for the coming year along with strategies for meeting these goals.

2. AFFIRM YOURSELF AND WHAT YOU WANT IN LIFE.

Affirmations are a powerful tool for manifesting what we want in our lives. See yourself healthy, happy, radiant, fulfilled, and engaged in meaningful work and relationships, enjoying your life on all levels. Affirm that this is your true self and that you are committed to living on this level of truth.

Write powerful affirmations for yourself and repeat them often in the course of the month. For example, "I am a radiant spiritual being who enjoys life fully" or "I am lovable and loving." Who we are and what we have in our lives is a reflection of our consciousness. Commit to changing your consciousness now.

Take note of the negative voice within, the inner critic or ego mind, which, in the guise of self-protection and rational thinking, is self-deprecating. This is the voice that tells you you are not worthy, you are inadequate, you are basically flawed, deficient, and not good enough. This negative voice is a product of your fears and is peripheral to you. It is not who you are! The Torah tells us that human beings are made in the image and likeness of God. Don't waste your time indulging in negative thinking or actions. This does not honor you or God, your Creator. Continue the repetition of your affirmations until they resonate deeply within you and you begin to live from them.

3. HEAL YOUR RELATIONSHIPS WITH FRIENDS AND FAMILY.

In the course of life, particularly in this last year, we may have been hurt or hurt people close to us. We may even be unaware of how we have hurt others, and we may not have shared with others how they have hurt us. The ten days between Rosh Hashanah and Yom Kippur are devoted to healing our relationships with others.

On Yom Kippur we ask God for forgiveness. Before Yom Kippur we are expected to make efforts to both forgive and seek forgiveness. It may be hard to make ourselves vulnerable, especially when we have been deeply hurt. Be gentle with yourself, but stretch yourself this month. Try to forgive others, even if they have not asked for forgiveness. Forgiveness is a gift you give to yourself. Blaming others keeps you stuck in a victim role that keeps you from opening to your true freedom and the new possibilities available in this coming year. Being angry is a waste of your precious vital energy. We cannot embrace fully the newness of this coming year if we are carrying the jealousy, anger, and resentments of past years. We cannot expect to receive God's forgiveness without first trying to forgive and to receive the forgiveness of others.

For example, you might say something like, "Please forgive me for anything I might have done to you or not done for you this last year. I love you, my relationship with you is important to me, and I want to start anew to strengthen it in this coming year." It is not necessary to stipulate specific offenses unless the person asks you to, because doing so often causes greater harm. Let's say you gossiped about a friend and your friend did not know. Because learning of your indiscretion would cause additional pain, it may be best not to reveal it.

In other scenarios, it may be quite clear to all parties what was done. Obtaining forgiveness might mandate some financial compensation or a commitment to act differently in the future. And it is possible that, when we ask for forgiveness, others might not be willing to give it to us. Our sages advise us to try three times, and even use intermediaries if necessary. The Rambam (Maimonides) recommended that you bring three friends with you when you approach a person you have hurt. But what happens if you have tried in all possible ways and are still unsuccessful? You may have to give the person some space and be patient. Pray for the person's welfare, and forgive yourself. Forgiveness is a process, and it is also a heavenly gift that comes through prayer and personal growth.

4. TRY TO MAINTAIN SILENCE AS MUCH AS POSSIBLE AND SPEAK ONLY WORDS OF PRAYER, BLESSING, LOVE, AND COMPASSION TO OTHERS.

Taking care with speech is a beneficial and powerful spiritual practice at any time of the year, but is particularly potent during this month and on Rosh Hashanah. This entire month is a time of judgment. As we judge others, so we are judged. Be watchful of your words and make an effort not to speak badly about other people, particularly on Rosh Hashanah. It is so easy to be careless and judgmental in our speech. When we speak badly about others, our spiritual energy is actually diminished and the negative inclination, known as the *yetzer hara,* is strengthened. The negativity we project onto others returns to us manifold.

5. MAKE AN EFFORT TO BE HAPPY, EVEN IF YOU FEEL SAD.

The great rebbe (rabbi) and kabbalist of the nineteenth century Reb Nachman of Breslov used to say that it is a great *mitzvah* (a good deed or commandment prescribed by the Torah) to always be happy. Being happy demonstrates our faith in the goodness of God.

This is not an easy *mitzvah* to do. Being happy does not mean that we are always jovial and smiling. It does not mean that we repress our real feelings and not allow ourselves to be sad when it is appropriate. Rather, it means that even when we're sad or heartbroken, we're still in touch with this place of inner happiness inside us, for we trust in God.

My rebbe, Reb Shlomo Carlebach, used to encourage us to dance and be happy on Rosh Hashanah, for by doing so we demonstrate our trust and faith in the goodness of God. And if, God forbid, it were decreed that we were not going to live to see the completion of the next year, we could actually change our fate by the joy we open up to on Rosh Hashanah. This is true for the entire month.

Astrological Sign: Libra

The astrological sign for the month of Tishrei is Libra, represented by scales. The energy of this month is one of deliberation, balancing, and weighing everything carefully. There is an inherent desire to find equanimity.

Tishrei retains its position as the seventh month also in astrology. According to astrology, the first six months focus on the development of the individual. Now in Tishrei a balance is found between the individual and the community, along with a new capacity and desire to bring harmony into the world.

Libra rules over the seventh house, which is that of marriage and relationships. Relationships are very important this month. Libra is ruled by the planet Venus, the goddess of love. Love, a primary force this month, is the energy that attracts and binds people together in harmony. This month brings people together to renew and strengthen relationships.

Hebrew Letter: Lamed

The Hebrew letter for this month is lamed, the tallest of all the Hebrew letters. Its height reflects the tremendous spiritual heights possible during this month. Jewish sages refer to the lamed as "a tower soaring in air." The lamed, the tallest letter, and the yud, the smallest letter, which represents Elul, the month immediately preceding Tishrei, together spell out "Le," which means "To Me." This indicates that Tishrei builds on the previous month, Elul, and is devoted to God. The significance of this word is taken from the high point of the wedding ceremony, when the groom says to the bride "*Harei et mekudesht le,*" which means "You are holy to me." The joining of a husband and wife is symbolic of the joining of God and people. The energy of this month is one of coming together, unifying in love. As mentioned earlier, the area of healing for this month is sex.

Looking at the size and shape of the lamed, we see a channel connecting the higher worlds to the lower worlds. The lamed, whose name literally means "to learn," reflects the human aspiration to ascend in knowledge. The lamed also means "to teach," which, according to kabbalah as discussed by Rabbi Yitzchok Ginzberg in his book *Aleph Beit,* reflects the "hovering mother" who offers protection and inspiration to those who truly aspire to know God. Energies of both learning and teaching are active this month. We also see an allusion to the healing of sex in the letter lamed. Sex in the Bible is called "knowing." When the Bible says that Adam "knew" Eve, it is referring to sexual relations.

Lamed is the first letter of the Hebrew word *lev,* which means "heart." The word lev consists of the letters lamed and *beit,* which has a numerical value of two. We could read lev as two lameds. If we put two lameds face to face, we see a heart. Tishrei is the heart of the year. Like the heart, it distributes the energies for the entire year. Tishrei is also time of the opening of the heart.

The lamed is also the heart of the Hebrew alphabet. The first half of the alphabet from aleph to lamed spells out El, which is a name of God associated with the divine emanation *(sephira)* of love *(hesed).* From the letters mem to tav, the second half of the alphabet spells out *met,* which means "death." Tishrei marks the end of the first half of the year that begins in Nissan and the beginning of the second half of the year.

Hebrew Tribe: Ephraim

The tribe associated with Tishrei is Ephraim, from the younger son born to Joseph while he was ruling in Egypt. About the naming of this son the Torah says, "And the name of the second he called Ephraim, 'for God has caused me to be fruitful in the land of my affliction'" (Gen. 41:52). "Ephraim" comes from the root *pri,* "fruit," and signifies fruitfulness and prosperity.

When Jacob, the father of Joseph, sees his grandsons, he says, "And now your two sons Ephraim and Menashah, who were born to you in the land of Egypt before I came to you into Egypt are mine, as Reuven and Shimon they shall be mine" (Gen. 48:5). Jacob's "adoption" of Ephraim and Menashah elevated them to the level of his other sons; the tribes named after them were thereby placed on equal footing with the other tribes of Israel.

Before his death, Jacob blessed Ephraim and Menashah, his brother, along with his other sons for whom the tribes were named. He blessed Ephraim, who was the younger, with his right hand and Menashah with his left. Thinking that Jacob had made a mistake in blessing his younger son over the firstborn, Joseph attempted to correct his father, only to find out that Jacob was insistent on blessing Ephraim over Menashah.

Ephraim was beloved of God. "Is Ephraim my dear son? Is he a darling child? For whenever I speak of him I remember him still" (Jer. 31:20). This echoes the beloved energy of Tishrei.

Divine Name Permutation: VHYH

The letter positions correspond to different spiritual worlds. The first and third positions are considered lights, and the second and fourth positions, vessels. In examining the permutation for this month, we note first that the hay (H) is in its usual position for YHVH. One hay is in the world of Assiyah, the fourth position, indicating an abundant flow of divine energy in this world. The hay in the second position, Beriyah, indicates expansiveness in the mind.

The yud (Y) in the world of Yetzerah, the third position, indicates that one should concentrate the heart into a yud, a small point. To receive the energy of this month, one must be very internally focused, directing the heart upward toward the higher worlds. The vav (V) in the world of Atzilut indicates that there is a great and direct flow from Ain Sof, the term for the infinite, unknowable God in kabbalah that is evidenced by all the holidays in this month.

Torah Portions

Special portions of the Torah highlighting the energy of the month are read during the holidays. On the first day of Rosh Hashanah we read the Torah story of Sarah giving birth to Yitzchok (Isaac) (Gen. 21) and the Haftorah, the selection from the Prophets of Hannah giving birth to Samuel (1 Sam. 1:1–2:10). Both women have difficulty conceiving naturally, and God intervenes. Both stories testify to the divine role in the birthing experience, reminding us that we need God to begin our lives anew.

On the second day of Rosh Hashanah, we read about the binding of Isaac and the willingness of Abraham and Isaac to sacrifice themselves to Divine Will (Gen. 22). It is said that this event actually took place on Rosh Hashanah, and the blowing of the shofar on Rosh Hashanah reminds us of the ram who was sacrificed instead of Isaac. We read this story not only to remind God and ourselves of the spiritual merit of Abraham and Isaac, but also, and more important, to recognize that our personal will is always to be subordinated to the Divine Will. In the coming year, we will be tested and we will have to make different kinds of sacrifices—how we respond is a demonstration of our faith.

The Torah portion for Yom Kippur is Leviticus 16:1–34, which recounts the death of the sons of Aaron and the service offered by Aaron, the high priest, to obtain atonement for the people. We read in this Torah portion God's establishing of this very day as a Day of Atonement for eternity. There are two interesting Haftorahs that are read on Yom Kippur. The morning one is from Isaiah 57:14–58. It is quite strange that although the Torah tells us to fast and "afflict ourselves" on this day and people generally do, we read in the Haftorah that God does not really want this; God wants us to dissolve groups that pervert justice, share our riches with the poor, and free the oppressed. If we do these things, God will be pleased with us.

During the afternoon service we read about the prophet Jonah, who was unwilling to share God's prophecy with the non-Jewish city of Nineveh. Escaping this mission on a boat that experienced turbulence, he was thrown into the water and swallowed by the whale. While inside the whale, when he had no other choice, Jonah prayed to God and agreed to carry out His will. As Jonah feared, the people of Nineveh repented and were spared destruction. This is a most important teaching for the Jewish people, who sometimes tend to be insular and unwilling to spread Jewish teachings to the world. In the beginning of the year, we need to recognize the spirituality of the other nations and commit to sharing ourselves with them in this way.

On Succot, we read Leviticus 23:33–44, the biblical commandment to observe the holiday of Succot. We also read the Haftorah of Zechariah (Zech. 14:1–24) and Haftorah of Ezekiel (Ezek. 38:18–39:16). Both, interestingly, forecast the war of Gog and Magog and the cataclysmic series of battles that bring about the messianic era. It seemed like a divine sign that we were reading these Torah selections at the very time, during Succot, that United States began its war on terrorism by bombing Afghanistan. Some of the details related in scripture are quite gruesome and frightening, but a good and happy ending is forecast.

Holidays

Rosh Hashanah

HISTORY   Rosh Hashanah marks the beginning of the new year and is the most universal of all Jewish holidays. Considered the birthday of humanity, Rosh Hashanah commemorates the creation of the human being by a Being who is One but who has many names, even within Judaism. Rosh Hashanah is a celebration of gift of life. We affirm that God created this world and creates it anew each year and at every moment. Life exists as an expression of Divine Will, and the celebration of Rosh Hashanah reminds us that we cannot take life or this world for granted.

Unlike most holidays, which occur at the full moon, Rosh Hashanah occurs on the new moon and consequently embodies the energies and mysteries of this phase. Just as what we open to at the time of the new moon shapes the entire month, what we open to during Rosh Hashanah shapes the entire year. In a passage in which Tishrei is numbered as the seventh month, the Torah instructs us: "In the seventh month on the first day, you shall do no laborious work, it shall be a day of shofar sounding for you" (Num. 29:1; also Lev. 23:24). Other than this reference to Rosh Hashanah, the Torah does not provide much information about the holiday. Most of what we know about it comes from oral tradition.

Rosh Hashanah is known as a day of judgment. We say repeatedly in the Rosh Hashanah prayers, "Today is the birthday of the world. Today all creatures of the world stand in judgment, whether as children or as servants . . ." We stand on this day with humility, not knowing what the upcoming year will bring. Jewish liturgy affirms that the destiny for each person, Jew and non-Jew alike, is determined on Rosh Hashanah and sealed on Yom Kippur, though some say it extends to the end of Succot or even Chanukah. Whatever our destiny, we can change it through *teshuvah* ("returning") to God by improving our character, *tefila* ("prayer"), and *tzedekah* ("charity").

OBSERVANCE   As we see from the Torah reference, the main event of Rosh Hashanah is the blowing of the shofar, which is a bent ram's horn. Oral tradition stipulates that we should hear a hundred blasts of the shofar on each day of Rosh Hashanah. The shofar blasts impart the essence and teachings of the holiday more directly and powerfully than words could ever do. The *Zohar*, an ancient book of Jewish mysticism, says "Happy is the people who know the *teruah* (the shofar blast)."

According to Saddia Gaon, a great rabbi of the ninth century, one of the main reasons for blowing the shofar on Rosh Hashanah is to coronate God as King. On Rosh Hashanah we acknowledge God as the Creator and the King of the world. Just as trumpets are blown to announce the arrival of an earthly king, so the shofar is blown to testify that God is King *(melech)* on the anniversary of God's creation of humanity. As we hear the shofar blasts, we reflect upon the questions, "How do I make God king over myself? What would the world look like if everyone recognized God as King of the world?"

Many people have difficulty with the metaphor of God as King and feel it is patriarchal, outdated, and alienating. However, when we say God is King, we do not mean God is a wise old man sitting on a throne, making judgments about our fate. That image may have been sufficient for us as children, but as adults it is limiting. Even though we may recognize this intellectually, it is sometimes emotionally hard to rid ourselves of childish images of God. For that reason, many synagogues have made an effort to eliminate masculine references to God. Some have substituted Queen instead of King, and some even alternate between the two. Some Jewish renewal circles substitute "Source of Life" for "King."

Even though I am a woman, I experience the metaphor of God as King as empowering. It awakens devotion in me and reassures me that in essence there is a unified underlying or higher reality of life. I want God to be King because God is the source of compassion, love, joy, ecstasy, wisdom, beauty, and all that is good. When I acknowledge God as King, I am empowered and strengthened because I am God's servant. I am transported to a higher consciousness, where I see the divine order underlying all the events in my life that may otherwise seem unconnected. This is the joy and blessing of

Rosh Hashanah. God as King is a metaphor for this highest spiritual awareness. Even those who have trouble with the metaphor of God as King believe, in the deep places within, on an intuitive level, in the unifying principle of God. This is the knowing that is awakened during the shofar blasts.

The shofar brings us to the deepest places within ourselves where we know there is a God. After the World Trade Center destruction on September 11, I experienced the shofar blasts differently. I imagined that I heard God's cry to humanity in the shofar blasts: "I made a world for love and joy, not for pain and suffering. Please take care of my world."

Rosh Hashanah is the first day of the ten days of Teshuvah, known in Hebrew as *aseret yemei teshuvah*. The Talmud tells us that these ten days are the days when God is closer than any other time: "Seek when God is readily found." Teshuvah, the returning to God, is facilitated by the shofar. The sounds of the shofar during Rosh Hashanah emulate the cry of our own souls and enable us to turn inward to our deepest core. A basic and primal sound issuing from the horn of the ram, the shofar blast instantly puts us in touch with what is true and real. It awakens our spiritual potential. It inspires us to change and become better people.

As we hear the shofar blasts, we find ourselves crying to God, "Here I am. I could have been better, I made mistakes, I am not complete. Please accept me. Please help me to be a better person. Please help me to be all I can be. Please guide me in Your ways."

Ritual observances and customs associated with Rosh Hashanah include lighting candles, saying prayers, and eating festive meals with friends and family. People eat round challahs (bread)—the circle signifying endless, continuing life—with honey, rather than the usual salt, to bless everyone with a sweet year. Apples with honey are eaten as well. Before the main meal, some have many different kinds of fruits, including pomegranates and dates, and vegetables such as carrots and cabbage as well as a fish head at their Rosh Hashanah table to convey special blessings. Prayer books such as *Art Scroll* outline the order and significance for the eating of these foods.

In one custom known as *tashlich,* which occurs on Rosh Hashanah afternoon, but can be done until Yom Kippur, people go to a natural body of water and symbolically cast their sins into the water. This ritual is designed to help people let go of the ways in which they have blocked themselves. This letting go prepares us to receive the blessing of Yom Kippur.

Yom Kippur

HISTORY   Yom Kippur, the holiest day of the Jewish calendar, is known as the Day of Atonement. The Torah says, "On the tenth day of the month (Tishrei) it is a day of atonement, a holy convocation, and you shall afflict yourselves . . . you shall not do any work on this very day, for it is the Day of Atonement to provide you atonement before God. . . . It is a day of complete rest for you and you shall afflict yourselves" (Lev. 23:26). Up until Yom Kippur, we have done whatever we could do on our own to purify ourselves. On Yom Kippur, we receive God's grace, love, and compassion, and are cleansed, forgiven, and liberated in a way we could never be on our own. As the Torah says, on Yom Kippur "You shall be purified from all your sins" (Lev. 16:30).

Yom Kippur commemorates the day when Moses descended from Mount Sinai with the second set of tablets and a message of forgiveness for the Jewish people after the sin of the Golden Calf. Yom Kippur is the culmination of the forty-day period of Teshuvah that began on the first day of the previous month of Elul. Yom Kippur is the tenth day of the more intensive period of Teshuvah that began on Rosh Hashanah.

Jewish sages teach that, although the first tablets Moses received were totally spiritual, the second tablets were material and enclosed in moral directives because the people were not able to absorb the pure spirituality of the first tablets. Unlike the first tablets, which were written by God, these second tablets were written by Moses and were born out of the hard work of repentance of the Jewish people and the intercession of Moses.

In the days of the Holy Temple in Jerusalem, Yom Kippur was the one day that the high priest entered into the Holy of Holies and said a particular name of God that ushered in forgiveness. The service the high priest engaged in on Yom Kippur is recounted in detail during the Mussaf service on Yom Kippur day.

OBSERVANCE   Yom Kippur is a day for meditation and prayer. As the Torah instructs, we "afflict ourselves" on this day. We do not eat, drink, wash, have sexual relations, or engage in worldly activities. We wear white clothes if possible and do not wear leather shoes. These restrictions enable us to attune to the heavenly transmission of love, forgiveness, and grace given on this holiest of days. Many times in the course of Yom Kippur we will chant the Thirteen Attributes of Divine Compassion that were given to Moses, recorded in Exodus 34:6–7. This ancient formula was handed down to us to as a means to invoke God's grace on our holidays.

During the entire day of Yom Kippur there are repeated requests for forgiveness and recitations of individual and communal sins. The requests are said in the plural, rather than the singular, to teach us about our interdependence and responsibility for each other. Too often in the course of the year, people feel alone and isolated from each other. On Yom Kippur, we are constantly reminded of our unity and connection with each other.

It is a tremendous gift to pray in a congregation on Yom Kippur, for what we can do together is greater than what we can do alone. To be in the company of people who are strong enough to acknowledge that they are vulnerable human beings and, as people, have all made mistakes is a powerful bonding experience. We also receive much more Divine Light and grace when we feel responsible for the community than we would as isolated individuals.

Yom Kippur offers us a special opportunity to attune to the experience of at-one-ment with the Divine in the most direct way. Because there are no distractions on Yom Kippur and the day is spent in prayer and meditation, it is easier to release all the ways we have blocked the flow of goodness into our lives. We do this in part by confessing our sins communally.

In Hebrew, "to sin" literally means "to miss the mark." In Judaism, because people are made in the image of God, there is no doctrine of original sin, as in Christianity. Human beings are not considered inherently sinful; rather, they may think, feel, and do things that are not in keeping with their true nature—this is what is meant by sin.

Because sin does not emanate from the true essence of human beings, but rather results from a false identification with the ego mind, it is easy to relinquish what is not attached to our true essence when we realize who we really are. Everything on Yom Kippur is designed to facilitate this kind of psychological and emotional release, which opens us to the clarity of who we really are. Out of our willingness to feel our broken-ness and vulnerability, we become stronger and more whole. We are in essence divine holy beings with pure, shining, loving souls. We simply need to let go of limiting, illusory, and false concepts of the self that we have misidentified as ourselves. That is why Yom Kippur is such a joyous day.

Succot

HISTORY   The Torah tells us, "You shall dwell in booths (*succot*) for a seven-day period, in order that your generations shall know that I caused the children of Israel to dwell in booths when I brought them forth from the land of Egypt" (Lev. 23:42). From this we learn that the holiday of Succot is primarily a holiday commemorating the divine protection the Jewish people received after the departure from Egypt.

Other biblical references to the holiday include Leviticus 23:33–36: "On the fifteenth of the seventh month shall be the festival of Succot to God, lasting for seven days. The first day shall be a sacred holiday when you may not do any work. For seven days then you shall present a fire offering. The eighth day is a sacred holiday . . . a time of retreat when you may do no work"; and Leviticus 23:39: "On the fifteenth of the seventh month when you harvest the land's grains you shall celebrate a festival to God for seven days. The first day shall be a day of rest and the eighth day shall be a day of rest." In addition to being a holiday commemorating the Jewish people's dwelling in little succot (huts), Succot is an agricultural holiday replete with prayers for rain, nature rituals, and gratitude for the harvest. The Torah tells us, "Celebrate to God for seven days in the place that God will choose, since God will then bless you in all your agricultural and others endeavors . . . so that you will be only happy" (Deut. 16:16). Though all Jewish holidays are times of joy, Succot is the one holiday that is called the time of rejoicing.

The Torah instructs, "On the first day, you must take for yourself an *etrog* (fruit of the citron tree), a *lulav* (palm branches), *hadasim* (myrtle branches), and *aravah* (willows) that grow near the brook. During these seven days each year, you shall celebrate to God" (Lev. 23:40–41).

When the Holy Temple stood in Jerusalem, the Jewish people brought offerings during the seven days of Succot in honor of the seventy nations of the world. According to Torah, there are seventy ancient nations that are the roots of all the diverse national groups and cultures. This number is derived from Genesis 10, which recounts seventy as the number of descendents of Noah. Rashi, the primary commentator on the Torah, explains that the purpose of these offerings was to seek atonement on behalf of the seventy nations, so that the entire world would merit rain during the coming year. "Rain" means actual rain, but it is also a metaphor for all that is needed for continued physical life and sustenance. These blessings are said even today for all nations, regardless of how they have treated Jews. How elevated and beautiful that the Jewish people pray and seek atonement even for their enemies. The Jewish people pray that all nations be able to receive the flow of blessings from the Divine. Perhaps if nations understood that the Jewish people pray and work for the perfection of the world, they would support them.

The sages have asked why we observe the holiday of Succot after Yom Kippur. The Israelites lived in these dwellings after the Exodus, which occurred in the spring. Why are Jews commanded to live in these dwellings in Tishrei, during the fall? One of the main reasons is that if the Jews lived in the huts in the spring, it would be experienced as a communion with nature, rather than a testimony to divine protection during the wanderings in the desert. Another reason is that the *succah* commemorates the clouds of glory that surrounded the Jews after the Exodus. The clouds of glory departed after the sin of the Golden Calf and returned after Yom Kippur, when forgiveness had been received. The clouds of glory then remained with the Jewish people for the entire time in the desert. It was the most visible sign that God was with them.

As we learn about the energy of this month, we understand that it is most appropriate for the holiday of Succot to be placed in Tishrei as instructed by the Torah. This month is a time to experience one's vulnerability and need for divine protection, which is best done in the fall when the weather is changing, when it is not too cold, but getting colder. Because the little *succah* provides shelter from the natural elements, it engenders a feeling of divine protection.

OBSERVANCE   The holiday of Succot is replete with many rituals and spiritual practices. Through these various rituals, the deepest teachings of Succot are imparted kinesthetically, for the entire body, mind, heart, and soul are engaged. As soon as Yom Kippur is over, Jews begin to construct hutlike dwellings reminiscent of the dwellings the Jews lived in in the desert. During the seven days, we sit, eat, drink, and even sleep in these huts. This is the main commandment of this holiday.

Being in the *succah* is a total body experience. People can talk a lot about God's loving protection, but when we are actually in the *succah* itself we feel it almost magically. When we sit in the *succah*, we experience our vulnerability, but we feel safe because we sense God's surrounding presence. Life is simple and joyous. We learn that all the external structures we build in our lives to protect ourselves from the experience of our own vulnerability are unnecessary. Furthermore, they separate us from our true selves, from other people, and from God.

Being in the *succah* is a time of intimacy. In the *succah,* I can be real, I can be totally myself, and I can allow others to be fully themselves as well. This intimacy with self and others brings happiness and awakens the child within. Sitting in the *succah* is fun, yet profound and mystical. The *succah* imparts a deep teaching more powerful than words alone could ever convey. In truth, all human beings are children of God and the world is God's house.

The holiday of Succot occurs during the harvesting time, when we rejoice in the plenitude we have been given. We draw to us many blessings during the time of Succot that will set the tone for the entire year. We sing Hallel, special songs of praise, every day during Succot. If sung in the proper spirit, these songs fill people's hearts with great joy.

We also read Koheleth (Ecclesiastes) during Succot to remind us of the temporal nature of human existence. In this book, King Solomon of ancient Israel guides us on a journey to discover the purpose of life. King Solomon, who had wealth, women, power, and knowledge, reviews all these things and concludes that none of them really matter. He tells us, "All is vanity." We read this book as we reap our bounty, when it might be easy for us to be full of pride and arrogance and attribute our harvest to our own efforts. Even though this is a time of bounty, it is also a time when we sense that the cold and barrenness of winter, whether we like it or not, will soon be upon us. There is a pervasive sense of the impermanence of life during this month that is reflected in this book.

We might think that the book of Koheleth is fatalistic and depressing, but King Solomon concludes it with an uplifting and empowering instruction. He tells us that in "the end of the matter, all is heard, you shall fear God, observe His *mitzvot*, for this is the whole of man." It is the God connection that is the most important possession we must acquire and earn during our brief time on earth.

During the holiday of Succot, Jews wave the *lulav* (branches of date palm), *hadas* (myrtle leaf), *aravah* (willow leaf), and *etrog* (lemonlike fruit) all together in all directions. These four species are said to represent the four personality types of people who are brought together at this time. The etrog is edible and fragrant and represents the refined person who is learned and also charitable. The *lulav* is odorless, but produces nourishing food; it represents the learned person who is not very sweet, because he or she is not doing beautiful things in the world. The hadas is fragrant, but tasteless; this person does good things, but is not very knowledgeable. The aravah (willow branch) is neither fragrant nor edible; it represents the ordinary person undistinguished by knowledge or good deeds.

Others say these species represent parts of a single person. The lulav is the spine, the hadas the eyes, the aravah the mouth, and the etrog the heart. By shaking these branches all together, a person brings these parts of the body into alignment and they are permeated with the joy of Succot.

Various meditations are to be undertaken when one is waving these four species in all six directions. Reb Shlomo Carlebach would say that we are bringing God's energy into the world. For example, when we shake to the right, we are drawing down God's loving-kindness *(hesed),* and when we go to the left, we are drawing down strength *(gevurah).* We wave and shake in all six directions, each one bringing down different blessings, clearing the path for greater contact with the Divine. It is an ancient shamanistic and magical practice.

Reb Nachman of Breslov said that the *mitzvah* of waving these four species brings about a revelation of Godliness and we can recognize that the whole world is filled with Godliness. He said that simply sitting in a *succah* brings purity of heart (*Likutey Moharan* 33).

Shemini Atzeret, Simchat Torah

HISTORY   Shemini Atzeret, the eighth day following the seven days of Succot, is considered a separate holiday. The Torah tells us, "On the eighth day shall be an *atzeret* [cessation] for you" (Num. 29:35). It is a day of stopping that allows us to make the most direct connection with God. In Israel, Shemini Atzeret and Simchat Torah, which literally means "Happiness of the Torah," are observed together on one day. Outside of the land of Israel, they are celebrated on two separate days. We do not find any reference to the celebration of Simchat Torah in the written Torah, but much of Torah is not written down, and many customs have been practiced for so long that they seem to have the same status as what is prescribed in the written Torah.

OBSERVANCE   Shemini Atzeret and Simchat Torah enjoy the usual rituals associated with a holiday such as candle lighting, Kiddush (blessing over the wine), and the prohibition of work. The She-hechi-yo-nu blessing is said again at candle lighting or Kiddush.

During Succot, the Jewish people pray for the whole world; the *succah* is open to anyone. Shemini Atzeret is a day for the Jewish people to be alone in their love and connection to the Holy One. As joyous as Succot is, Shemini Atzeret is even more so. A special powerful energy and special blessings are given to those who celebrate this holiday. Though Shemini Atzeret is one of the most joyous times of the year, unfortunately, it is one of the least known or celebrated of Jewish holidays.

There is a question whether people should eat in the *succah* during Shemini Atzeret. Most people do not, but Reb Shlomo Carlebach would make Kiddush one last time in the *succah* during Shemini Atzeret. There are special prayers and practices during Shemini Atzeret. At the time of the Mussaf service, we do an extended prayer for rain. When Jews pray for rain, it is never simply for just rain. Rain is a symbol of all of God's blessings.

On Shemini Atzeret and Simchat Torah, the yearly reading of the Torah is completed. The Torahs of the synagogue are all taken out and danced with in seven circlings known as the seven *hakkafot*. These circlings are reminiscent of the circling of the bride around the groom at the traditional Jewish wedding. There is the feeling of a wedding between God and the Jewish people.

Reb Shlomo Carlebach used to give out blessings and books of Torah along with the actual Torah scrolls for both the men and women to carry on Shemini Atzeret. We would sing and dance for hours. There were usually fewer people there than on the next day of Simchat Torah, so it was a time of intimacy with the rebbe, the community, and God.

Simchat Torah is a total celebration of the Torah. As on Shemini Atzeret, we again dance seven circles around the Torah, rejoicing that we have received the Torah and through the gift of the Torah we have a special way to connect with the Holy One.

Meditation

This month is a time of blessing. The following meditation will help you to both give and receive blessing.

Assume a sitting or standing position. Take a few long, deep breaths to relax and center yourself. First, breathe in through the nostrils and exhale through the mouth to maximize the release of tension. Then inhale and exhale through the nostrils. When you are relaxed and focused, imagine that you are transported to the Garden of Eden, a place where the Divine Presence is fully manifest. Soak up the vibrations of this place. Imagine that you are a righteous person, a holy person, which is who you really are inside, on the level of your soul.

You have been entrusted with the power to bless. To do this, it is necessary to nullify yourself, get out of the way, and allow the divine energy to be channeled through you. You know how to do this. It is a great pleasure to give way to God's energy and allow it to be expressed through you. Continue to take deep breaths. Feel that you can breathe into the top of your head.

Imagine that the light of the Shechinah, the Divine Presence, is above your head, entering you and surrounding you. Open to being a channel of blessing. Visualize on your inner screen the image of a person you would like to bless. Consider what this person wants and needs and open to bless him or her in ways even beyond what he or she might request. Formulate a blessing in your mind and then pronounce it: "May God bless you with . . ." or "You are blessed with . . ." If the person is not physically present, visualize the person happy to receive your blessing. Say "Amen" and ask the person who received the blessing, if present, to also say "Amen" to seal the blessing.

Practical Recommendations

1. BLESS PEOPLE EVEN MORE THIS MONTH THAN EVER BEFORE.

Blessing other people is a most important Jewish spiritual practice, particularly during this month. As you bless others, so you will be blessed. The more you bless others, the more blessings you will receive from others and from God.

Beginning on Rosh Hashanah and extending until Yom Kippur, it is a common practice to bless people with a happy, healthy new year. This can be done in a perfunctory way, or it can be done with feeling and focused intention. Our words are powerful. Just as God created the world with words, so we can change reality with our words. Our blessings make a difference.

Be sure to bless the people closest to you, but also extend blessings to people not in your immediate circle. Extend blessings to people who need them. Think of all the people you know who need blessing in their lives. Call these people to mind and take time to bless them in your meditations and prayers.

Bless those who are childless and want to be fruitful and multiply with children. Bless those who are without a partner with meeting their soul mates. Bless people who are poor with the means to earn a good living. Bless those who are sick with a speedy and complete recovery. If you really want to be empowered by the practice of blessing, bless someone for whom you may still harbor negative feelings.

It is not necessary for you to be in the physical presence of people you bless. (See this month's Meditation for instruction.)

2. GIVE CHARITY.

We say repeatedly during this month that *tzedekah* (charity) can literally change your destiny. It makes you worthy of receiving more blessings. It atones for negative actions. Charity is always considered an antidote to suffering.

Charity is important year-round, but it is especially important this month, prior to Yom Kippur. Giving charity places one in the flow of blessing and expands one's capacity to receive. *Tzedekah* in Hebrew means "to bring into order." This is the month to not only give *tzedekah*, but to make a plan of what you can and will give for the coming year. Even if you do not have much money, it is still important that you give something. It is a known spiritual principle that the more you give, the more you receive. Many organizations solicit funds for the coming year during this month. Think about where you can make your greatest contribution.

3. IMMERSE YOURSELF IN THE *MIKVAH*.

The *mikvah* is a ritual bath used for purification. There is a *mikvah* in most Jewish communities. A natural body of water may be used in lieu of a constructed *mikvah*. Prior to immersion in the waters of *mikvah*, one showers or bathes and removes all makeup or nail polish, focuses one's consciousness, and then dunks, fully immersing the entire body under the water several times. One can read about the mikvah, but reading about something cannot compare with the actual experience. Don't deprive yourself of this wonderful and powerful ancient ritual.

The great Jewish prophets and heads of the ancient Torah academies obligated people to purify themselves in a *mikvah* either before Rosh Hashanah or Yom Kippur or both. It is a common spiritual practice for both men and women even today.

A Tale to Live By

Because this month has more holidays than any other month and eating is an integral part of the celebrations, even on Yom Kippur, when we eat a festive meal before and after the fast, a story about holidays and foods seems appropriate. I heard the following story from Rabbi Simeon Jacobson, who said it was told originally by the Baal Shem Tov, the founder of the Chassidic movement. It conveys important kabbalistic teachings about the purpose of life that we should be particularly mindful of during this month.

The king was concerned that his son, who had lived all of his life within the confines of the palace, would not have the sensitivity and skill necessary to rule the kingdom. Spoiled and having lived a life in which everything was provided for him, he was sent out of the kingdom to acquire the kind of learning he needed so that one day he could return and rule wisely. He left the palace to explore the kingdom, but he could not reveal his true identity. Even if he tried to tell people he was the king's son, they might not believe him. And if people were told and they believed him, this knowledge would compromise the purpose of the whole mission. Dressed in ordinary clothes, he was able to travel freely among the people because no one knew who he was. Sometimes he himself even forgot that he was the king's son.

A few times a year, the king would send him a letter and he would be so happy. The letter caused him to remember who he really was, that he was the king's son and that the king loved him. He could not really tell the people in the town why he was so happy, but he wanted to celebrate with them. So he would have a party and serve wonderful food and drink for everyone in the town, and they would all rejoice together.

This story illustrates a very important kabbalistic teaching about the purpose of the human being and the power of Jewish holidays, particularly the holidays of this month, to remind us who we are. We are all the king's son. Before entering into this physical world, we lived in the palace of the spiritual worlds where we were spoiled. We basked in the light of the Divine Presence. We entered into this physical world, where there are hardships that force us to grow. Being in a physical body, we sometimes forget who we really are, that we are this pure soul, God's child.

Several times a year, the king (God) communicates directly with us, and when this happens, it is a holiday. Holidays remind us of who we really are. The holidays that occur in this month are opportunities for the most powerful communications to our soul. We want to celebrate this message to our soul, but our body is not interested and does not understand the message. So we give the body lots of special food during the holidays so it is also happy and made healthy and we can celebrate the holidays body and soul together.

Cheshwan

MONTH: *October-November*

ENERGY: *The Inner Work of Personal Transformation*

AREA OF HEALING: *Smell*

ASTROLOGICAL SIGN: *Scorpio*

HEBREW LETTER: *Nun*

HEBREW TRIBE: *Menashah*

DIVINE NAME PERMUTATION: *VHHY*

HOLIDAY: *None*

fter a recent illness, Diane was more anxious than usual. The holidays had busied and distracted her, but somehow as she entered this month, the anxiety resurfaced. One evening, when she was out to dinner with a casual acquaintance, the topic of conversation turned to Israel. She was surprised and horrified to hear from this woman, whom she had known for several years, rhetoric that was actually anti-Semitic and anti-American. Though the acquaintance was a physician, an intelligent woman, beneath the sur-face she was apparently an old-fashioned, run-of-the-mill, card-carrying anti-Semite. Diane allowed her to rant and rave about the Jews and then walked away from her and their friendship.

This episode unsettled Diane and triggered a deep exploration of woundedness in her life. Diane chose to be with and explore these feelings. She found herself remembering and reexperiencing the fear she felt as an abused child, but also recalling the particular closeness to God she had felt then as well. As she was willing to be with these feelings, she saw how she had disowned parts of herself to guard against feeling these fearful feelings. In an important insight, she realized that she never wanted to make waves, avoided conflict, and always wanted to please people, even if it was at her own expense.

I instructed her to imagine that she was standing before gates to a realm of greater well-being. I told her to tell God, directly and out loud, that she wanted to enter these gates and to ask for guidance on actually doing so. This was a powerful practice for her. In subsequent visualizations we worked through her fears and resistances. Through deep feeling work and the meditation practices of this month, Diane was able to re-claim herself in a way that she never had before. It was not easy, but she felt stronger and found that she could set boundaries with people rather than compromising herself or selling herself short. She radiated a confidence that people found attractive, and she received several job offers.

In this month of Cheshwan, we are all challenged, like Diane, to let go of those things that do not support the newness in our lives. This may mean that we need to let go of friends or work, certainly of old, limiting expressions of self. This month offers an invitation to go into the depths of ourselves and uncover and reclaim the inner riches.

Energy: The Inner Work of Personal Transformation

In Cheshwan, we begin to do the hard inner work of spiritual and personal transformation. It is a time of review, reflection, and integration. As we begin to translate into reality the visions we received in Tishrei, we need to let go of the old, of what is not essential, and purify ourselves so that we are really able to contain the new. We do this letting go, this purifying, and this integration during this month of Cheshwan.

In many places in the world, the leaves have now mostly turned to beautiful colors and fallen to the ground, and the temperature is becoming colder. As we view the barren trees, we become aware of the cycles of life and of the cycles in our own lives, and we find that our attention is naturally directed inward, to the life that is below the surface reality.

In Cheshwan, we reenter the normal routine of life. True, it was during Tishrei that schools reopened and people returned from summer vacations with new energy and newly conceived projects, but many holidays occurred in Tishrei. It is in Cheshwan that people settle into their routines and the real work begins.

Because there are no holidays in Cheshwan, it is sometimes called Mar Cheshwan, which means "Bitter Cheshwan." It is, however, predicted that this month will inaugurate the Third Temple at the time of Messiah. This signifies that this month will be transformed into a very joyous time in the future.

If we celebrated the holidays of Tishrei in their true spirit and depth, we have opened and received many blessings. We have been inspired to make changes in ourselves and our lives. As we begin to consider the implementation of these changes and even begin to implement them in Cheshwan, we encounter our resistances to change. As much as we may want to change, forces within us are frightened of change and want things to remain the same. As we come up against these ego defenses and resistances, we become aware of deep-seated beliefs that shape our feelings and emotions and make it hard for us to change in the way we want. We may become discouraged and even question our capacity for real change during this month.

When this occurs, we need to contact the even deeper resolve of the soul to go forward in our lives, even if it is painful and difficult. Sometimes this commitment to go forward in our lives is possible only when we realize that we are up against the wall, that we are so unhappy in the way we are living, we are ready to do whatever it takes to change. This is often a significant turning point. When we recognize that there is no escape, nowhere to run, there are not even any holidays to help us transcend, we will settle down to do the work of this month. This is the spiritual opportunity and challenge of this month.

Without the anchor of holidays, there is a sense of falling in this month. We naturally identify with the leaves that have fallen and feel that we are also shedding parts of ourselves. Loss is a theme of this month. There is a noticeable increase in the breakup of relationships and the loss of jobs during this month. Do not be alarmed. This is not necessarily negative if we realize that falling is part of going forward. Each ascent is often preceded by a descent. When we can be with this process of falling without fear, we will ascend and be cleansed of what has limited us in the past. And it is through this process that we gain greater faith in ourselves and in God.

As we find ourselves becoming more aware of and contacting the shadowy parts of ourselves during this month, we can begin to transmute them into light. What we know about, what is in our awareness, will change even by virtue of our awareness and acceptance of it. What we resist, what we deny, will continue to occupy psychic space within us, and we will be at the mercy of our own unconsciousness.

This month healing is through the sense of smell. The sense of smell is the one sense that was not involved in the sin of Adam and Eve in the Garden of Eden. They saw, they touched, and they ate of the tree, but it does not say that they smelled the tree. The sense of smell is the most refined and spiritual of all the senses. The sense of smell is likened to the intuition of the soul. It is this sense that needs to be heightened during this month.

In purifying the sense of smell, we become sensitized to the inner essence of things. And when we do this, things become clear. We need to develop our capacity to "smell," to penetrate to the essence of what is before us. Our minds tell us many things, our emotions tell us more, but the sense of smell that informs us about the essence of things is what we need to listen to during this month.

Kabbalah teaches us that fragrance is not really a physical thing, but is connected to the soul. The more alive, the purer something is, the better its fragrance. During the Havdalah service that marks the separation of the Sabbath from the weekday, we smell pleasant spices to ease the soul's pain as it leaves the sanctity of the Sabbath.

Cheshwan is also called Chodesh Bul. "Bul" is taken from the word *mabul,* which means "flood." The flood that we read about in the Bible began on the seventeenth of Cheshwan and continued to the twenty-seventh of Cheshwan in the following year. It is said that every year until the time of the building of the First Temple in Jerusalem by King Solomon, which was completed in this month, it rained for a forty-day period that included the whole month of Mar Cheshvan.

Even today, it rains a lot during this month in Israel, and even in New York. Prayers for rain are recited daily. Water is a prominent element in the cleansing and preparing of the environment for the upcoming winter. Characteristic of this month of Scorpio, a water sign, water is the purifier and cleanser. Water removes what is not essential.

General Guidelines and Goals

The following guidelines and goals enable us to direct our energies in the ways that are optimal for our growth and transformation in accordance with the energy of this month. It is recommended that you read and meditate upon them often in the course of the month. Reflect on their applicability to you, and allow them to direct and inspire you often this month.

1. ENGAGE IN SELF-INQUIRY.

Give yourself time this month to observe your negative thinking patterns. What kinds of negative thoughts do you repeat to yourself? When are they triggered? How much time do you spend in negative thinking? How often do you feel depressed? To what do you attribute the depression?

Upon observation and inquiry, we may find that the negative thoughts we repeat in our minds reflect many beliefs about ourselves and life that are not true, yet we live our lives as if they were. If we are feeling sad, depressed, angry, or confused, it behooves us to examine what our underlying beliefs are behind the feelings. We need to consider whether these beliefs are essentially true. For example, a person may attribute her unhappiness to not having the right job or earning enough money. This, however, may not be the true basis for her unhappiness, for it is quite possible for a person to be happy regardless of the work she does. Another person may say he is unhappy because he does not have the kind of intimate relationship he wants with another person. This may also not be the true cause of his unhappiness, although he believes it is.

> *Our true happiness does not come from outside of us. It is not determined externally or artificially.*

Our true happiness does not come from outside of us. It is not determined externally or artificially. It is not true that we need to have personal achievements and possessions to be happy. This may be the desire of the ego, but it is not that of the soul. Begin to differentiate between the needs of the ego and those of the soul. Affirm that you have what you want and are able to receive in your life right now.

2. OWN YOUR OWN PROJECTIONS.

If we see something we do not like in someone else, we often need to rectify that quality within ourselves. For example, if we are angry at others for not loving us the way we want to be loved, we need to look at whether we are loving ourselves the way we need to be loved. If we see others as judgmental and critical of us, we need to practice loving and accepting ourselves as we are right now.

Generally, people waste a lot of energy thinking about and blaming other people. We want others to change, so they will meet our needs, rather than change ourselves.

When we blame others, we are weakened, and we are unable to truly move forward. We need to focus on ourselves, not on others. Make an effort in this month to assume responsibility for your own life. Investigate the ways that you sabotage yourself, but be careful not to blame yourself.

3. DEVELOP GREATER TRUST AND FAITH.

As we move forward, we become aware of the fears that have limited us in the past. What we fear often points to the direction we need to go in to experience more expansiveness and freedom in our lives. Interestingly, we do not fear things we have no connection to or possibility of achieving. For example, I have no fear of becoming the president of the United States, but I might fear buying my first house; the former is highly unlikely, but the latter is within my reach.

Fear is most often a barrier we need to cross on our path of growth. Trust in God and in ourselves enables us to go through these barriers more easily. The mind can give us many reasons to not do what we are afraid of doing. What enables us to go through our fear is faith. Faith is not just the passive belief in a Being external to us, but rather the experience of this Being within us. When we go through our fears, we feel so much more energy and freedom.

4. LOVE YOURSELF UNCONDITIONALLY.

Loving ourselves unconditionally means accepting ourselves as we are right now, with all our imperfections and shortcomings. Unconditional love is the willingness to be with ourselves fully, to feel our feelings without having to change them or do something about them. We do not need to do something to be loveable; we are intrinsically loveable. We need to know and experience that about ourselves.

Loving ourselves unconditionally is new for many of us because we received negative messages and internalized them as children. We do not feel worthy of being loved as we are and we continue to judge ourselves, others, and even God harshly. We often compare ourselves to others and fall short in our estimation, or we project our short-comings onto others and blame them for the feelings we have inside ourselves. We fail to turn to God because we feel that God will not think us worthy of His love or that God will punish us. Take note of this tendency this month and be gentle with yourself. Many shadow parts of yourself and others will surface this month, asking to be loved and redeemed. Practice unconditional love this month—of yourself and others.

Astrological Sign: Scorpio

Cheshwan corresponds to the astrological sign of Scorpio. Pluto, the ruler of Scorpio, was known in mythology as the lord of hidden wealth. Many of the earth's important resources, such as iron, gold, silver, oil, and minerals, are hidden below the ground. To find the resources, one needs to be willing to dig deeply, to get down in the dirt and mud to uncover and sort out the inner riches. This is what the energy of this month of going beneath the surface is all about.

In the inward journey to the depths that occurs this month, be aware that the energy of Pluto is sometimes very intense and often ruthless, forcing us to let go of at-tachments, sometimes those we hold most dear. We are often thrown out of our com-fort zone this month.

Scorpio is also a water sign. Unlike the astrological sign of Cancer, which is also a water sign, whose emotions ride the waves and tides of the moon, the emotions of Scorpio are intense, underground, and steady. The sign of Scorpio is associated with the scorpion, the eagle, and the phoenix, the mythological bird that rose from the ashes of destruction. The scorpion is dangerous, the eagle soars high, and the phoenix renews itself from death—this is the emotional range of Scorpio reflecting the energy of this month.

As we witness the workings of the mind this month, we may become aware of the destructive thoughts of the poisonous scorpion and feel its sting. It is generally known that you do not want to hurt a Scorpio because he or she will seek revenge and not easily forgive being slighted.

Scorpio is also represented by an eagle. This month our consciousness can soar upward to new heights and swoop down to new depths as an eagle. The deeper we go inside, the more we will uncover and the more expanded we will feel.

And, most important this month, what was destroyed may take new inner and outer forms like the phoenix. Cheshwan is a month of transformation and change. As the ruler of the dead, Pluto symbolizes the transcendent forces that cause death to the old and give life to new visions.

People born under the sign of Scorpio are said to have an extremely emotionally sensitive disposition. If emotions are channeled positively, they have the potential to penetrate the depths of life; if not, they can fall easily into depravity. Such ultrasensitivity may cause them to be withdrawn and hidden.

Hebrew Letter: Nun

 נ The Hebrew letter for Cheshwan is the nun. In Aramaic the word *nun* means "fish." In kabbalah, fish have great significance. The *tzaddik* (the righteous, perfected person) is said to reincarnate as a fish. When I asked my teacher why this is so, I was told the following: Fish swim in water, and their eyes are always open. All their needs are met and they are said to be pure, with no self consciousness. The nun directs us to acquire the attributes of the fish particularly this month.

Kabbalah divides souls into two categories: *leviathan* ("fish") and *behamot* ("animal"). Through *gematria,* the kabbalistic practice of assigning numerical value to letters and making connections between words having the same numerical value, we discover that the words *leviathan* and *malchut* ("kingdom") have the same numerical value. That informs us that there is a connection between these words. Understanding the connection between these words sheds light on the energy of this month. The *sephira* (divine emanation) of *malchut* is represented by King David. This is an allusion to the Messiah, for the Messiah comes from the House of David. This is further corroborated by the fact that the nun is the fourteenth letter of the Hebrew alphabet and the numerical values for the letters in the name David equal fourteen. As mentioned, it is said that the Third Temple, in which the Messiah will be revealed, will be established in this month.

The nun is associated with the word *nefilah,* "falling." Kabbalah teaches the concept of descent for the purposes of ascent. Because of the descent, a person can rise higher than before. We see this principle demonstrated in the way people grow and become better people through the mistakes they make. But it is also true ontologically. The soul's entry into the physical world is a descent for the purpose of ascent. The soul enters into a physical body to raise itself up, to purify, to do good, and make rectification in a way that can only be done in the physical world. In so doing, the soul can go higher than if it remained solely in the spiritual world.

Interestingly, the Messiach, the Messiah, the highest person, the redeemer of the Jewish people and the world, comes from lowly and impure origins. We learn from the Torah and kabbalah that the Messiah is of the lineage that began with the illicit affair that Yehuda (Judah), the fourth son of Jacob, had with his daughter-in-law, who was disguised as a prostitute, and also from the incestuous affair of Lot and his daughters. Given the emphasis that Judaism places on sexual purity, you might not expect the redeemer of the world to have these soul roots. This is, however, in line with the energy of this month and the Jewish perspective that negativity will ultimately be transformed and redeemed. Because the Messiah represents the highest form of spiritual evolution, his origins are in the lowest place.

Hebrew Tribe: Menashah

Menashah was the firstborn son of Joseph, born to him when he was in Egypt. When Joseph named him, he said, "For God said He has made me forget all my toil and all my father's house" (Gen. 41:51). The birth of Menashah gave Joseph perspective and the ability to release the pain and suffering he had experienced earlier in his life.

Having been born in Egypt, a word translated to mean "narrow straits," a place of impurity and limitation, Menashah had the unique ability to uproot negativity and evil, characteristic of the energy of this month. The unique capacity to defeat evil within oneself and in the world was demonstrated by Menashah's descendent Gideon, who led a victorious battle against the Midianites (Judg. 6–8). The Midianites had posed a threat to the integrity of the Jewish people. The word Midian relates to the word *madon,* which means "strife." It refers to the psychic force within us that causes strife and disunity.

The army of Gideon circled the Midian nation, carrying shofars and earthen jugs with torches in them. They blew the shofars, broke their jugs, and waved their torches, lighting up the sky, overwhelming and defeating the Midianites, and winning the battle without raising a sword. During Cheshwan, we must fight our own negativity by remembering the divine call of the shofar, break our earthen jugs, which represents the opening of our hearts, and wave our torches of spiritual awareness, and the negativity within us will be dissolved.

Though Menashah was the firstborn of Joseph, he did not receive the blessing of the firstborn. That blessing was given to his younger brother, Ephraim, who represents the previous month of Tishrei. Unlike the animosity that occurred between Jacob and Esau over the blessings of the firstborn, there was no jealousy or anger on the part of Menashah. This represented a tremendous fixing of the jealousy between Esau and Jacob and between Joseph and his brothers, who sold him into slavery.

The letters of Menashah, when rearranged, spell *neshama,* which means "soul," or *neshima,* which means "breath." Breath and soul are bound up with each other: "God breathes into us a pure soul." Both are connected with the sense of smell, the area of healing for this month. Though we smell by breathing through the nose, smell is a sense of the soul that refers to our intuition and ability to discern the essence of the matter. This kind of discernment is a primary mode of transformation for this month.

Divine Name Permutation: VHHY

In reviewing the Divine Name permutation for this month, we see that the yud (Y) occupies the position of the world of Assiyah, this physical world, indicating that the activity in this physical world is reduced. It is not particularly a time to go forward in major ways. It may be difficult to do so now, so be patient. The hay (H) in the worlds of Yetzerah and Beriyah indicates that the flow of light is greatest in these worlds. So the focus this month is for expansion in one's thinking and in the heart, in one's emotions. The vav (V) in the world of Atzilut, the first position, indicates that there is a great influx of divine energy in the highest world of Atzilut, the spiritual world closest to Ain Sof (the kabbalistic term for unknowable God). Indicators from the permutation align with what has been said about the energy of this month—working through one's thinking and feelings.

Torah Portions

The Torah portion for Cheshwan begins with Noah and the Flood in Genesis 6:9–11:32. This flood caused the destruction of the world except for Noah, his family, and representatives of the animal species who would begin the world anew. Even though it was only in the last Torah portion that the story of creation was related, human beings engaged in such wicked behavior that it was necessary for the world to be purified. As we read about Noah and the Flood, we are reminded that we need to let go and be cleansed of the parts of ourselves that are not in alignment with our true nature and what we opened to in the last month.

It is interesting that God told Noah to build an ark, which took time to do. People had an opportunity to investigate what was happening and be included in the ark if they desired. The ark provided the sanctuary for maintaining the purity of the divine intention. Similarly, in this month, we must build an ark within ourselves to afford us that safety and security. We must go deep inside ourselves to find that place where we are in contact with the purity of our soul. There will be floods in the forms of challenges in the course of one's life, and particularly during this month. Our internal ark will serve us through these times. Through crisis, we can let go of negativity and be purified and strengthened.

The Hebrew word for ark is *teva,* which also means "word." The arks we build in our lives are the words of prayer and blessing. Such positive words provide a sanctuary for us, and we need to fortify ourselves with them. We need to be aware of our thoughts and the conversations we have with ourselves this month. What thoughts do you allow into your inner sanctuary? Many thoughts may enter the mind, but they do not gain a foothold in the self unless we give them energy.

The Torah portion of Noah is followed by the Torah portion of Lech Lecha (Gen. 12). This portion contains a powerful and important message for this month. *Lech lecha* literally means "come to yourself." These were the first instructions that Abraham received from God. He was told, "Leave your land, your family, and your father's house to the land that I will show you" (Gen. 12:1). These words contain important instructions for those of us who are committed to a spiritual journey as well.

People have to leave the external influences that have had an impact on their identity if they are to discover their true selves. Unless we inquire into those influences and exercise discernment, it is quite possible that we will live the life that other people want for us and not the life that expresses our potential and essence. For example, people sometimes get married or choose a profession not because it is what they really want, but because they think it will give them the parental love and approval they want. Though this choice may not have been a conscious one at the time, sometimes later in life they realize they are living a life script written for them by someone else.

Abraham models the steps a person takes on a spiritual journey. Like Abraham, who had to let go of all the attachments that shaped his sense of self and be in a state of not knowing to be a true servant of God, we also need to let go of the physical and emotional attachments that do not support the expression of our true essence. Like Abraham, we also need to contact the soul within and trust our own inner voice to guide us forward in our lives. This takes great faith, because there is not always clarity.

We have to transcend the mind. It is not always easy, but that does not make it impossible or inessential.

If the journey outlined by God for Abraham was intended to be a purely physical one, the instructions would have been phrased differently. Abraham would have first been told to leave his parents' home, then the birthplace, and finally the land. In fact it was the reverse: Abraham was first told to leave the land, then the birthplace, and then his father's home. The journey God directed Abraham to take was essentially a spiritual journey, one that mirrors the journey we each must take out of our own subjectivity.

It is easier to leave the external influences of one's land or one's culture than to leave the influences of one's family. Because we were so impressionable and vulnerable as infants and children, the impact of the family upon us is the greatest. This level of subjectivity is much more difficult to separate ourselves from because we often associate it with our intrinsic selves. We often believe the messages we received about who we were as children and continue to live from them. As a therapist, I see that often these messages are negative, limiting, and not true in essence. Much of therapy involves discernment and insight into our true nature through separating ourselves from the influences that have externally and internally affected our experience of ourselves. With this insight comes greater objectivity. With objectivity come freedom and choice.

In the next chapter of the Torah, *Veyara,* Abraham is worthy to receive the visitation of three angels (Gen. 18). Interestingly, the portion begins with "God appeared to him." It doesn't even mention Abraham's name. This indicates that Abraham had entered a state of *bittul,* a nullification of ego self, which made it possible to have the kind of revelation of God that he did.

Each angel who visits Abraham has its own mission. One heals him from his circumcision. Another angel prophesies the birth of Isaac, which soon comes true. The third informs him of the pending destruction of Sodom and Gomorrah. The Torah recounts in detail the pleading and bargaining that Abraham engages in on behalf of the people of these towns. This is a powerful demonstration of the *hesed* (loving-kindness) of Abraham, who prays for the most wicked of people.

Abraham continues to grow through many tests. He has to send his son Ishmael and his wife Hagar away, but his hardest test was the sacrifice of his son Isaac. This act went against everything Abraham stood for, yet he was willing to do it because it was what he thought God wanted. We each have our own tests, maybe not as dramatic as Abraham's, but, nevertheless, they are challenging and we grow through them.

The last Torah portion of the month is Chaya Sarah, the Life of Sarah, which is really an account of her death. In the midst of a Torah portion that begins with the death of Sarah and concludes with the death of Abraham (Gen. 23:1–25:17) is the marriage of Isaac. The Torah describes in much detail the selection of Rebecca as well as their meeting. The Torah tells us that Isaac married her, loved her, and that he was comforted in the loss of his mother. Here the cycle of life continues. The parents, Abraham and Sarah, die, the son, Isaac, marries, and a new generation will come into being.

The Torah portions outline a path for self-transformation characteristic of the energy of this month. First, it is necessary to find and build a place of safety within ourselves, which develops ego strength. We then have the strength to discern areas of subjectivity, and gaining objectivity then enables us to make real choices, as demonstrated in the Torah portion Lech Lecha. We gain the capacity to meet challenges that further refine and strengthen us. Through this process, we learn to nullify the ego and, as in the Torah portion Veyara, we begin to have God revelations and gain clarity of life purpose. Though the old will die, new life will be born, as in the Torah portion of Chaya Sarah.

Meditation

The following meditation will support your growth in accordance with the energy of this month, introspection and mindfulness.

Sit in a meditative posture comfortable for you and give yourself the time and space to be with yourself. Begin by taking deep breaths. Breathe in through the nostrils and exhale through the mouth. After a few minutes, breathe in and out through the nostrils. Let this be a time of self-inquiry, a time to be present to yourself as fully as possible.

Begin by observing the thoughts in your mind, your mental body. What is the conversation in your mind when you are not focusing on anything else? Witness the thoughts that pass through the mind. What thoughts grab your attention? What are the beliefs underlying these thoughts? What are the feelings accompanying these thoughts? Breathe into these thoughts and explore the emotions or feelings that come with them. Breathe and contact any emotions that are present, your emotional body. Give yourself the psychic space to be with any feelings that are occurring within you. Refrain from judging these feelings as good or bad, desirable or undesirable. Simply breathe, feel, be with, and release. Feelings do not need to be understood or make sense. They are not rational. Give yourself the time to be with your feelings, whatever they are. They contain deep wisdom within them.

Take time to explore the physical body. Take note of any sensations that are present for you on a physical level. The body does not lie and speaks to you in the form of sensations and tensions. Breathe and relax. You are a very large container. It is safe to feel your feelings.

When you feel complete for this seating, focus again on the breath and allow yourself to focus on the space between the breaths. Allow the mind to quiet. Simply be with the breath and experience the expansiveness within you. Appreciate the different states of consciousness.

Practical Recommendations

1. REVIEW THE GOALS YOU SET FOR YOURSELF IN THE PREVIOUS MONTH OF TISHREI.
   In Cheshwan, we begin to implement the vision we received in Tishrei. Reflect on whether you are taking the steps to realize the goals you set for yourself. What progress have you made toward realizing your goals and what resistances have you encountered either within yourself or in the external world? Make a note of this, and share it with a friend or write it in your journal.

2. UPDATE YOUR PLAN TO GO FORWARD IN YOUR LIFE IN THE WAY THAT YOU WANT.
   You may find that you now have more information than you did in Tishrei when you formulated your goals and strategies and you should consider making adjustments and modifications as needed. You may now have greater clarity about what you truly want and the capacity to articulate it to yourself as well as to others.

3. GIVE YOURSELF TIME TO MEDITATE AND FIND A PLACE OF REFUGE WITHIN YOURSELF.
   Finding a place of quiet and healing within yourself is important at all times, but is even more so now during this month. It is easier to go forward in your life if you are centered and relaxed. Make a schedule and commit to a daily practice of meditation. A meditation session can be very brief or extended. You can also meditate as you go

about your errands. Take deep breaths, quiet the mind, and allow yourself to be open and present. Be aware of the Divine Presence that surrounds you and is within you.

4. TALK TO GOD.

Talking to God is a powerful practice. This very cathartic experience helps people uncover broken and wounded parts of self and bring them into higher awareness. This is a potent practice any time of the year, but now, as we are shedding the old and not clear about the new, we need to receive higher guidance. God is a healer, God is a guide. When we make a God connection, our consciousness is lifted upward in ways that we might not have even imagined possible. Talk to God, then quiet your mind, and listen deeply.

5. SPEND TIME IN THE NATURAL WORLD, PARTICULARLY IN PLACES THAT EXHIBIT THE NATURAL CYCLES.

Spending time in the natural world aids in learning how to let go and flow with the cycles of life. This year I spent several days in the country during Cheshwan, and I had occasion to watch the trees as their leaves turned and fell to the ground. Witnessing how the trees gracefully shed their leaves and then stood tall and barren inspired me and helped me to accept the changes that were occurring within me at this time of the year.

A Tale to Live By

The following is a favorite story about the power of unconditional love to transform and redeem the negative and shadowy parts of ourselves and others. Let this story remind us to love fully and unconditionally during the times when we might tend to judge harshly.

There were three rebbes-in-training with the mission of raising money for the dowry of a poor bride, one of whom was Reb Shneur Zalman of Liadi, who later founded the Lubavitch movement. In the town was Moshele the miser. Though he was a wealthy man, he had the reputation of never giving money to anyone. When Reb Shneur Zalman suggested that they all go to ask Moshele for the money, his companions laughed and told him it would be a waste of time. He insisted, and they were soon knocking at his door.

Moshele graciously invited them in, surprised that rabbis would be visiting him. After brief formalities, Reb Zalman explained the purpose of the visit. Moshele was inwardly disappointed and felt that these rabbis only visited him and professed to care about him because they wanted money from him. Though he did not express his disappointment directly, he angrily criticized them and called them hypocrites for being only interested in the money.

In his anger Moshele threw one penny on the floor and haughtily said to Reb Zalman, "This is for you." The other rabbis were angry, but Reb Zalman quieted his companions, bent down to pick up the penny, and thanked Moshele profusely. As they left with penny in hand, he thanked him again, looked him in the eye, and told him that he was a good man.

They were only a few feet from the house when Moshele ran out to stop them. He then threw another penny on the ground in front of Reb Zalman. The other rabbis were again protesting, ready to beat Moshele up for being so disrespectful, but Reb Zalman quieted them once again, telling them that Moshele was a good man. He again bent down to pick up the coin, looked Moshele in the eye, and thanked him profusely. This went on a few more times, and each time Reb Zalman thanked Moshele from his heart. Soon Moshele was giving larger amounts to Reb Zalman, who thanked him each time as if it were the first time.

Soon Moshele was lifted up so high by his encounter with Reb Zalman that he asked Reb Zalman if he could give him all the money he was looking to raise for the poor bride. And he did that. No longer a miser, transformed by this experience, Moshele became a generous benefactor of Reb Zalman.

Kislev

MONTH: *November-December*

ENERGY: *Rekindling Dreams*

AREA OF HEALING: *Sleep*

ASTROLOGICAL SIGN: *Sagittarius*

HEBREW LETTER: *Samech*

HEBREW TRIBE: *Benjamin*

DIVINE NAME PERMUTATION: *VYHH*

HOLIDAY: *Chanukah*

Many people have a vision of what they want to do in their lives, yet they hold back, fearing rejection or failure. They consequently feel depressed that they are not realizing their potential or life purpose. Because they are doubtful of their capacity to be successful, their self-esteem plummets. This phenomenon is all too common. If this is true for you, take heart. This is a month of going forward. I see with so many of my therapy clients as well as in my own life that tremendous leaps in growth are possible during this month.

One of my clients, Marcy, a senior in high school, was feeling overwhelmed about the process of applying for college for next year. She had always assumed she would go to college, but now she was questioning this assumption—and everything else. Feeling intimidated and frightened by the prospect of leaving home for the uncharted territory of college and fearing rejection from colleges, she delayed completing the applications in a timely fashion. This only compounded her anxiety and made the task harder. She felt overwhelmed, incompetent, and powerless. She wished that someone would tell her what to do and then do it for her. She felt very alone, embarrassed to share her feelings with her parents and teachers.

Marcy was counseled to avail herself of the energies of this month. Opening to God's support through prayer, meditation, and affirmation, she realized that she was not alone. She could draw on this support and be calmed and comforted. She practiced affirmations and affirmed that she could do what was in the realm of her own capabilities and then trust in God for the right outcome of her efforts. Learning to relax and trust empowered her to do what she needed to do. She was able to ask for help. She selected a variety of colleges, a few of them far away and others close to home, so that she would be able to make choices at the appropriate time. Through this process, she gained greater self-confidence and self-esteem, which enabled her to express herself in other areas of her life as well. She was more open and playful this month as a whole.

Energy: Rekindling Dreams

The days are getting shorter and the nights longer. It is one of the darkest times of the year, yet Kislev is a time of expansiveness, travel, and going forward in life. The energy of this month is about actualizing dreams and visions and going forward in one's life with trust and faith. Natural optimism, hope, confidence, and faith are easily accessible during this month to support rekindling dreams. This is a month of miracles and redemption.

Tishrei saw us opening to newness and reflecting on what we want in our lives, and in Cheshwan we did the hard inner work of shedding the past and letting go. Now, in Kislev, is the time to rekindle our deepest dreams, to embrace all the possibilities before us, and be empowered to go for what we want. I know so many people who are going for what they want in this month. Sheila went to China. Elliot began a new business. David applied for a grant for independent study. Look around at those you know this month and you will see that people are on the move.

We are able to go forward and take risks this month because Kislev is actually a time of deepening faith and trust in God. Kislev is an auspicious time to meditate on one's life purpose and receive important guidance. It is a time of clarity. Because there is a God in this world, life is always full of synchronicity, but particularly in this month we see the Divine Hand in what happens to us and in the world. One of the signs that we are living in accordance with our life purpose and Divine Will is that we are happy and are experiencing the magic and abundance of life. We receive many signs from the universe providing feedback that we are on course. Small miracles seem commonplace, an everyday occurrence. This awareness fills us with gratitude. The whole month is a time of thanksgiving. It is no accident that the secular American holiday of Thanksgiving occurs during this month.

The whole month is shaped by the holiday of Chanukah, the holiday of miracles that occurs at the end of the month, the darkest time of the year. As we celebrate this holiday with the lighting of candles, we learn experientially a most important and deep truth about life: there is light amidst the darkness. At the darkest time, there is light and there will be light. Actually, the light in the darkness shines even more brightly because of the darkness that surrounds it.

Chanukah is the celebration of the rededication of the Holy Temple in Jerusalem in 164 B.C.E. At that time, the Temple, the site of the most holy, intimate place of divine connection, had been violated by Greeks. Foreign practices and influences infiltrated the psyche of the Jewish people, threatening belief in the divinity of God. The Greeks believed in the reasoning powers of the mind, what is logical and rational, and used this philosophy to undermine the intrinsic faith of the Jews in the Divine.

Like the Maccabeans, who redeemed the Temple in ancient times, during this month we redeem the Holy Temple within us. Much more than a physical place, the Holy Temple represents to us today the holiest and most pure dimension within us. It is the seat of our deepest hopes and our visions of life, which are beyond the mind, not bound by the laws of reason or logic. The oil used for the rededication of the Temple was pure and undefiled, reminding us of the possibility of returning to a state of original purity. The miracle of the rededication was that, although there was only enough oil to burn for one day, it lasted for eight days. It was not logical, but God is beyond logic.

During this month, we too leave the shackles of the limiting logical Greek mind and open to greater faith. When we are limited by the mind, we are always tied down to what is known and familiar; we seek to understand why and how. Faith by definition is beyond the reasoning powers of the mind. Faith enables us to be present, to not dwell in the past or worry about the future, but live moment to moment fully with trust and fearlessness. It is faith, not the mind, that opens us to new possibilities and new dimensions, enabling us to go forward in ways that we could not do solely on our own.

> *It is faith, not the mind, that opens us to new possibilities and new dimensions, enabling us to go forward in ways that we could not do solely on our own.*

This month is a time when we go beyond what is logical, and go for what we really want. This may be different than what we feel we want. In determining what we really want, we may still need to sift and distill our visions to make sure they are not contaminated by the ego mind and come from the purest place within us. To know what we really want inside, we have to listen to what God wants for us.

By a simple allowing and deep listening on our part, this deep part within us, the light of our highest soul connection with the Divine may emerge to shine upon us and guide us during this month. When we do this, we may experience miracles. This is the month of miracles. With the light of Chanukah, we see even the ordinary aspects of life as miraculous.

Though the name Kislev itself is Babylonian in origin, the word *kis* in Hebrew means "pocket" and *lev* means "heart." This has been said to refer to the capacity to be a vessel for what your heart desires. Very often people may want and want, but they do not know how to receive what they want into their life. They therefore stay in a place of wanting. During this month we have a greater capacity to actually receive what we want, by just a small allowing within ourselves. By the way, according to the Talmud, Kislev has also meant a time of unexpected money.

The first letters of Kislev (kuf, samech) spell out *khes,* which means "hidden," and the last two letters, lamed and vav, equal thirty-six. This is a reference to the thirty-six candles that are lit during the holiday of Chanukah, as well as the hidden thirty-six righteous people who sustain the world. Though this is physically a dark time, there is a hidden, inner light shining brightly this month.

The healing area of this month is sleep. Though we sleep every night, it is still a mystery how we sleep and what occurs to us during sleep. Though we have some choice about when and how we sleep, we all have to sleep whether we want to or not. Just as we feel trust in God to go forward in our lives this month, we also demonstrate our trust in God through sleep. When we can let go into the mystery of sleep and sleep deeply, we emerge rested and renewed. So much healing occurs during a sleep state. Though sleep is likened to one-sixtieth of death, it is also a time of vision. When we sleep, we are told, our soul is able to ascend to the higher worlds. Those who have purified their consciousness may receive true vision and understanding through dreams. Many dreams may be prophetic.

This is the time to pay attention to your dreams. We read the Torah portions this month about Joseph, who was a master of prophetic dreams as well as of interpreting dreams. King Solomon was also said to receive much prophecy during a sleep state. When I first began teaching Jewish meditation, I used to receive instruction when I was in a sleep state. Before teaching, rather than preparing and thinking about what I would do, I would go to sleep and have spiritual conversations with my teachers.

As the nights get longer and it gets cold outside, you may find yourself wanting to sleep a little longer, which is fine. It is even good to allow yourself to sleep longer than usual. Sleep is not a waste of time, but provides an opportunity to live in another dimension.

The healing of sleep also means that this is a time when we should wake up from the sleepy dimension that we usually live in. When we sleep, we should sleep deeply. When we are awake, we should not be sleeping.

General Guidelines and Goals

The following guidelines and goals enable us to direct our energies in the ways that are optimal for our growth and transformation in accordance with the energy of this month. It is recommended that you read and meditate upon them often in the course of the month. Reflect on their applicability to you, and allow them to direct and inspire you often this month.

1. GIVE YOURSELF TIME TO DREAM YOUR DREAMS.

You have the right to dream. Your dreams speak the messages of the soul. They need not be logical. This is the month of paying attention to your dreams, listening to the part of yourself that is beyond the rational mind. During this month, we reclaim the pure faith of the child within who believes in miracles.

Close your eyes and allow images and visions to emerge about yourself and your life. Quiet your mind and listen to what you really want in your life. Who are you? How do you live your life? What kind of work do you do? What kinds of relationships do you have?

As a child, you may have had many dreams for yourself. What were they? Some of these dreams you may have realized, some you may have abandoned, as you thought they were not practical or possible, and others you partially fulfilled through improvisation and compromise. Some of these dreams you may now want to revisit in a different form. Give yourself time this month to pay attention to your dreams and hopes.

2. MEDITATE ON DIVINE LIGHT EACH DAY.

In Kislev we celebrate the miracle of light in darkness. We meditate on lights during Chanukah and Shabbat (the Sabbath), but the practice of meditating on Divine Light is not to be confined to just those times. God's light is always present for those who yearn for it. It will heal and transform you. It will cleanse you of negativity and impurity. Meditating on Divine Light is a foundational practice of Jewish meditation.

When you sit down for meditation, open yourself as if you were a vessel and ask to be filled with Divine Light. Ask to be aware of the Divine Light that surrounds you all the time. The experience of God's light is very accessible, but you must want it sincerely. Whenever you have a free moment, feel your yearning for Divine Light and allow yourself to visualize and draw this experience to you.

When you find that your mind is filled with negative thoughts, wherever you are, even if you are out on the street doing your errands, stop for a moment, take a few deep breaths, and be aware that God's light is everywhere. Breathe in God's light.

3. SEEK HOW TO GO FORWARD IN YOUR LIFE RATHER THAN UNDERSTANDING WHY YOU CAN'T.

The mind always wants to understand; it seeks answers, reasons, and justifications. It is not often a fruitful inquiry. I believe a limitation in some talk therapies is that they are confined to talking, seeking to understand the reasons for a person's suffering with the very mind that is the cause of the suffering. Understanding does not necessarily change things. It may be interesting, but it doesn't always make a difference.

Note the tendency in the mind to try to understand, explain, and justify why you are not living your dreams and assert your intention to not be limited by the mind. Breathe and connect with God. Know that when we align our intention with the Divine, we are not limited. Tap into the natural faith within, for faith enables us to leave the place of limitation within the mind without even knowing how or why. Transformation is the bottom line.

4. STRENGTHEN A "CAN DO" ATTITUDE WITHIN YOURSELF.

This is the month to go forward. Know that often when we live our vision and bring new things into our life, fears of the unknown or of failing may surface. As much as we want change, as much as we want more light and joy, we are resistant and frightened by change. This is natural. Don't let your fear or your resistances stop or limit you now.

Strengthen your belief and trust in God with prayer and meditation. Strengthen yourself with affirmations. Strengthen yourself by doing *mitzvot*. A *mitzvah* is a good deed prescribed by the Torah. Each time we do a *mitzvah,* we make a connection to the Divine. This gives us strength that we would not have on our own.

5. REDEDICATE YOURSELF TO THE PURITY OF THE HOLY TEMPLES IN YOUR LIFE.

There are many holy temples, those places where the divine presence lives, in our lives. For example, our body is a holy temple for the soul. Our intimate relationships with our spouse, our parents, our children, our friends are holy temples. Our synagogues, places of communal worship, are also holy temples. This month is a time to purify these places. Relationships may easily be strengthened at this time. As we purify our consciousness, we are able to receive clearer vision.

6. PRACTICE GRATITUDE.

The whole month of Kislev is a time for thanksgiving and praising God. Sometimes in our lives we experience God's hand very directly, and at other times it is very subtle and we may be unaware or take for granted all the miracles, growth opportunities, and blessings we are given each day. Make a conscious effort to practice gratitude. Savor all the blessings that are part of your life. Keep a journal to record insights and experiences of gratitude on a daily or weekly basis.

Astrological Sign: Sagittarius

Sagittarius is represented by the centaur, a mythological creature that is half man and half horse. The horse portion represents animal energy and the drive for freedom; the human portion poised with a bow indicates the ability to direct consciousness above the instinctual animal level. Sometimes Sagittarius is represented by an archer. The glyph for Sagittarius is also plainly an arrow. The arrow expresses the desire to go forward, to explore and reach beyond oneself. A new vision is possible in Sagittarius.

Sagittarius is a fire sign. The energy of the month and the people who are born in it are fiery, inspirational, and expressive. Enthusiasm and passion are directed upward and outward in a way that has not occurred in the previous months.

Sagittarius is ruled by the planet Jupiter. In mythology, Jupiter (also called Jove, Zeus) was the king of the gods. The energy of Jupiter is expansive, beneficent, and optimistic. Jupiter sees the larger vision and opens doors to new plans, aspirations, and growth opportunities. There is an adventurous and freedom-loving spirit and the willingness to take risks this month. Travel is indicated.

The energy of Sagittarius encourages us to explore other cultures, to pursue advanced studies, and formulate ethical, philosophical, and religious principles to build life upon. Sagittarius rules the ninth house, which is the house of philosophy, religion, and higher education. People born under this sign are generally exuberant, positive thinking, good humored.

Hebrew Letter: Samech

The samech looks like a circle and is one of two letters that are totally closed. The shape of a circle has many important properties. First, a circle is a closed system; one feels protected in a circle. Second, a circle reminds us of the transcendence of God, for each point on the circle is equidistant from the center. All souls are in essence equidistant from or equally close to God.

Third, a circle is continuous. You can't tell the beginning from the end of the circle. Every point in the circle is both a beginning and an end. The samech, through its circular shape, reminds us that life is an endless cycle. Things may seem to be breaking down, but they are really continuing in another form, and this form will change yet again. This symbol has particular meaning during this month when there continue to be so many changes occurring on the physical plane. The samech is also likened to a wedding ring, which also reminds of the covenant between God and the Jewish people.

The word *samech* means "to support." Significance is found in the fact that the samech follows the nun, last month's letter, which means "falling." In King David's psalm of Ashrei (Ps. 145) it says, *"Samech Hashem lecol hanoflim,"* "God supports those who fall." Support means being with, descending so as to lift upward. Everything in life goes through a cycle, of falling and being lifted upward. Kislev lifts up the month of Cheshwan. The word *smeicha* also begins with a samech. *Smeicha* is a support whereby the teacher lifts the student to become a teacher himself.

Together the nun and the samech spell out *nais,* which means "miracle." This month is truly a month when there is divine support to go forward, to experience miracles within our lives.

Sefer Yetzirah, an ancient book of mysticism from which this material derives, says that "God coronated the samech with the attribute of sleep." The samech helps us to overcome our spiritual slumber and awaken to go forward and realize our dreams. The healing of this month is through sleep. The numerical equivalent of samech is sixty. It is said that sleep is one-sixtieth of death, and a dream is one-sixtieth of prophecy. This is also an allusion to the importance of dreams this month.

Hebrew Tribe: Benjamin

After many years of infertility, Rachel gave birth to a second son (her first son was Joseph). Knowing that she was dying, during the birth she cried out his name, *"Ben oni,"* which means "son of affliction" (Gen. 35:18). Though she died, her son lived on, echoing the theme of light in darkness of this month.

Not wanting his son to bear such a negative name, Jacob changed it to *Ben yamin,* which means either "son of the south," "son of the right," or "son of days." South refers to "love," for the emanation of *hesed* ("loving-kindness") emerges from the south, according to kabbalah. "Right" also refers to *hesed,* as *hesed* is on the right side of the Tree of Life.

Benjamin was the only son of Jacob born in the land of Israel. Just as Israel is associated with a higher level of divine providence than any other place, Kislev receives a higher degree of divine providence than any other month. The way the Torah speaks of Benjamin informs us about the energy of this month: "And of Benjamin he said, The beloved of the Eternal shall dwell in safety by him. He shall harbor him all day long and he shall dwell between his shoulders" (Deut. 33:12). The Torah is telling us that this month of Kislev is a beloved month and there is a special sense of divine protection available this month.

The land of Benjamin included the Temple Mount, the location of the Holy Temple. The Temple, rededicated this month, was the site of the greatest vision and dreams for humanity, ultimately, a place of worship for all nations. Worthy of containing this holiest site, Benjamin was seen to be the tribe of great vision, as is this entire month.

Divine Name Permutation: VYHH

In examining the permutation for this month, we see that there is expansiveness in the world of Assiyah, the physical world, and in Yetzerah, the world of the heart and angels, by the positioning of the hay (H). This is a time of action in the physical world as well as a time of opening and allowing the heart to guide you. The yud (Y), which is a small letter, in the world of Beriyah indicates that the mind must be contracted, focused, and made small, so the light from above may shine through. The vav (V), the letter that makes connections, in the position of the world of Atzilut indicates that there is abundant light being drawn through the higher worlds. The drawing of the light initially comes from the world of Assiyah, which is a large container and vessel for Divine Light.

Torah Portions

The themes of this month are echoed in the Torah portions, which provide important and relevant spiritual guidance for this month. The Torah portions for this month begin with Vayetze (Gen. 28:10–29:35), which recounts Jacob's departure from his parents' home after stealing the blessings from his brother Esau. In keeping with Kislev as the month of dreams and visions, the Torah portion includes Jacob's dream vision of a ladder, standing on the ground and reaching up into heaven, with angels ascending and descending it. Through this vision Jacob receives a prophecy about the future of the Jewish people, how long and how many times they will be exiled from the land of Israel and how they will ultimately return. He is assured that God is with him and that he will be blessed to continue in the lineage of his grandfather, Abraham, and his father, Isaac. He says, "God is truly in this place. . . . How awe-inspiring this place is. It is a gateway to heaven" (Gen. 28:16–17). This is the consciousness that we need to open to this month. Like Jacob we need to go forward as we are guided.

Representing the energy of this month, Jacob goes forward and soon marries. His wives, Leah and Rachel, and their maids, Bilhah and Zilpah, all bear him children. He also works hard and business thrives. Abundance is a theme this month.

Jacob had wanted to marry Rachel—he loved her upon seeing her—but he is deceived into marrying Leah. Just as he had deceived his father to receive the blessings, so he was deceived. There is always karma in all our actions, but that does not mitigate the blessings.

In the next Torah portion, Va Yishlach (Gen. 32:4–37), Jacob is returning to Israel and is afraid that his brother Esau will kill him. Even though he is afraid, he does not let the fear stop him. He prays, but he is also practical and makes various contingency plans for dealing with Esau. He will bribe him or fight him if necessary. This is seen to be a model of how to deal with a possible enemy: pray, bribe, and prepare for war. In a life-transformational struggle with an angel Jacob's name is changed to Israel. In this way, he earns the blessings he originally stole. As a result, the meeting with Esau was positive and healing.

The next Torah portion, *Vayeishev,* focuses on Joseph, the first son of Rachel (Gen. 37:1–40:23). Again we see the theme of dreams, for Joseph's prophetic dreams so enraged his brothers that they conspired to kill him. Ultimately they sell him into slavery and Joseph has to undergo many tests.

The month usually ends with Joseph in prison interpreting the dreams of the baker, the butler, and then of Pharaoh. Joseph then is lifted up to a high government position in Egypt, demonstrating the miraculous energy of this month. Second only to Pharaoh, Joseph is responsible for administering the distribution of food during the famine. The famine causes the brothers of Joseph to travel into Egypt and they are soon in front of Joseph, who recognizes them.

People wonder why Joseph does not reveal his identity to his brothers at this time. Why does he put them through so many tests? The Rambam (Maimonides) said that Joseph understood that his initial dreams that made his brothers so jealous of him had to be fulfilled and he would have to let things happen in a more hidden way. He also wanted to see if his brothers regretted selling him into slavery and whether they had changed. He knows that they have when Yehuda (Judah) offers to replace Benjamin as a captive.

The theme of redemption is found in the Torah portions of this month in two interesting stories providing the antecedents of the prophesized two messiahs Messiach ben Dovid and Messiach ben Joseph. Both Joseph and Yehuda, who represents the lineage of Dovid, faced sexual temptation. Joseph resisted the temptations of the wife of Potiphar and ended up in prison. Joseph represents the *tzaddik,* the pure, righteous person who suffers on behalf of others. Yehuda succumbed to his daughter-in-law, who was disguised as a prostitute, and fathered a child with her. Yehuda represents the *baal teshuva,* the person who does wrong, but acknowledges his or her guilt and repents.

Holiday

Chanukah

HISTORY   The conquest of Israel by Alexander the Great in the fourth century B.C.E. brought with it a blending of Eastern traditions and Greek culture that was called Hellenism. Hellenism was very revolutionary, cosmopolitan, and intellectual movement that attracted many Jews. A century later, Palestine was captured by the Seleucids of Syria.

By the second century, the divisions within the Jewish community about how it wanted to relate to the Seleucid Empire became delineated. The Hellenists, who favored assimilation, were generally the educated, wealthy, and powerful. The Chassidim, who favored separation and religious piety, were the poor farmers who did not mix with the Greeks.

When Antiochus IV became the ruler of the empire, he wanted to further hellenize the Jews and forbade the study of Torah as divine, as well as other ritual practices like circumcision, Sabbath observance, and sanctification of the new moon. He did not necessarily want Jews to convert to his religion, but only that they not take Judaism so seriously as a religion.

Needing money for his military campaign against Egypt, he sold the position of the high priest in the Jerusalem Temple, installed a Jew sympathetic to himself, introduced idols into the Holy Temple, and instituted foreign practices like pig sacrifice and sacred prostitution. These practices spread throughout the entire empire. The Chassidim accepted these violations as evidence of divine punishment, believing that martyrdom was preferable to disobeying the commandments; they were fervent pacifists. A much smaller third group began to emerge, the Maccabeans, who were also observant, like the Chassidim, but believed that that humans should be active partners in the covenant, even fighting on the Sabbath if necessary to protect it.

What spurred the Maccabeans into battle were not, interestingly, the religious violations, but an ordinance stipulating that Jewish virgins had to have sexual relations with the Seleucid governors prior to marriage. Though most people got married secretly, the marriage of Yehudit, the daughter of Yehuda the high priest, however, became public. The story I heard is that she challenged the Maccabeans to defend her honor by actually disrobing in front of them. They were ready to stone her, but she retorted that they were worse than the Greeks. She was prepared to die rather than submit herself to the Greek general. She called the Maccabeans hypocrites who thought they were holy because of their study of Torah, but they were not because they allowed Jewish woman to be sexually violated. Her arguments hit home, provoking them to battle.

Initially small in number, the Maccabeans engaged in a guerilla war. They knew the terrain well. Soon their numbers swelled as moderate Hellenists and militant Chassidim joined their ranks. The Jewish masses for the most part were sympathetic to the cause of the Maccabeans. Another Yehudit, a shy beautiful widow, played an important role in this military victory by seducing the Greek general Holofernes and beheading him. Though it is not talked about much, this war was also civil war between the Jews. Devout Hellenists sided with the Seleucids and Jew fought against Jew.

The holiday of Chanukah celebrates the military victory of the Maccabeans. Previously a day of cult sacrifice, the twenty-fifth of Kislev was chosen as the most appropriate day to rededicate the Holy Temple by lighting the menorah, the symbol of the Divine Presence. Any oil could have been used in the menorah, but they wanted a vial of oil that had not been defiled and, quite surprisingly, they found a buried one. Looking for a vial of oil that had not been contaminated was an expression of the desire to return to the original purity of their connection with God. And as the legend goes, the oil burned miraculously for eight days rather than the expected one day. The Maccabeans ruled in the Holy Temple for only one year, after which they were defeated by the Hellenists led by Lysias.

King Antiochus then appointed a new regent over his kingdom, and a new agreement was negotiated that allowed the Jews to maintain control of the Holy Temple and practice their religion as they wanted. When Israel was occupied by Rome many years later, the holiday of Chanukah became more important and gave hope and inspiration to the masses.

OBSERVANCE   The holiday of Chanukah begins on the twenty-fifth of Kislev and continues until the second of Tevet. The main observance of Chanukah is the lighting of the menorah. At this time, we recite blessings that remind us of the military victory as well as the miracle of the oil burning for eight days. There was a debate between rabbis Hillel and Shammai about whether one candle should be added each day so that eight candles are lit on the last day or whether eight candles should be lit on the first day and one extinguished each night. Hillel won.

In lighting the menorah, one begins on the first night by lighting the candle on the extreme right. The next night an additional candle is placed immediately to the left and lit first. Then the candle to the right, from the previous night, is lit. This procedure is repeated for the eight days. In the case of Shabbat, the Chanukah candles are lit first. At the conclusion of Shabbat, the Havdalah candle that marks the end of Shabbat is lit first and then the Chanukah candle.

The purpose of the candle lighting today is to publicize the miracle, so it is recommended that the candles be near windows, so people on the street can see them. One menorah may be lit for an entire family, or individuals may have their own. It is suggested that the candles be lit as early as possible after the appearance of the stars, but it is not prohibited to do it later.

In the course of the holiday, thirty-six candles are lit. The Talmud says that there were thirty-six hours when Adam and Eve could see from one end of the world to another. They were illuminated by Divine Light. There are also said to be thirty-six elevated souls in every generation that sustain, nurture, and guard this light. Special Hallel prayers of praise and thanksgiving are sung in synagogue every day.

Chanukah is a joyous holiday with great mass appeal. It does not have the restrictions associated with the biblical holidays. The holidays prescribed in the Torah have certain restrictions, things we must do and not do, which acts like a container for the light of divine revelation. On Chanukah, there are no restrictions, for as my teacher Reb Shlomo Carlebach said, on Chanukah we get both the vessels and the light together. It is a complete gift. One simply lights the Chanukah menorah, and one is plugged into Divine Light.

Chanukah is often considered a holiday for children. Whether you are an adult or a child, Chanukah is a delight, awakening the child within us to play. Chanukah parties are many, gifts are exchanged, and children spin dreidels. On the dreidel are written the Hebrew letters nun, gimmel, hay, and shin for *"Nes, gadol hayah sham"* ("A great miracle occurred there"). People eat donuts and potato latkes, made with oil to commemorate the miracle of the oil.

The holiday of Chanukah has increasing relevance for the Jewish people in modern times. Once again, the Jewish people, such a small group, and the state of Israel, such a small state, have such large enemies both inside and outside that threaten its integrity and identity. Chanukah reminds us that, though we may suffer, we as a people will prevail. We are reminded that the Jewish people live on a level of miracles. It is not logical that the Jewish people have survived from antiquity, facing the kinds of persecutions they have in almost every generation. The holiday of Chanukah and the energy of this month teach us that life is miraculous, and with faith and trust we can go forward in our lives in ways that transcend the logical.

Meditation

The meditation this month is for lighting candles at Chanukah. It can be modified for Shabbat candle lighting or even a weekday candle meditation. The light of the candle provides a glimpse into the light of God and the light of the soul. This light enables us to see the miraculous nature of life and the holiness and purity of God and the human soul.

In lighting the menorah for Chanukah, read slowly the Al Nissim blessing, found in Jewish prayerbooks, in which we praise God for all the miracles. Then we light the candles and say the following Chanukah blessings:

> *Baruch atah, Adonai Eloheinu, melech ha'olam, asher kidshanu b'mitzvotav*
> *v'tzivanu l'hadlik ner shel Chanukah.*
> (Blessed are You, Adonai, our God, King of the universe, who makes
> us holy through the commandments and commanded us to light the
> candle of Chanukah.)

Baruch atah, Adonai Eloheinu, melech ha'olam, sheh'asah nissim la'avoteinu ba'yamin ha'heim ba'z'man has zeh.

(Blessed are You, Adonai, our God, King of the universe, who performed wondrous deeds for our ancestors in those days and at this season.)

(On the first day only)
Baruch atah, Adonai Eloheinu, melech ha-olam, she-hechi-yo-nu v'ki-y'manu v'higiyanu la-z'man ha zeh.

(Blessed are You, Adonai, Our God, King of the universe, who has given us life and sustained us and enabled us to reach this season.)

After you have said the blessings slowly and consciously, stay in front of the menorah or the Shabbat candles. Gaze at the light; be with the light. Let it enter deeply into your heart.

Although it may be a little uncomfortable, keep your eyes open as much as you can and let the light fill your screen of vision. This light has the power to purify and transform us, and we all have varying degrees of resistance to change or to seeing ourselves from a different vantage point.

Be gentle with yourself and loving, allowing space for any discomfort without running away. Just be with yourself and the light. Imagine that you can cast into the light anything you want to be rid of. The more you are able to let go, the brighter the light is. Allow yourself to be present, let go of the distractions, and steadily focus on your breath.

This candlelight provides a glimpse into the eternal light of God, the hidden light, the holy light. This light has burned forever and will burn eternally. This is the light of creation, before creation. This is the light of God made manifest. Repeat these phrases silently to yourself or meditate on them.

After a while, allow your eyes to close and visualize yourself as a Chanukah or Shabbat candle. Your body is the candle and your soul is the light. Visualize the light of your soul radiating and shining brightly in this world. Stay with this as long as possible and alternate between keeping your eyes open and closed.

Practical Recommendations

1. PAY ATTENTION TO YOUR DREAMS THIS MONTH.

If you take time to read spiritual books, meditate, or pray before sleep, you will transform your dream life during your nightly sleep. Your sleep will be deeper and your dreams will be a source of inspiration and guidance. Keep a journal by the bed and record your dreams. Recording dreams sends an important message to your subconscious mind that your dream life is important. As you pay attention to your dreams and record them, you will find that your dreams will be richer and you will remember more and more detail.

2. FIND A DREAM BUDDY.

Share your dreams with a close friend you love and who loves you. In the process of sharing, you will gain more understanding of what your dreams actually mean and what their messages to you are. Share your hopes and visions with your dream buddy as well. Together, you will support and encourage each other to fulfill your visions and the dreams of your hearts. Listen deeply to each other and encourage each other.

3. PRAY FOR THE HEALING OF THE SICK.

When people are ill, it is often hard for them to dream, to vision, to be free to do what they want. Illness is such a prison. This is a month of liberation. When you pray for someone who is ill—yourself or another—you send the ill person love and surround him or her with light and blessings. See the person as healthy and strong in your vision. Remember that God is the true healer, and God is not confined to the laws of cause and effect. Miracles are possible whenever we make a true God connection. There is much blessing available this month to be channeled for healing.

4. PRAISE GOD AND YOURSELF FOR YOUR VICTORIES.

On Chanukah we celebrate the victory of the Maccabeans. Reflect on your current life, your work, and your relationships and acknowledge the growth and victories you have had in your life in recent years. What are you able to do now that you could not have seen yourself doing years ago? What challenges have you overcome? Praise yourself and praise God for the growth that has occurred in your life. Celebrate your victories with a friend. In our life we are constantly challenged, waging many battles. We need to pause to savor our victories and celebrate them with others. This will give us strength and courage for the battles ahead.

A Tale to Live By

Every time we do a *mitzvah,* we connect to the Source of all, and kindling Chanukah lights enables a powerful connection. As Chanukah is a time of miracles, what follows is a story about the miracles and Chanukah lights.

Reb Aaron Roth was reported to be on his deathbed. His doctors had consulted with his students and told them that their rebbe had only a few hours to live. Many of his closest students gathered around his bed. As it was the first night of Chanukah, he whispered that he wanted to fulfill the *mitzvah* of lighting the Chanukah candles. The students prepared the menorah on a table by the window. The frail, weak old man gazed lovingly at the menorah. How could he light the candles? his students wondered.

The students tried to pick up the table and bring it to the bedside, but the rebbe asked to be brought to the menorah instead. They lifted him up, sat him in a chair, and brought the chair to the window. In preparation for the act, he asked that his hands be washed, and that the garments he wore for Shabbat and holidays be put on him.

The *shamash,* the head candle, was lit and placed in his hand. One of the students held the candle with him, because his hand shook so. The rebbe began to say the blessing, *"Baruch . . ."* He said it so softly, it was barely audible. He paused to catch his breath, and after a minute or so he said the next word, *"atah,"* much more clearly. With each word in God's name—*"Adonai Eloheinu, melech ha'olam,* Our God, King of the universe"—his voice became noticeably stronger. The words empowered him. God is the King of the world, and surely God is stronger than any illness or disease. The rebbe's hand became steady. *"Asher kidshanu b'mitzvotav v'tzivanu l'hadlik ner shel Chanukah."*

He completed the first blessing, and then he rested. What a privilege to fulfill God's commandment, he reflected. He no longer looked as if he was dying; his eyes sparkled and his face had a certain radiance. For the second blessing, he held the candle by himself, and with each word he grew visibly stronger. After he completed the second blessing, he again rested. He then said the third and final blessing, thanking God for allowing him to live to this day. The blessings completed, as he gazed at the lit candle, he pushed himself off the chair. Reb Aaron Roth began to sing a joyous hymn, and then he began to dance! He danced and danced, and then went on to live many more years. Such is the power of the Chanukah lights in this month of Kislev.

Tevet

MONTH: *December-January*

ENERGY: *Purification and Transformation of Negative Emotions*

AREA OF HEALING: *Anger*

ASTROLOGICAL SIGN: *Capricorn*

HEBREW LETTER: *Ayin*

HEBREW TRIBE: *Dan*

DIVINE NAME PERMUTATION: *HYHV*

HOLIDAY: *Last Days of Chanukah, the Tenth of Tevet*

evet is one of the darkest and coldest times of the year and these qualities are often reflected in our personal lives as well. For example, during this month, Danny felt lonely and isolated and found himself withdrawing socially. He reported that he felt dead inside and had no inspiration, no creativity, only a deep and pervading feeling of depression and listlessness. He judged himself harshly because he had begun so many projects, but they all stayed on his desk, because he was unable to carry on with them. He couldn't understand why he could not accomplish what he saw others doing. Though he did not like to admit it, he resented and was jealous of other people. These feelings depleted him further.

As Danny continued in therapy, he discovered that underneath his sadness were deep feelings of anger, rage, and guilt. He explored the roots of his anger and found them to be very early and very deep. As a child, he felt ignored and unappreciated. Though highly intelligent, possibly brilliant, he thought he was stupid and was afraid that others would discover that about him. He recalled that his parents had even ridiculed his creative projects as a child. He was afraid to put his work out to the public, for he feared rejection or ridicule, which would confirm what he had suspected about himself.

As part of his treatment, he was encouraged to contact and release these deep feelings he had buried inside as well as to deepen his relationship with God through prayer, meditation, and doing *mitzvot*. As he opened himself more to God, prayer, and meditation, he found that there was a new space and a quiet joy within him. As he contacted his center, his self-esteem grew. He began to let go of the excessive concern he had about other people's reactions to his work. He felt a new freedom and self-acceptance. He began to make a plan for making his work available to others.

Energy: Purification and Transformation of Negative Emotions

Tevet, the darkest month of the year, brings challenges that force us to tap into our inner resources and become stronger. The winter solstice occurs during Tevet. Though the days begin to grow longer and the nights shorter, in our part of the world, it is still very cold, frost or snow covers the trees and the ground, and the sky is gray, making us spend more time inside than outside. These physical conditions reflect the spiritual themes of this month. Unlike the expansiveness of Kislev, when we contact our dreams and our visions, in Tevet we uproot the remaining negative forces that keep us from realizing them. There is a natural tendency to restrict oneself, to be cautious, prudent, and focused during Tevet. This month is a time not so much to go forward or start new projects, but to be with oneself, to be reflective, to process deep feelings, and to purify. What we can witness and release during this month will provide the openings and opportunities that will be available for us during the remainder of the year.

Kabbalah divides the months between Jacob and Esau. Tevet is one of the three months kabbalistically said to belong to "the other side," that of Esau. The other months are Tammuz (June-July) and a part of Av (July-August). In Jewish history, Tevet was a time of great trial and calamity. On the tenth of Tevet, the walls of Jerusalem were breeched, which led to the destruction of the first Temple in 586 B.C.E. and of the second Temple in 70 C.E. The completion of the translation of the Torah into Greek was said to take place on the eighth of Tevet, around 250 B.C.E. during the period of the second Temple. Though non-Hebrew speakers might not feel that translation is a matter of great concern, at the time it was seen as a terrible travesty, for the holiness of the Torah was compromised in the translation. Although some religious people fast on the eighth day of Tevet, the tenth day of Tevet was established as a general fast day to transmute the negative energy of the month. The essence of a fast day is not simply to feel grief and restrict oneself, but through fasting to awaken the heart to overcome the negative inclination and to do good.

Kabbalistically, this month is devoted to the healing and transformation of anger. Most likely, there will be numerous opportunities to see the many different faces of anger and explore them. I have noted in my students, therapy clients, and myself that as soon as Tevet comes, anger increases. Knowing about the energy of the Tevet, I still find it amazing to witness how anger becomes prominent in so many people's lives during this month.

Among ten clients during the first days of Tevet, everyone reported an incident of anger, and in many cases it was actually an episode of rage. Joyce became enraged when her husband did not get the theater tickets she had asked him to. Marlene became enraged when her husband went to help a friend in the middle of the night. Dick found himself feeling impatient and irritated and yelled at his wife for no reason. Everyone was angry this month. In most conflict between people, particularly marital conflict, the real issue underlying the conflict is always much deeper than the initial trigger to the disagreement and often points to the need for the healing of early childhood wounding.

Many of my clients and students had real challenges in the work arena this month as well. Recently I ran into two former students who both reported that they had lost their jobs. When I asked when this happened, I was not surprised to discover that it happened in Tevet. Another client of mine, Harold, faced a significant decrease in revenue due to a business competitor. Stewart had worked three years on his doctoral dissertation, only to find that it was totally rejected in Tevet. In Tevet, Joan, a very close friend in Israel, lost her job after six years of employment. She initially felt angry and betrayed, but then recognized that being unemployed for a period of time with a large severance pay was actually a blessing. I could go on and on.

It also seems as though many more people become ill in Tevet than in other months. Tevet is a challenging month, so try to relax if you find yourself becoming angry in your relationships with others or if you are confronted with negative events that naturally might make you angry. It is the energy of the month. When it is cold outside, people get heated up inside.

During this month, many things will trigger your anger. There most likely will be challenges in the work or relationship areas of your life. Accept them as gracefully as you can. Nothing happens by accident. There will be goodness within every challenge you face. You may even find that people appear unexpectedly from your past and you have an opportunity to heal unresolved conflicts and let go of anger. During these meetings, make a conscious effort to let go of the need to be right and attempt to see everything and everyone in the best light. You will know how you are progressing spiritually by observing your anger level. Becoming angered easily is a sign that you need to purify yourself.

Our sages say in *Ethics of the Fathers,* "Anger, jealousy, and idolatry drive a person out of this world." These three things are all connected to each other. If we're honest, we have to admit that jealousy is often the root of anger. Anger is like idolatry in Judaism. Idolatry is the belief in forces other than God. God is the true reality, yet because of our self-love and subjectivity, we often distort reality with illusions and become angry when reality does not conform to our needs and desires. It is like worshiping idols—we want life and God to be in our image. The inward tone of this month forces us to see reality as it is. Though this process may be painful and disillusioning, it actually strengthens us. Through this kind of introspection, we touch the essence of truth, which brings an inner joy and goodness with it. We experience God more as God is and not as a projection of what we want God to be.

This month we have an amazing opportunity to heal the anger we carry inside that continues to limit us. It may not be an easy process, but working through it will yield greater well-being, freedom, and joy in our lives. We must begin with the awareness of how we limit ourselves through our anger. It does not matter if the anger is directed at ourselves or toward other people.

We must make a decision to work on anger, because being stuck in anger has so many negative consequences. It renders us victims who are powerless and unable to go forward in our lives. When we are angry, we are not free. We are slaves to our emotions. We are out of control. We lose our center when we blame other people or events for our own unhappiness. That is why during this month the Torah portions we read are all about slavery. Long before the holistic movement made the connection between the mind and the body, kabbalah said that anger was the root cause of illness, because it actually disconnects us from God's energy and from our true selves. If we want to heal ourselves from illness, we have to heal and transform the anger we feel inside.

As we go through life's challenges this month and throughout the year, it is important to remember that nothing is coincidental, things don't just happen, and that the deepest pain often precedes the greatest awakenings. I have seen this so many times with my clients and experienced this in my own life. Sometimes the pain that we experience in life is so overwhelming that we are brought to our knees, forcing us to surrender and call out to God in a new way, for a new way. Take heart, for God does answer the sincere calls of the heart and soul.

General Guidelines and Goals

The following guidelines and goals enable us to direct our energies in the ways that are optimal for our growth and transformation in accordance with the energy of this month. It is recommended that you read and meditate upon them often in the course of the month. Reflect on their applicability to you, and allow them to direct and inspire you often this month.

As we go through life's challenges this month, it is important to remember that nothing is coincidental, things don't just happen, and that the deepest pain often precedes the greatest awakenings.

1. EXPLORE THE NATURE OF YOUR ANGER.

In the course of this month, you may find yourself becoming angry. Allow yourself to feel anger when it arises and explore its nature. Feeling your anger is different from expressing it. As you open to the feeling of anger, observe it and consider the following questions: What is the source of the anger? Does it come from the ego or the soul? What is the difference? Does the anger empower me to make positive changes or does it weaken me?

Anger is usually derived from arrogance and pride, from the ego mind demanding that we be treated better or honored more. We want things our way. We may become angry when we do not have what we perceive others as having. When we are angry, we often fail to take responsibility for what we have created or allowed to occur in our lives. We blame others, we blame God, and we even blame ourselves, and in so doing, we become paralyzed, unable to change.

Sometimes people think that if they are angry enough at themselves, they will change and become better people. It does not generally work that way in the long run. Anger may enable a person to make changes that are reactive, but not integrative. Real change occurs through love and self-acceptance. We may regret certain behaviors, but be careful not to identify these behaviors with the self, which we must love unconditionally.

If you find that the anger you are experiencing is resulting from the ego mind, its source is the wounding of the inner child. The child within is vulnerable and may be easily hurt. This inner child needs our love and compassion. When we are angry at others for not nurturing us the way we want, it is a sign that we need to nurture ourselves more.

There is, however, a kind of anger that has a positive side—righteous anger, which comes from the soul. This anger enables us to take back our power. The expression of this kind of anger actually liberates, motivates, and inspires us to make positive changes within ourselves and in the world. For example, Miriam was in a relationship with a man who imposed himself on her in ways that were not comfortable for her. She found herself becoming angry at him. Not the kind of person who easily expresses anger, Miriam initially stuffed these feelings inside herself. She ate more than normal, and she was depressed and often tired. Owning and expressing her feelings of anger enabled her to leave a relationship that was not satisfying to her and regain her physical vitality and emotional well-being.

2. ASSUME RESPONSIBILITY FOR YOUR FEELINGS.

Transformation begins with the recognition that, to a large extent, we are responsible for what happens in our lives and most definitely for the responses we have as a result. When we acknowledge this, we are empowered and able to forgive others. For example, if we are hurt, we need to recognize that we are hurt because we are hurtable. If we feel betrayed by others, often it is because we have betrayed ourselves. We also need to recognize that God is behind everything that happens as well. Nothing happens by chance, Divine Will is ever present, and there is good in everything.

We often get stuck in trying to understand why things happen to us. There are so many questions we ask ourselves and others: "Why does God make it so hard for me? Why did this person hurt me? Why do bad things have to happen to me? Why me?" Do these kinds of questions sound familiar to you? Sometimes people repeat these questions to themselves like a mantra, but these kinds of "why" questions are basically disempowering. They make us feel helpless. What would be more helpful and honest than asking ourselves why is to take responsibility for our feelings, to be compassionately with ourselves as we allow ourselves to feel our feelings and ask how we can grow through the challenges we are now facing. Often the anger we feel is covering a deep hurt and early woundedness that needs healing and love.

3. PRACTICE HUMILITY.

The great kabbalist Rabbi Yitzchok Luria, in his book *The Gates of Holiness,* tells us that when we refrain from anger, we engender in ourselves a spirit of humility. When we humble ourselves, the spirit of the Shechinah can rest upon us. The more we negate our anger and our sense of self-importance, the more Godliness can be revealed to us. We experience ourselves in a more expanded way. Humility is very different from low self-esteem or self-deprecation. In our tradition we are taught that the greatest men, like Moses, were the humblest. Be grateful for opportunities to practice humility.

In Jewish liturgy, the following silent prayer is included to limit the expression of anger: "My God, guard my tongue from evil and my lips from speaking deceitfully. To those who curse me, let my soul be silent. And let my soul be like dust to everyone." Of course, actually living these words represents a very high level of spiritual attainment and degree of humility. The sentiment, however, does signify a direction for us. Becoming indifferent to praise or insult is considered a prerequisite to entering higher states of spiritual attainment. Be mindful of this goal.

4. SEE THE GOOD IN EVERYONE AND EVERYTHING.

We have the ability to penetrate and transform darkness with the light of our awareness. The Baal Shem Tov says that because God's light is so powerful, it needs to be concealed in darkness. Great light and goodness can be experienced this month. Tevet does begin with a tet, which is also the first letter of *tov*, which means "good."

In this dark month, it is important to see the light within every person and every event. In this way, we remove the concealment of darkness. Whatever we see is reflected back to us. Everything is a mirror. If we see the good, the good is reflected back to us; if we see the negative, the negative is reflected back. Make an effort to see the good in everyone and everything. Make an effort to suspend judgments about other people. The letter this month is ayin, which is about seeing.

Astrological Sign: Capricorn

The sign of Capricorn is named for the goat constellation. Like the goat climbing the mountain, according to astrology, we should be methodical and focused this month. Capricorn is an earth sign, indicating that the physical world is the arena of focus and challenge. Capricorns are said to be focused on their career and have a desire to amass material wealth.

The goat, according to Nachmanides, is associated with evil. In ancient times the sins of the Jewish people were symbolically placed on the goat (Lev. 16:20–22). The Talmud says that the goat is brazen, always wanting to be first. This trait can be positive if it is directed toward holiness or negative if directed toward impurity.

While Jupiter, the planet that ruled the previous month of Sagittarius, is about expansion, largeness of vision, optimism, and faith, Saturn, the ruler of Capricorn, is about restriction, establishing boundaries, discipline, and pragmatism. Saturn brings challenge. Saturn is a taskmaster, seen also as a teacher, who forces us to do our greatest learning through hardships.

Saturn also rules over Saturday, the Sabbath. The Sabbath is a time of restriction; however, when embraced as a spiritual practice, the Sabbath can be a time of transcendence and contemplation. The inward and restrictive focus of this month enables one to go deeply inside and transcend limitations.

In Roman mythology, Saturn was the god of agriculture, yet Capricorn, the sign it rules over, is in the winter when the growing season is over. Saturn is depicted as holding a sickle used for cutting grain and corn. He represents the physical work that we must do on our own, the organization, all the hard efforts, all the toiling that does not show immediate fruits. Hard workers, serious, and disciplined, those born in Capricorn also have a tendency for loneliness, depression, and isolation.

The ancient Greeks called Saturn Kronos. Kronos was a father figure who, unlike Jupiter, did not encourage his children to grow. His jealousy of his children kept them confined and restricted. Saturn is Father Time, the Grim Reaper, reflecting the seriousness and darkness of this month.

Hebrew Letter: Ayin

ע The name of the letter ayin means "eye." Ayin is associated with perception, insight, discernment, and understanding. When we say "we see," we mean that we understand. According to *Ethics of the Fathers,* a good eye is one of the greatest human achievements. The ability to see the good in every person and thing is a worthy goal for this month and one that will offer protection. As we grow spiritually, we see the interconnectedness of everything. We see "God's hand," or "God's signature," in all of creation. The letter ayin seeks to teach us to see God in everyone and everything. Meditate on the letter ayin this month.

In the Mishnah it is said, "Whoever has the following three attributes is a disciple of our patriarch Abraham, and whoever has the following three faults is a disciple of the wicked Balaam. . . . The disciples of Abraham have a good eye, a humble soul, and a low [humble] spirit" *(Tractate Aboth).* A good eye means that one is not jealous of others and is as considerate of a friend's honor as one's own. According to the Rambam, a good eye means one is satisfied with what one has and does not pursue excesses. The "evil eye" is the opposite of the "good eye." The evil eye is jealous, haughty, and demanding.

Cultivate a good eye this month. Before we judge ourselves and others we should be aware that our eyes may deceive us and that what we see may not true. People become jealous of others because they only see the externalities. They think that if they had the material possessions or external achievements of another, they would be happier than they are. This is most likely not true.

When we judge others in a negative light, we see only the *klippah,* the negative shell of a person or event, and not the underlying Godliness. When we judge others harshly, we are often projecting our own negative qualities onto them; projection is a defense mechanism we use to protect ourselves from the experience of our own essential vulnerability. Even when projection is not involved, when others have qualities of their own that we are critical of, we can still take a cue: the reason those qualities bother us so much is that they are mirroring something within ourselves that needs healing.

The numerical value of ayin is seventy, an important number. The Torah tells us that there are seventy nations that are the root of all the nations in the world. Seventy elders received a divine revelation, described in Exodus 24:9. This is the only recorded mystical experience in the Bible. Also, in Numbers 11:16 God asks for seventy elders to receive the Holy Spirit to ease the burden of Moses because the people were complaining and Moses also felt that the burden of leadership was too great for him. There are seventy faces to the Torah. Seventy was the number of Jews who originally entered Egypt escaping the famine in Canaan. There are seventy names of God. There are seventy holy days in the year, including Shabbat and festivals.

Hebrew Tribe: Dan

When Rachel was not able to become pregnant and her sister, Leah, has already borne Jacob several sons, Rachel became jealous and angry and decided to give her handmaid Bilhah to Jacob, as was the custom then. Through her handmaid, Rachel would bear a child. When Bilhah gave birth to a son, Rachel named him Dan and said, "God has judged me and has also heard my prayer. He has finally given me a son" (Gen. 30:6). The name Dan has the same letters as the Hebrew word *din,* which means "judgment." From this name, we see the attribute of judgment that is prevalent this month.

Perhaps because of the negative energy underlying Dan's birth, the tribe of Dan was the most vulnerable to idolatry, sorcery, and forbidden sexual relations. When the Jews traveled in the desert, the tribe of Dan marched in the rear, on the periphery of the clouds of glory that protected the Jewish people. They were known to find and return lost objects left before them, which is reflected in the blessing that Jacob gave to Dan. On his deathbed, Jacob blesses Dan and says, "Dan will be serpent on the highway, a rattlesnake on the path, that bites the hoof of the horse and the rider falls backward" (Gen. 49:17). The horse in kabbalah represents licentiousness. Though the snake in kabbalah is usually associated with evil inclination, Dan is the holy, clever snake that can weaken the power of evil inclination.

Though the tribe of Dan was not blessed with the strength of Judah, it produced the famous Samson, who single-handedly fought against the Philistines. Out of weakness and vulnerability comes the greatest strength. Samson was a forerunner of the Messiah. Samson took a Nazirite vow, which meant that he did not cut his hair or drink wine. Samson's strength was compromised, however, by his intense and overwhelming attraction and marriage to Delilah, a Philistine who was bent on undermining him. His "eyes" deceived him. He told her his secrets and she betrayed him.

According to the kabbalist Rabbenu Bachaya, the nation associated with this month is the Philistines. The Philistines are kabbalistically associated with sexual desire that seeks to wound the holiness of Israel. This is a month of tests, particularly in the sexual arena. The eyes make one vulnerable, particularly this month, and one must make an effort to guard against this.

The tribe of Dan occupied the north of Israel. According to the ancient kabbalistic text *Sefer Yetzirah,* the energy of *gevurah* emanates from the north. *Gevurah* is the energy of judgment, strength, and discipline. The north was also the place of material wealth, enabling the tribe to amass gold. There is a rabbinic proverb that says that anyone who wants wealth should face north; many people place their beds facing to the north for this reason.

Divine Name Permutation: HYHV

The divine name permutation for this month is a little more challenging to understand. The reversal of the first two letters, yud hay (YH) to hay yud (HY), is indicative of judgment and tests, which are reflected in the energy of this month.

The hay in the worlds of Atzilut, the first position, and Yetzerah, the third position, indicates that there is expansiveness and blessing in these worlds. The heart, which corresponds to the world of Yetzerah, should be a focus of opening for this month. The mind, represented by the world of Beriyah and the letter yud, should be concentrated and focused during this month. The vav (V) in the world of Assiyah, corresponding to this physical world and our bodies, indicates that our efforts should be channeled directly into the physical world. We may not see expansiveness immediately, but we set the stage for it in the future by what we do this month.

Torah Portions

It is in the Torah portions for this month that Joseph reveals his true identity to his brothers (Gen. 45:1–46). The brothers are beginning to understand that all the challenging events they underwent in Egypt were divine punishment for selling Joseph into slavery. They are full of regret and plead to Joseph for mercy on behalf of their father, who continues to suffer over the loss of his son Joseph. When Yehuda (Judah) offers himself in place of his brother Benjamin, it is a sign that the brothers have done complete *teshuvah* (repentance) for selling Joseph into slavery so long ago. When Joseph hears this, he can bear it no longer and reveals his true identity. I imagine that the brothers were happy to find that Joseph was alive, but it most likely was not easy confronting the person they once sought to harm. Forgiving his brothers, Joseph tells them not to feel bad about selling him into slavery. He says, "God sent me ahead of you to insure that you survive in the land. . . . It is not you who sent me here, but God" (Gen. 45:7–8). Joseph is the model for the transformation of anger this month. When we really understand that everything happens according to divine plan, our anger is diminished.

The Torah portions for this month include the entrance of the Jewish people into Egypt and Jacob's blessings to his sons (Gen. 46–49). Even though Egypt is part of the prophecy that Abraham had received, Jacob is afraid of leaving Israel, but he receives a vision that God will be with him. This is itself an important teaching, reminding us that God is with us in the midst of our suffering. Before his death, Jacob blesses his sons, as well as the children of Joseph, whose descendants become tribes in their own right. Jacob states what he sees and feels about each tribe, although it is sometimes highly critical and condemning.

In this month we open to a new book of Torah that in Hebrew is called Shmot, which means "Names." Why is this book called the book of Names? The name in kabbalah is a definition of a person's potential. This book is a journey toward uncovering potential, which is sometimes done through suffering. In English the book is called Exodus because it traces the Jewish people's departure from Egypt. Kabbalistically Egypt is seen as a place of constraints, limitation, and impurity.

While Joseph lived, the Jews enjoyed a special status in Egypt and prospered in wealth and numbers. But now, as the book of Exodus begins, the Jewish people are seen as a threat. Over time, a new Pharaoh had emerged who feared their power and sought to weaken them. The plight of the Jews became dismal; they became enslaved and persecuted.

As we read these Torah portions, the energy of this month invites us to revisit what it means to be in Egypt, what it means to be in exile, what it means to be a slave. The concept of being in exile has not only national ramifications, but existential overtones as well. The most painful exile people experience today is separation from their own soul and God. When people experience their soul, God, and the world in alignment with each other, all flowing together, there is a well-being and joy. Without this alignment, there is suffering, confusion, and unhappiness. All emotional problems, disorders, anxiety, and depression come from this separation.

Exile can be self-imposed. People exile themselves from God's world when they see only the worst in themselves, in others, and in life. When they cannot access their own goodness and are trapped in their own negativity, this is truly exile. Such people look outside of themselves for the feeling of aliveness, for power and identity. This is what Egypt represents to the kabbalist.

People also exile God from their world when they do not believe in Divine Providence. They believe only in what they can see, what they can understand; they do not believe there is a God they can call out to in times of crisis. This is a dark form of exile. As Reb Shlomo would say, we have to admit that we are all still a little bit in Egypt, but we have hope, because there is a God who is pouring out love and compassion to take us out of Egypt.

There are many great teachings about how to meet the challenges that are imparted in the Torah portions of this month. The redemption of the Jewish people from Egypt reflects our own redemption from our personal exiles. Moses is born in the Torah portions we read this month (Exod. 2). He is saved from the water where all Jewish male infants were placed to drown and is even raised in the house of Pharaoh. The birth of Moses is an important reminder that during times of greatest darkness, there is light and goodness.

The strength of the Jewish people in Egypt came when they saw that God was talking to them through the adversity they faced. Their suffering was not random or without meaning. They called out to God, and God heard their cry. All the hardships, all the challenges were opportunities for purification and growth.

In the Torah portions of this month, we see the development of Moses as a leader and prophet (Exod. 3–5). Though initially reluctant, Moses assumes leadership of the Jewish people. He meets with Pharaoh, there are many plagues where God's power is demonstrated, and yet Pharaoh's heart remains hardened. Reality is shattering before their eyes and yet the Jews are forced to remain in slavery. With each plague, there was a deeper revelation of Godliness. We see from these Torah portions that this month is less about moving forward than about purification and cleansing.

Holidays

Last Days of Chanukah

Much has been said about Chanukah in the previous chapter, Kislev. Chanukah is the one holiday that occupies two months, Kislev and Tevet. The last night of Chanukah is the beginning of Tevet. Since the essence of the holiday of Chanukah is about revealing light in the midst of darkness, it radiates its light and message into the month of Tevet, the darkest month. The light of Chanukah brings clarity, hope, and strength into Tevet that enables us to see the hold that anger has in our lives and helps us to release it.

The Tenth of Tevet

HISTORY   The Tenth of Tevet commemorates the breeching of the walls of Jerusalem by the Babylonian king Nebuchadnetzar that resulted in the exile of the Jews from Jerusalem in the month of Av (Jer. 52). Beginning on the day the Jews entered the land of Israel under the leadership of Yehousha (Joshua), the Jewish people inhabited the land for over 850 years. When the Jews were exiled from the land and their Holy Temple destroyed, they understood that this was not a random act. They took responsibility for what had happened. The prophets of Israel had told them that they would be exiled if they did not follow the commandments of God that had been given to them earlier. They were particularly admonished for the practice of idolatry. In Leviticus 18:24 they were warned: "And you shall observe all my statutes and all my judgments, and you shall do them—so that the land may not spit you out, where in I bring you to dwell in it."

OBSERVANCE   The Tenth of Tevet is observed as a fast day, although it does not have the same mandate or restrictions as the fasts of Yom Kippur or Tisha B'Av. One can wash, wear shoes, and eat until daybreak. Those who do not fast easily or are weak or ill need not fast on this day. People are, however, asked to refrain from eating in public or overindulging; only moderate portions of healthy food are recommended. Fasting is recommended for a community undergoing a hardship, such as a drought, or for individuals undergoing personal trials. Fasting is a powerful spiritual practice if done with the proper intention.

Meditation

In accordance with the energy of this month, the following meditation is offered to transmute the negative feelings stemming from hurt, anger, or regret that may still be stuck within. As you begin this meditation, reflect on the following question: What inside you needs healing?

Take a few minutes to center yourself and relax with the breath. Scan the physical body and take note of any sensations, tensions, and numbness in the body. Imagine that you can direct the breath to those places. Continue to breathe deeply; breathe into any sensations.

Now begin to gently open to the feelings that have been buried in the tensions of the body. To the degree you feel comfortable, explore the range and depth of feeling that remains associated with a past painful experience. Do not judge yourself. All feelings are valid and acceptable. Allow yourself to be present to your feelings in a most loving and compassionate way. This facilitates the release of negativity from your body. Stay with the breath, and keep breathing deeply. It is okay to feel your feelings. It is safe to feel your feelings. Do not make any decisions about any actions you will take because of your feelings; simply stay with the feelings that are present for you as fully as you can.

Now enter into a dialogue with God. Talk to Him in your own words about the pain, suffering, guilt that you continue to have. Ask God for the healing you need to be able to move on and the insights to appreciate the growth contained in this painful experience. Observe the responses and shifts in awareness that occur as a result of this meditation.

Practical Recommendations

1. BE MINDFUL OF YOUR SPEECH.

In the midst of anger, people say things they regret, things that can never be taken fully back. When you are angry, make an effort to calm yourself and not speak or act impulsively. Speaking rashly will only escalate the situation. Before you speak, consider whether your words will contribute to the other person's growth and healing. It is not that you should repress your thoughts and feelings; rather, you should express them in a way that loves, honors, and is of service to others as well as to yourself.

Train yourself to take long deep breaths and visualize the release of tension through the breath. Think before you speak. Make a habit of speaking in a soft, gentle voice, so even when you are angry you will not raise your voice too much. When you do speak, as much as possible make "I" statements, such as "I feel this when you do that . . . ," rather than accusatory "you" statements, such as "You did that . . ."

2. DILUTE YOUR ANGER.

When you are angry, it may be helpful for you to vent your anger, but not directly to the person you are angry with. If you need support, find a friend, a therapist, or write a letter to the person you are angry with. Rabbi Kalonymus Kalman Shapiro of Piaseczno, who was the rebbe of the Warsaw ghetto, suggested that you write such a letter at the peak of your anger and read it aloud to yourself frequently for a month. Also, speak to God about your anger and hurt and ask for guidance and healing.

3. PROTECT YOURSELF FROM THE ANGER OF OTHERS.

When you are confronted with the rage of another, you may need to place yourself in a protective bubble of white light or imagine yourself behind the shield of

Abraham, the first patriarch, who defended all people as mentioned in the first blessing of the Silent Amidah prayer in the standardized Jewish prayerbook. In most cases, you are not responsible for the anger directed at you. This anger is often not even about what is happening in the present. Usually, it is an expression of early woundedness and is indicative of an unresolved problem within the person who is angry. The most helpful quality to call forth is compassion *(hesed)*.

When a person is angry or raging, it is not hard to see the two-year-old child within him or her who felt ignored and learned to make a lot of noise to be noticed. As two-year-olds need limits for their own protection, an angry person also needs to have a limited space in which to ventilate his or her feelings, but under no circumstances should physical or emotional abuse be tolerated. Once the rage has been released, the person may be spoken to calmly and firmly and instructed in more effective ways of communication.

To acquire a feeling of detachment and objectivity in a heated situation, imagine yourself on a mountaintop looking down. How does this change your perspective? To avoid being pulled in by the anger and becoming angry yourself, raise or heighten your own vibration by doing something nurturing or enjoyable. When we are happy in ourselves, we are less vulnerable to becoming angry. Though angry individuals may be presenting a very unattractive side of themselves to you, look to see the good in them and remind them that the good person you see is who they really are.

4. BE HAPPY FOR WHAT YOU HAVE.

Make a list of what you feel grateful for in your life. Look at your list often. When we are grateful, our anger is reduced. Take moments each day to acknowledge the gift of life and all the blessings you often take for granted.

5. NURTURE YOURSELF.

When we get angry, it is a sign that we need to nurture ourselves. We are often angry at another for not giving us what we should give ourselves. During this month particularly, it is important to give yourself time and energy. I often instruct my therapy clients to literally give themselves a hug, open fully to the experience of being embraced, and tell themselves silently and also out loud, "I love you."

A Tale to Live By

The following is a story told by my teacher Reb Shlomo Carlebach while performing for people who were in jail facing long periods of incarceration. As he looked around, he only saw angry and unhappy people—most people who commit crimes are angry people—and told this story to transform their anger. When we focus on what we do not have, we become angry. When we focus on what we have, we are happy. Even in jail, one has much to be grateful for.

A young boy around the age of nine was seen singing and dancing in a poor town where everyone was suffering. This young man himself had not eaten in three days. He, like most of the people in the town, had been so angry at God. For days, he cried, "Why do I have to suffer so much? What did I do so wrong that I should be so hungry?" When he had no more tears left to cry, on the third day he began to look around at what he did have. He had a mother, a father, and a house to live in. He had so much to be grateful for. When he realized what he did have, he could not stop dancing and singing, thanking God for what he did have.

A few famous rabbis were traveling through his town and were attracted by his singing and dancing. When this young child explained to them why he was so happy, they were amazed by his spirit. They went to his parents and told them that their child was such a holy soul they wanted to educate him. They gave money to his family and took this young man with them. This young man became the great Rebbe Mendele of Rimanov.

Shevat

- MONTH: *January-February*
- ENERGY: *Inner Renewal*
- AREA OF HEALING: *Eating*
- ASTROLOGICAL SIGN: *Aquarius*
- HEBREW LETTER: *Tzaddi*
- HEBREW TRIBE: *Asher*
- DIVINE NAME PERMUTATION: *HYVH*
- HOLIDAY: *Tu B'Shevat*

y most beloved uncle died in Kislev of last year. In Tevet I was given the overwhelming task of clearing out his apartment, and I had to complete it in a month's time. It was a most difficult time. I cried every day as I went through his belongings. I was terribly heart-broken and extremely vulnerable. In the process of dealing with both the mundane details and the emotional upheaval, I made many mistakes. On top of it all, I was basically swindled by an unsavory estate buyer. I had lots of opportunity in Tevet to confront deep feelings of loss and anger, characteristic of the energy of that month.

In Shevat, I returned to my life, which had been on hold for many months since my uncle's illness. I began to teach a small number of people again and was looking forward to my Tu B'Shevat seder, which is always the most fun and well attended event I do in the course of the year. I wondered where I would hold it, whether people would come, and if it would be as wonderful as it had been in previous years. During moments of sadness, however, I wondered whether I should even hold it this year.

I mentioned my concern to a friend. Encouraging me, he immediately put me in touch with a person who had a large apartment and who was very eager to host this event. She and her husband had been searching for meditation and increased Jewish spirituality, and she was absolutely ecstatic at the prospect of having this event in her home. She would invite her friends. This was a sign of new beginnings. I began to feel the flow of God's light in my life again.

When I received a call from a grand niece of a very famous kabbalist from Morocco, I knew that God was again with me. It turns out that Tu B'Shevat was the *yahrzeit* (or anniversary of the death) of her uncle, and she wanted to donate the food to my gathering in his memory and speak briefly about him. I was amazed that word of my small gathering had somehow reached her, but I took it as a sign of God's participation in the event. What a privilege to do a Tu B'Shevat seder and a *yahrzeit* celebration for such a great saint!

Needless to say, it was a wonderful gathering. The niece was such a delight, and through her and her amazing stories about her uncle, we felt connected to this wondrous *tzaddik*. Not only did we have a kabbalistic seder, we felt as though the spirit of this great kabbalist was with us. For many of the people there, the experience was extraordinary on many levels. Many seeds were planted that night. For some, it was their first Tu B'Shevat seder. For others, it was their first exposure to kabbalah or Judaism.

The room was completely filled with interesting people of all ages and backgrounds. There were married couples, singles, young people, old people. There were Russian, Israeli, American, French, and Dutch Jews. Some were religiously observant Jews, others nonobservant; there were even Buddhist Jews and non-Jews. Some people attending the gathering had met several unaffiliated Jews on the elevator who were curious about what was happening in their building and invited them along. Usually I might be bothered by having strangers brought into a gathering, but I saw that this was God's event, not mine, and I later found out that those people really had to be there.

Many people told me they had made important connections that evening. I never do a follow-up about how an event affects attendees, but I knew that many people had received a great deal more than fruit and wine that night. In the course of the evening, I was amazed at how strangers had so easily opened to each other and to themselves in very new ways. The evening was very full. There were moments of deep meditation and moments of deep, beautiful silence; there was laughter, lots of hugging, singing, dancing, and a great feeling of love in the air. It felt magical, almost perfect. For me, it was truly a time of inner renewal. I felt once again that I was doing what God wanted me to do. I knew then that I would heal and live my life in a new way. I thanked God that I had survived Tevet and that Shevat was now here.

Energy: Inner Renewal

It may still be the heart of winter in many places, but Shevat marks a hidden and mystical time of new beginnings and rebirth. This month is a time of new inspiration and creativity. It is a time when it is easy to come close to God. The first part of the month may still feel dark and harsh, but that all changes according to kabbalah after the fifteenth of the month.

The renewal that occurs in Shevat is not yet manifest on the physical plane, but the process has begun and is occurring on the inner and hidden planes. This month is pregnant with new possibilities. We may have lived through a cold and challenging winter this year in our lives, but spring is coming. As a metaphor, winter represents the time when it is not always easy to see the fruit of one's labor; indeed, in our lives there may have been long periods of time when it felt like winter. But be patient and never lose hope. Shevat is here.

In the previous month, Tevet, we fought the negative forces that were limiting us and keeping us from realizing our vision and dreams. But even though the purpose of the challenges we faced may not have been clear, the work we have done to meet and overcome them has not been in vain. The seeds of our vision have been planted deeper within us, and we have been strengthened; now, in Shevat, the seed is sprouting. A little more patience is needed. Something new is going to come forth within you. Believe that you will bear new fruit and you will. We will bring forth our visions into reality. This month of renewal is the time to go deep inside and contact the creative energy within you. Open to a new beginning. Say yes to newness of life once again, and allow the potential within you to come forth.

The energy of this month is best represented by the holiday of Tu B'Shevat, which is the fifteenth day of Shevat, the time of the full moon. Though not widely known or celebrated, like the renewal energy of this month that is not yet manifest, Tu B'Shevat, the New Year for the Trees, is kabbalistically one of the most spiritual and joyous days of the year. At this time the trees are still barren, but we are told that the sap has begun to flow, and we trust in the cycle of life to produce new leaves, fruits, and flowers. The Torah tells us that the human being is likened to a tree, so we can think of it as another Rosh Hashanah for us, yet a more spiritual and hidden one than the one we celebrated in September. It is a celebration of and opening to the potential within the human being, which is infinite. Shevat is a time of conceiving new projects, planting new seeds, and beginning anew. Like the sap of the trees, our creative juices begin flowing, so we too will bear new fruit and flowers in the spring.

By honoring trees this month, we are reminded of the theme of the cycles of life. Many trees go from barren in the winter, to full and vibrant in the spring and summer, and then to leafless again in the fall. Similar changes occur within the individual and within the Jewish people as a whole. There are times in our personal lives and in the life of the Jewish people when we are shining and expressing ourselves fully, when our branches are full; and there are times when we are emptying ourselves, when we are

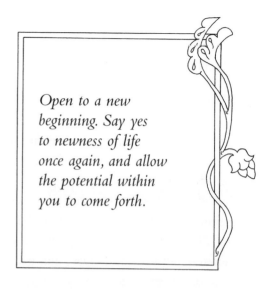

Open to a new beginning. Say yes to newness of life once again, and allow the potential within you to come forth.

leafless and humbled. Knowing that there is a cycle to life enables us to flow with and accept these changes gracefully.

We also learn something important about the creative process by witnessing these changes. In the creative process, there also has to be an emptying, so inspiration can be received and something new can be brought into being. Creation begins first in the spirit, then in the mind, and then in the heart before it manifests on the physical plane. For example, an author empties her mind and conceives of a new book. The vision becomes clear, and the strategy for translating this idea into reality becomes apparent, but there is as yet no book. This is what Shevat is about. The internal creative process begins, but it is not yet visible on the physical plane.

This month the area of healing is eating. Eating is also a mysterious inner process of renewal. How we eat, digest, and gain energy to animate, sustain, and heal our bodies and souls is still a great mystery. We do not just eat physical food; we ingest all kinds of "food." What we do for recreation, the movies and television we watch, the books we read, the music we listen to, the friends and acquaintances we associate with, the work we do—everything we take into ourselves is food and has the ability to strengthen or weaken us. This month asks us to become more conscious of what we take within us.

The redemptive energy of this month has shown itself historically. Zerach, the daughter of Asher, the ancestor of the tribe that represents this month, informed Jacob that his son Joseph was alive on Rosh Chodesh Shevat, the first day of Shevat. What a joy that must have been for him. Not only had he suffered the loss of his favored son, but because of his depression, he no longer experienced the presence of the Shechinah. This was restored to him when he found out that Joseph was alive. This month is associated with the oral Torah, which is the fruit, the blossoming of the written Torah. Moses began to explain the Torah he had received in his own words on the first day of Shevat.

The energy of Shevat connects to the energy of Nissan (March–April), a time of newness and freedom. Not only do we read the Torah portions relating to the Exodus in Shevat, both Tu B'Shevat and Passover (in Nissan) have a seder with four cups of wine. Passover is the most outwardly celebrated of Jewish holidays, and Tu B'Shevat is the least known. As wonderful and transformational as Passover is, Tu B'Shevat is a more hidden celebration of the potential within life. Because the potential within us is infinite, the celebration of it is very great. There are forty-five days from Rosh Chodesh (the first day) of Shevat until Purim, and forty-five days from Tu B'Shevat until the month of Nissan.

General Guidelines and Goals

The following guidelines and goals enable us to direct our energies in the ways that are optimal for our growth and transformation in accordance with the energy of this month. It is recommended that you read and meditate upon them often in the course of the month. Reflect on their applicability to you, and allow them to direct and inspire you often this month.

1. OPEN TO NEWNESS.

This is an optimal time to conceive of new projects, to open to newness in your life in general. Breathe out the old and breathe in the new. It may not be clear what the new is for you, but simply agree to open to the process of renewal in your life. Say yes to the process. Be open to surprises, meeting new people, and doing new things.

Renewal begins this month in the spiritual and unconscious dimensions. Give yourself some time this month to relax, to let go, and to receive inspiration. There is much blessing available this month. Believe that the future holds much hope and joy for you.

2. EAT CONSCIOUSLY TO SUPPORT YOUR GREATEST WELL-BEING.

This month is devoted to healing through eating. As human beings, we eat to sustain our lives. What and how we eat is an expression of who we are and what our relationship is to God. Food is a contraction of Divine Light, and by eating with the proper consciousness the Godly sparks within the foods are elevated and returned to their source. Eating provides an interface between the spiritual and the material. When our spiritual and physical dimensions are unified, there is balance and joy.

We need to reflect on whether what we eat and how we eat supports our well-being. Reflect on the following questions: Is your diet filled with fresh, organic foods that include lots of vegetables and fruits or is your diet filled with processed foods, heavy on carbohydrates, and laden with chemicals and hormones like those found in milk products and meat? Do you eat when you are hungry or do you eat to stuff down negative feelings? Do you eat slowly, chewing your food carefully, blessing your food before and after, or do you eat on the run, gulping your food down unconsciously? Make a commitment to eat consciously this month to support your well-being on all levels.

3. IDENTIFY THOSE THINGS THAT SUPPORT AND NURTURE YOU AND DEVELOP A PLAN TO INCLUDE THEM IN YOUR LIFE.

In addition to looking at the quality of our physical food, we need to look at love and work in our lives, the main areas that either nurture or deplete us. For example, we may find that relationships we have with some people are literally draining. These people seem to eat off us, demanding and taking whatever they can with little thought of what they can give. Other relationships are healing and life-affirming. Choose to let go of draining relationships, and cultivate and strengthen life-affirming and nurturing ones. Positive life-affirming relationships are the foundation and source of creativity in life.

In previous months, we have worked hard to heal, transform, and redeem negative relationships, but sometimes we simply have to let go. There is no need to feel guilty about this or to continue to allow ourselves to be manipulated by others. We may feel we cannot let go of such relationships because we have to take care of others, but there are times in our caregiving when we are simply enabling others to be dependent, so we are not serving them or ourselves by maintaining the relationship.

Take time this month to also look at the work you do. Is your work meaningful, life-affirming, expressive of who you are? Or do you spend your days toiling for money, feeling alienated, doing work that is disconnected from who you are and what you hold as important in life? If you do not love your work, what kinds of work do you love and want to do? If you cannot change your work, how can you change your attitude and find joy in what you do?

4. GUARD THE ENVIRONMENT.

This month we should be mindful of the *mitzvah* of *shomrei adamah,* guarding the environment. As we celebrate the new year of the Trees, Tu B'Shevat, this month, we have to extend our acknowledgment and caring to the whole physical environment. God created a beautiful world, where everything was in harmony. The waters were clean, the air was pure, and there were enough resources to go around to feed everyone. But what have we done to the world?

In a powerful midrash, a story from the oral Torah tradition, that is relevant today, God shows man the trees in the Garden of Eden and says to him, "See My works, how beautiful they are. Now all that I have created, I created for your benefit. Think upon this, do not corrupt and destroy My world, for if you destroy it there is no one to restore it after you."

Because of our greed, we currently face real threats to our survival. The purity of our air, our water, our oceans, our soil, our forests, and various species are endangered. Even many of the foods we eat have been tampered with. Who knows what the outcome of genetically engineered food will be?

During this month, make a commitment to learn more about the problems that affect the health of our environment and make a commitment to do something.

Astrological Sign: Aquarius

Aquarius is ruled by the planet Uranus. Uranus was only discovered in 1781, which coincided with a time of great social change. Until Uranus was discovered, Aquarius, along with Capricorn, was thought to be governed by Saturn. Kabbalah thought of Capricorn (Tevet) and Aquarius (Shevat) as two eyes. With the eye of Capricorn, we see the past and the negative; with the eye of Aquarius, we see the future and the positive.

In astrology, Uranus is associated with new directions, inventions, independence, and sudden change. Under the influence of Uranus, one suddenly sees things in a new way, and new possibilities, new vistas, are available. One sees the greater picture. There is a waking up to greater consciousness, along with the desire to translate this inner vision into action during this month.

Mythologically, Uranus is associated with the Ouranos, a primeval god who stole fire from the gods to enable humans to grow in knowledge. This shows itself in the willingness this month to break down rigid, old structures that do not serve the higher good. Much like the energy of this month, people born in this sign are said to be the most unconventional and open-minded of people.

Aquarius is an air sign that has the capacity to be both objective and expanded, reflecting the expansive nature of the energy of this month. Uranus is also known in astrology as the planet of the "higher mind."

Aquarius is represented by the water pitcher, a symbol that indicates a willingness to contain and share blessings with others. This month is surely a water pitcher pouring out blessings for the entire year. Water in kabbalah is a symbol of Torah, written and oral. In the Torah are several stories illustrating that worthiness as a mate was determined by the willingness to offer water. We see how Rebecca was selected to be the wife of Isaac by her willingness to fetch water for Eliezer and even for his camels. Moses also draws water for the daughters of Jethro, and he marries the eldest. Moses is also associated with this month, for he is seen as the water pitcher giving spiritual water to the people.

Hebrew Letter: Tzaddi

This month's letter, the tzaddi, is the *tzaddik,* the righteous, perfected one. Though often hidden, the *tzaddik* is considered the foundation and conduit of blessing for the world. The *tzaddik* is connected to the highest worlds and brings down the blessings to the people, much like the astrological sign, the water pitcher. Hidden like the *tzaddik,* this month of Shevat is also a foundation and source of blessing for the entire year. The *tzaddik* represents the hidden potential of every Jew, because, as it says several times in the Torah, all of Israel are *tzaddikim.*

The word *tzaddi* means "to hunt." The *tzaddik* "hunts" in order to redeem and elevate fallen sparks. This is referred to kabbalistically as the act of eating for the *tzaddik*. According to kabbalah, in the act of eating there is the raising of the fallen sparks of Godliness. So similarly the tzaddik raises the fallen Godly sparks within a person as he connects this person to God. The redeemed sparks elevate the *tzaddik* even more. This is an allusion to the area of healing, eating, that is prominent this month.

The letter tzaddi is the first letter of the word Tzelem, which refers to the Divine Image in which God created humankind, and is the second letter in the word *etz,* which means "tree." We see in the *tzaddik* the Divine Image and we experience the *tzaddik* also as a tree. Planted firmly on the ground, the *tzaddik* extends into the heavens, providing shelter from the sun. We refer to the Torah as Etz Hayim, a Tree of Life. We will learn more about the mystical significance of trees in the holiday section of this chapter for in this month we celebrate the New Year of the Trees.

Hebrew Tribe: Asher

Asher was born to Zilpah, the handmaid of Leah. When he was born, Leah proclaimed, "'Happy am I, for the young girls will call me blessed,' and she called him Asher" (Gen. 30:13). Asher was born after Leah had already given birth to four sons. Her first sons were born when Leah felt the pain of being loved less than her sister, Rachel, and these sons carried the scars of her pain. This pain is reflected in the energy of the months these tribes represent. As Leah develops spiritually, she emerges as a powerful woman in her own right. By the time she gives birth to her fourth son, Yehuda (Judah), she no longer begs for her husband's love with each new son, but praises and thanks God.

When Leah stops bearing children, she offers Jacob her handmaid Zilpah, who bears first Gad and then Asher. It is significant that Leah is now strong and self-confident enough to share her place with another woman. She is more interested in expanding her role as a matriarch of the Jewish people by having more sons. Asher is a source of great joy for Leah; he was not born out of pain, but out of the joy of bringing forth more life.

The Torah says a few additional things about Asher that shed light on the wonderful energy of this month. When Jacob blesses him he says, "Out of Asher shall come the richest foods and he shall provide the king's delights" (Gen. 49:20). Moses blesses Asher and says, "Blessed among sons is Asher. Let him be acceptable to his brothers and let him dip his foot in oil. Your shoes shall be iron and brass and as your days, so shall your strength be" (Deut. 33:24–25). What powerful affirmations and blessings!

The land Asher inherited was rich and full of oil derived from olives. Oil is said to kabbalistically represent the oral Torah, which gives a special blessing to the Jewish people and to this month. Although most if not all of the oral Torah has now been written down, it is still considered more hidden than the written Torah. The oral Torah is the expansion, the flowering of the written Torah. Oil also represents purity, for the oil never blends with another liquid, but always rises to the top. Oil is made from pressing the olives. There is a similar psychic pressing within us that puts us in touch with the oil within us, which represents what is pure and cannot be contaminated. This pressing most likely will occur during the first part of the month.

According to the oral tradition, the members of the tribe of Asher never showed their age. I have also noticed that righteous people never show their age. Their spiritual radiance keeps them looking young, no matter how old they are. It is also said that the tribe of Asher never wandered in search of what they did not have. They were happy with their portion. They also had the most children. All these qualities of Asher, the youthfulness, the contentment, the abundance and productivity, are expressive of the energy of this month.

Divine Name Permutation: HYVH

At first glance, we note that the first two letters are in an inverted order and the last two letters are in their natural placement in the tetragrammaton, YHVH. From this we are told that the month is divided between judgment and grace, judgment for the first part of the month and grace for the second. The placement of the first hay (H) in the world of Atzilut indicates a great heavenly influx of light this month, and the yud (Y) in the second position indicates that the mind must be contracted and concentrated so as to receive. The influx is then channeled through the heart into the physical world.

It is interesting to note that when the work of transformation primarily relates to consciousness, as during the months of Cheshwan and Tevet, the hay will appear in the second position, in the world of Beriyah, corresponding to the mind. When the energy is more about manifesting in the physical world, a hay will be in the fourth placement, in the world of Assiyah, the physical world.

Torah Portion

The Torah portion for Shevat often begins with Bo in the book of Exodus (Exod. 10), recounting the story of the exodus of the Jewish people from Egypt. This event is very much in line with the energy of this month, a time of breaking free from the past and beginning anew. In this Torah portion, we see the final plagues that were given to demonstrate God's power and finally take the Jews out of Egypt.

Interestingly, there are ten plagues, Ten Commandments, ten sayings used in creation of the world, and ten *sephirot*. These are all connected to each other. As we read the text on the literal level, we only see the plagues. When we understand the connection of the plagues to the *sephirot* and to the Commandments, we see clearly that with each plague, God is revealing the deepest secrets of creation and revealing the nature of God to the world.

Sometimes Shevat begins with the Torah portion of Beshallach (Exod. 13:17). In Beshallach, the Jews cross the Red Sea in the most miraculous way. The Jews have left Egypt, but they now find that the Red Sea is in front of them, making it impossible for them to go forward, and Pharaoh's army is quickly approaching from behind. There is confusion about what to do. Should they return to Egypt, should they fight the Egyptians, or should they drown themselves in the sea and so commit suicide? They pray to God and God tells Moses in so many words, "Don't cry to me. Go forward into the sea. Raise your staff and I will split the sea." God offers them a solution they never would have imagined possible. The key here is to pray, to move forward, and trust in God, an important teaching for us in our lives in general and particularly for this month.

When we are faced with what appear to be insurmountable challenges, we should move forward with faith, even if it doesn't make sense to our rational mind. If we fight the negativity, we often become mired in it. If we retreat, we lose and deny a part of ourselves, and to some extent we will have to deaden ourselves to accept this retreat. As the Jews cross the sea, it parts; Moses sings and Miriam sings; and the connection with God was so strong that even the simplest person was said to be a prophet. The crossing of the sea continues to be a source of great joy, because for that brief time, God was not hidden in nature, but revealed through it. This is the highest awareness that we yearn for deep inside.

Farther on, we read about the complaints of the Jews for water and then for meat. Again the concern about food reminds us about the energy of healing through eating of this month. God gives them the manna in these Torah portions and the Jewish people have the opportunity to have a very close relationship with God at this time, which is also reflected in the energy of this month. If they could open to this kind of closeness, there would be no need to be tested. But alas, people have to go through so many tests until they truly wake up.

In the next Torah portion, Yitro (Exod. 18–20), the Jews receive the Ten Commandments. The Jews have reached such a high level of God awareness, they are surrendered and declare that they will do whatever God asks of them, and then they will understand. This kind of surrender is the prerequisite to a close relationship with God.

In the following Torah portion, Mispatim (Exod. 21–24), they receive the laws by which to maintain the holiness of the nation, after the peak experience of Sinai. The laws regarding slavery are discussed in detail. In Judaism, slavery was an act of kindness given to an unfortunate person who may have committed a crime and needed some rehabilitation. All the Torah laws protect the human soul, enabling a person to grow and realize his or her awesome potential. For this reason, we read about this during Shevat.

The Torah portions read during Shevat connect us to Passover, the exodus from Egypt, which occurs in Nissan, the receiving of the manna, which occurs in Iyar, and the receiving of the Torah, which occurs in Sivan. Even though Shevat occurs in the winter, we are reading about the spring in the Torah portions. This supports us in opening to a vision of freedom and newness that is characteristic of this month.

Holiday

Tu B'Shevat

HISTORY   The holiday of Tu B'Shevat, the fifteenth of Shevat, the time of the full moon, is biblically a halachic demarcation, formerly used to determine which year a crop belonged to for the purposes of *smittah,* the practice of allowing the land to rest every seven years. If a tree began to flower before the fifteenth of Shevat, it was included in the tithe for the previous year; if after the fifteenth of Shevat, it was counted in the following year. One explanation for this date was that in the land of Israel most of the annual rain has fallen by the fifteenth of Shevat, the sap has risen in the trees, and the process of bearing fruit has begun. Another opinion was that a tree that blossomed before Tu B'Shevat did so with the rainwater of the previous year, before Rosh Hashanah, so it should be counted in last year's tithe. At the time of the Holy Temple, Tu B'Shevat was a date to regulate the giving of tithes.

In the Talmud, Tu B'Shevat is called the New Year's Day for the Trees. Much like our Rosh Hashanah, it became a day marking a new beginning for the trees, and a day of gratitude for the fruits in the land of Israel. There is much testimony in Jewish writing of the appreciation for the benefits we receive from trees. Recognizing a mystical connection between the trees and humanity, the kabbalists of Safed in the 1500s revealed that Tu B'Shevat is a spiritual and mystical Rosh Hashanah for us, a time of new beginnings, even a time of ushering in redemption for the world.

In the Mishnah, Tu B'Shevat is actually called the New Year of the Tree, rather than Trees, a reference to the original Tree of Good and Evil that Adam and Eve ate of in the Garden of Eden story in Genesis. Because eating of this particular tree was forbidden, humanity was cast out of the Garden of Eden. Adam was initially commanded to eat from all the fruit-bearing trees except this one tree. When he sinned, he was told to eat the grasses of the fields like animals and toil working the ground to grow vegetables. This was originally a humiliation and a curse upon him. The fruit of the tree is the most perfect food. The tree surrenders its fruit gracefully, and when we eat it, the integrity of the tree is not compromised. The tree is planted once, and then it goes through cycles and bears fruit every year. Vegetables have to be replanted every year.

The eating of fruit on Tu B'Shevat is a symbolic rectification of this original sin, a return to the consciousness of being in the Garden of Eden, the place of the original and total connection that humanity had with God. The kabbalists developed the custom of a kabbalistic seder, comparable to the Passover seder, which revealed the deepest kabbalistic secrets of creation. As Tu B'Av is forty-five days before Rosh Hashanah, so Tu B'Shevat is forty-five days before Nissan.

OBSERVANCE   The way the holiday of Tu B'Shevat is celebrated has developed over time, and varies in different communities. The most popular form is as a day of gratitude for all the fruits in the land of Israel, which helps to deepen one's connection to the land of Israel. It is often a day of picnics, a time to be outdoors, surrounded by trees. For some it is a day to focus on ecology, celebrating our partnership with God, and remembering our responsibility to take care of the land. In Israel, it is Jewish Arbor Day, when trees are planted.

I celebrate Tu B'Shevat in kabbalistic custom and find it to be the most joyous, ecstatic day of the entire year. For many years, I have conducted a kabbalistic seder with my students. During this seder we drink four cups of wine and eat more than fifteen kinds of fruits. Through this experience, we learn kabbalah in a kinesthetic way and have a taste of the great joy that God experienced in creating this world. We also understand the process by which creation occurs as relevant to our lives. It is hard to outline the seder in detail, because there are so many nuances, songs, and stories, but what follows are the basics. (Please see my *New Age Judaism* for a deeper explanation of the kabbalistic worlds and the secrets of creation and plan to join me once for a kabbalistic seder.)

My kabbalistic seder begins with a journey in one's imagination, going back to a place before there was time and space. We can't really imagine such a place, but before there was time and space, there was God, Ain Sof, as God is called in kabbalah. There arose a desire within Ain Sof to bestow goodness, to love and be known. We know this desire because it is the deepest desire within us. As there was only Ain Sof, there was nothing to give to, nothing to be known by. Ain Sof withdrew, so to speak, and created an empty space where worlds would be brought into being. The seder is a journey through these worlds. By drinking different kinds of wine and eating different kinds of fruit, representing the various worlds, we gain direct insight into the nature of these worlds, their purpose, their gifts to us. Needless to say, the eating of the fruits takes place in silence.

The first cup poured, of white wine, is for the world of Atzilut, the world of nearness. We say the blessing over the wine, drink it, and meditate on the world of Atzilut, the world of the most intimate connection with Ain Sof, touching the highest level of our soul. Atzilut is in such proximity to Ain Sof that it is absorbed in the domain of the *sephirot.* We meditate on the *sephirot,* for it is through the *sephirot* that we interact with Ain Sof. We meditate on the letter yud, which represents this world. There is no fruit, for there is only absorption in oneness with Ain Sof in this world.

The second cup is for the world of Beriyah, the world of creation. Creation is separate and outside, so to speak, of Ain Sof. This is the beginning of the seeming separation between the human being and God. Here we drink a second cup of wine, white wine with some red wine mixed in. We say a blessing over the fruits associated with this world. The fruits are completely edible, such as grapes, figs, carob, oranges, and blueberries. This is the world of the highest angels, and the world that corresponds to the level of soul known as *neshama,* the seat of the higher self. Like the fruits of this world, the soul is pure and open. We meditate on the letter hay. We welcome the highest angels, and open to the level of soul of *neshama.*

The third cup is poured for the world of Yetzerah, the world of formation. Here we drink a cup of red wine with some white wine mixed in. In this world there is increasing differentiation, because it is further removed from the direct light of Ain Sof. The fruits corresponding to this world are olives, dates, peaches, cherries, and pears. These fruits are edible on the outside, but have a protective covering for the seed, which is not edible. This world corresponds to the level of soul of *ruach,* which is seated in the heart. The heart is more fragile and delicate and needs a protective shield. We meditate on the letter vav in the heart, and open the heart to the blessings of the angels of this world.

The fourth cup is poured for the world of Assiyah, the world of action, corresponding to our physical world. Here we drink a cup of completely red wine. The fruits of this world—pomegranates, almonds, avocado, walnuts, mangos, and so on—are the most vulnerable; they have an outside protective covering and in some cases an inside covering as well. We really have to work hard to eat the fruits of this world. We have to crack the nuts, we have to peel the fruits. This is our physical world in which we have to do things, and what we do makes a difference. We meditate on the letter hay.

We meditate on the Divine Name, the yud (visualized outside of the body, six to twelve inches above the head), the hay (visualized close to the head), the vav (visualized in the heart), and the hay (visualized in the waist and legs) and recollect the worlds that they represent. We do this several times, carving out the letters deeper and deeper. The meal concludes with a blessing for fruits and wine.

Meditation

In honor of Tu B'Shevat, two meditations on trees follow.

In the first, imagine yourself in a beautiful wondrous garden with every kind of fruit-bearing tree in the world. See yourself beholding all these beautiful trees, smelling all the beautiful aromas, dancing joyfully in this garden. It is said in the Talmud that the trees were created for the pleasure of humans and that in former times Adam could actually converse with the trees. As you visualize yourself in this wondrous Garden of Eden, imagine that you have a dialogue with a tree. Which tree do you feel attracted to? Tell the tree how beautiful it is, how you so much appreciate its fruit. What does the tree say back to you?

Do this meditation with a partner, so afterward you can share the messages you received, or write down your experience. You will find that the tree you are attracted to varies depending on what you are experiencing in your life. What world does the tree belong to? This will indicate the kind of opening needed in your life at this time.

In the second meditation, imagine yourself as a tree. Your branches are now barren, but your roots are hidden, strong, and very deep into the earth. Go deep inside, and open to the new creative energy that is stirring within you now. Breathe deeply and open to this new flow. What potential do you feel within you that has not been expressed? Open to a new beginning. Keep breathing deeply as you do this simple opening to the new. You will bring forth beautiful flowers and new fruit.

Practical Recommendations

1. DO NEW THINGS.

This is a month of new creativity, so add new activities to your life that will open you, nurture you, and enable you to be creative and expressive in new ways. For example, during this month, Neal began drum lessons, Erin took acting lessons, Jean took singing lessons, and Susan took a writing class. Each of these activities was new and fun and helped to stir the creative juices within each person.

2. LEARN TORAH.

According to kabbalah, the water pitcher in the sign of Aquarius is a symbol of Israel and the water is Torah. The oil of the tribe of Asher for this month is a symbol of the oral Torah. This is also the month of the trees, and Torah is called the Tree of Life. Learning Torah will open your mind and heart to newness and inspiration. Give yourself time to learn this month. Go to a Torah class and find inspiring books to read.

3. BE MINDFUL AS YOU EAT.

This month the area of healing is eating. In selecting the foods for a meal, take a moment to get in touch with what your body wants right now. This may be hard to discern at first, but as you listen to your body more, you will have a greater insight into what your body needs.

Before you eat, take a moment to breathe, say the appropriate blessings, and then breathe again for a moment or two. Be aware that this food has been given to nurture you in the ways that you need right now. Eat slowly and consciously, chewing each bite of food many times so it becomes almost liquid. Be present with your eating as much as possible. Delight in the sense and taste sensations in all the foods that are on your plate. After you complete eating, take a moment to relax, to allow the food to digest, and say the appropriate blessings after the meal.

Sometimes I have Shabbat gatherings at which I ask people to eat silently and consciously for most of the meal. It is a wondrous, holy, sensual, and intimate experience. When we talk while we eat, we are not fully present to the experience of eating. You may want to experiment with this when you eat with others on Shabbat and even when you eat alone. Often when people eat alone, they read or watch television and are similarly distracted.

4. BECOME KOSHER OR VEGETARIAN AND EAT HEALTHY FOODS AS MUCH AS POSSIBLE.

Our consciousness is influenced by the foods we eat. The Torah provides clear instructions regarding the kinds of foods that will nurture us spiritually. We may not understand the reasons behind the rules, but if we want to grow in the Jewish path, we will need to accept this higher wisdom. For example, the Torah prohibits the eating of milk with meat. There is no logical reason why we shouldn't mix the two, but the Torah is very clear about this. It must mean that we cannot easily digest the energies of these two foods together. When we do eat these two foods together, we may become spiritually blocked and not be able to receive the influx of divine energy.

Although we may like to eat foods like pork, lobster, or scallops, the Torah forbids it. For some food items there may have been actual hygienic reasons for their prohibition in the past, which protected observant Jews from illness and disease; for other items, the reasons are not yet clear. We have to assume that the prohibited foods do not support us spiritually.

I personally recommend that people become vegetarians, and if that is not possible, they should eat kosher, organic, free-range chicken or meat. At least with kosher meat, one is assured that the animal was healthy when it was slaughtered and it was slaughtered in a way to minimize pain. However, today now even in kosher factories, animals are given antibiotics and hormones, and the long-term health hazards of such practices are not known. Also, animals are now kept locked up in cages and not allowed to roam and get the exercise needed to maintain health. This is not in keeping with the Torah rules of compassion toward animals. It is therefore best to limit the intake of meat.

Eating vegetables and fruits that are fresh brings more life to people. Foods that are processed and dead do not have the same life-giving properties within them. Feed your body with life-giving foods.

A Tale to Live By

Micah lived at the time of the Second Holy Temple. The following is a tale told about him in relation to Tu B'Shevat.

Micah was a Jew who had a dream of world peace and built a special house to embody his dream. How he built the house reflected its purpose. His house was built out of stone, because he did not want destroy any trees in the building of his house. He also did not want to use metal tools to carve the stones, for metal tools can be used as weapons that destroy life. So he did it all with his own hands, like the altar in the Holy Temple. He then planted a fig tree outside of the house and placed a table in its shade.

Like the Holy Temple, he envisioned his house as a place for all people. People would visit him from everywhere and he would feed them under the fig tree. He would leave the crumbs remaining from the meals and the birds would fly down to eat them. Micah, of course, was a vegetarian, an ardent one.

One day a prophet visited Micah, though Micah did not know that the man was a prophet. After staying in Micah's house a few days, he said that he had to leave and wanted to pay him. Micah did not take money for his hospitality, but he did not want to make a big fuss in front of the man, so he accepted it and then slipped the money back into the pocket of the prophet's coat.

The prophet, however, knew what Micah had done and gave him a blessing. He said to Micah, "In heaven they are so impressed with your house. I'm here to tell you that one day a child of yours will eat a fig from the tree outside of your house and this will bring the Messiah." Micah at that time did not have any children.

The next day the Romans invaded Jerusalem. They destroyed the Temple and Micah's home. Micah went into exile along with many other Jews. But the dream of Micah and the story of Micah continue to be told to this day. Throughout time, for thousands of years and even today, people serve figs to their children, because maybe, just maybe, one of their children is a child of Micah and maybe, just maybe, one of these figs is from a tree that grew from a seed of another tree that can be traced back to Micah's fig tree. So one day, the prophet's words may come true, that the Messiah will indeed come when one of Micah's descendants eats a fig of Micah's tree.

Adar

MONTH: *February-March*

ENERGY: *The Joy of Oneness*

AREA OF HEALING: *Joy and Laughter*

ASTROLOGICAL SIGN: *Pisces*

HEBREW LETTER: *Kuf*

HEBREW TRIBE: *Naftali*

DIVINE NAME PERMUTATION: *HHYV*

HOLIDAY: *Purim*

oy and laughter have great healing properties this month, especially when they result from insight into the underlying unity in what seems on the surface to be incongruous or disparate. In thinking about joy and laughter, I was reminded of a memorable experience of a Purim with Reb Shlomo over twenty years ago. I had been a student of Reb Shlomo for about five years, and Shlomo had been invited to do a Purim concert at Studio 54, one of the most popular trendy discotheques in Manhattan at the time. People used to wait in line for hours to get into Studio 54, and then only get in if they were chosen. Movie stars frequented Studio 54, and it had quite a wild reputation, even by New York standards. That was why it was so popular. I believe it was eventually closed down by the police or FBI years later for a combination of drugs, sex orgies, and tax evasion.

I was organizing events for Reb Shlomo, so I was one of the few people to accompany him on this adventure. This was, however, at the beginning of the most religious period in my life. I was wearing long skirts, praying three times a day, not going to discotheques, not doing mixed dancing, not even listening to secular music. I remember that I was immediately hit by the energy. I had been to discotheques before, but this was my first time in a place of this magnitude. It was overwhelming.

Before the concert, with the music blasting so loud I could barely think, I wondered how Shlomo would celebrate Purim in such a place. Needless to say, the people at Studio 54 were not attending synagogue on a regular basis; many were not even Jewish. These people did not come to see Shlomo; he would be an unexpected treat. Most did not know that it was Purim or even what Purim was. How would they respond to Shlomo?

I had no real doubts or concerns, because I had seen Shlomo work in many differ-ent settings. I knew my rebbe, and I knew he would transform this discotheque. In a short time Studio 54 would be a synagogue. I had accompanied Reb Shlomo to many concerts and adventures, and I often did outreach for the synagogue at those times. People we met at these events started to come to the shul (Shlomo's synagogue). I looked at Studio 54 as another opportunity for outreach. As I handed out leaflets I had prepared about our synagogue I told people, "Everything is one! This discotheque will be a synagogue, and if you come to our synagogue you will see that it is like a disco-theque. We dance, sing, and get high there as well." When I think back about this, I was somewhat of a missionary at the time.

And that is what happened. We danced, we sang, we got high (naturally!). And we turned that discotheque into a synagogue. Reb Shlomo was given a limited time to perform. The loud music stopped, Reb Shlomo took the microphone, and soon all that was heard was the strumming of his guitar and his soft, sweet voice singing and telling stories. I couldn't believe it was actually quiet. In a short time, these sophisti-cated New Yorkers were dancing in circles as if they were at a Jewish wedding, wishing each other Good Purim, and there was such a heavenly holy energy in the air. It was like being in shul. I don't remember whether anyone we met that night came to our shul, but perhaps some did. But for those moments, I tasted such exquisite holiness I might have been in Jerusalem. Even before we left, the loud music had already re-sumed. As I exited, I looked at the discotheque and it appeared that everything had immediately reverted back to what it had been before Shlomo's concert. Everything in the physical world seemed so transient to me, but still I felt that this event was carved into my soul. I carried the joy of Purim inside of me in a deeper way than ever before, and I laughed.

Energy: The Joy of Oneness

The sages in the *Gemara,* the commentary on the Torah, have said, "Joy is increased in the month of Adar." There is a heavenly flow of joy this month, but we must also do our part to claim it as well as increase it. In other months such as Tammuz and Av, we talk about the growth and healing that occurs through pain and suffering. This month is all about learning how to grow and heal through joy and laughter. According to kabbalah, joy is the greatest healer. Reb Nachman of Breslov said it quite simply: sickness comes from a lack of joy and healing comes from joy.

The joy of this month comes from embracing the materiality, the mundaneness, the physicality of the world and experiencing its inner divinity. When we can see that the physical and the spiritual dimensions are separate but also together, we are filled with joy and laughter. This joy is epitomized in this month's holiday, Purim, when we are told to feast, drink to the point of becoming drunk, wear costumes, play, and be happy. Kabbalah says that the holiness we can experience on Purim is even greater than that on Yom Kippur.

Just as the Eskimos have many names for snow to distinguish its varieties, the Hebrew language has as many words for "joy" as there are many different experiences of joy and laughter. One of the Hebrew words for "joy" is *simcha. Simcha* is when something good happens that makes you happy. For example, you buy a new car, you get a new job, you meet a new man or woman, and you are happy. You got what you wanted. *Sasson* is a term connoting an unexpected joy. Reb Shlomo used to explain *sasson* in the following manner. Imagine you go to the store to buy a suit and expect to pay about two thousand dollars. When you arrive at the store you find that there is a special sale going on, and the suit you wanted now costs you five dollars. You are more than happy—you start laughing. This is *sasson*. In the Bible, when Sarah was told that she would bear a child when she was old and no longer menstruating, she laughed. God is hidden in many ways this month, but in the experience of *sasson* we experience a message of such tremendous blessing that we feel God is playing a wonderful game with us. The story we read on Purim is filled with so much unexpected joy. May we all be blessed with *simcha* and *sasson* this month.

The joy of this month comes from embracing the materiality, the mundaneness, the physicality of the world and experiencing its inner divinity.

In Adar, we are told to destroy Amalek. "Remember what Amalek did to you. . . . You shall erase the memory of Amalek from beneath the heavens, you shall not forget" (Deut. 25:17–19). We read this in a Torah portion on the Shabbat before Purim, and the rabbis have asked that everyone be present to hear it. The scripture sounds very heavy, and one might naturally wonder what it has to do with the joy of this month.

Historically, Amalek was a descendent of Esau who had sworn to hate and kill Jews. His tribe, the Amalekites, waged war on Jewish people as they wandered in the desert. The Amalekites went out of their way to battle the Israelites because they could bear that the Israelites had a connection with God.

No longer confined to a specific Bedouin tribe, the faces of the Amalekites have changed, but the energy of Amalek has remained the same throughout history. The energy of Amalek is so bent on the destruction on what is positive and good, on destroying the spiritual entity and integrity of the Jewish people, even if its proponents receive no benefit from Israel's destruction and it costs them their lives. The hatred that

Amalek feels toward the Jewish people is not logical and cannot be placated with bribes. Haman in the Purim story of this month was considered a descendent of Amalek. Hitler is considered the Amalek of the last generation. An interesting gematria that I read states that the numerical value of the letters composing the name Adolf Hitler equals that of Amalek and Gog. Today, I wonder whether Amalek is being expressed by the militant Islamic fundamentalists.

In common usage today from a kabbalistic perspective, Amalek refers to the negative force, the *yetzer hara,* the evil inclination within humans. Amalek has the same numerical value as the Hebrew word for "doubt" *(safek).* The energy of Amalek causes us to doubt ourselves and our capacity to accomplish what we want to do, especially in regard to spiritual growth. It is the evil inclination that makes us self-critical, judgmental, and vulnerable to depression.

Amalek is anti-God. It is the energy of Amalek within us that says, "Things just happen" or "Everything is random." Amalek is that negative inclination within people that is spiteful, jealous, and willing to do harm to oneself or to others even though it serves no purpose and will bring no benefits. Amalek may be at the root of drug addiction.

The final destruction of Amalek will take place in the messianic time. But each year, during Adar, the energy of Amalek is erased a little more by the joy that we open up to this month. Joy is actually a powerful weapon. Adar hosts the holiday of Purim, the day of the greatest joy. On Purim, we feast, we drink, we wear costumes, we give gifts to each other, all of which wipes out Amalek in the most fun way. There is a great feeling of unity on Purim and that is part of the joy. We are so happy if we feel close to one person. Imagine how happy we are if we feel close to everyone. This is the joy that we can easily experience on Purim.

Adar is a very positive and auspicious month for good things to happen on the material plane. The *Gemara* says that if a Jew has to go to court, he should go during Adar. I told this to a friend who, after a divorce, was involved in terrible litigation over custody. After many years of custody battles, he went to court in Adar and got everything he wanted. The *Gemara* also says, "Someone who wants a fortune should plant it in Adar." Sounds like a good time to invest in the stock market.

According to the Torah and astrology, Adar is considered the twelfth month, the last month of the year. It is less a time to start projects than to attend to existing projects and complete them as quickly as possible. The energy of Adar expresses the fulfillment of the original divine intention, which was to create a dwelling place for the Divine Presence in the physical world. The joy of Adar comes from the unification of the material world with the divine. If we count Tishrei as the first month of the year, as we do in this book, Adar is the sixth month. Six in kabbalah is indicative of the weekday, material world. So we also see that Adar is the elevating of the mundane physical world to the divine.

The joy of Adar is increased every seven years with an additional month of Adar. In those years, Purim is celebrated in the second Adar so as to link it with Passover. In this way, the Jewish calendar assures that Passover will occur in the spring as prescribed in the Torah.

General Guidelines and Goals

The following guidelines and goals enable us to direct our energies in the ways that are optimal for our growth and transformation in accordance with the energy of this month. It is recommended that you read and meditate upon them often in the course of the month. Reflect on their applicability to you, and allow them to direct and inspire you often this month.

1. COMMIT TO INCREASING JOY IN YOUR LIFE.

Take time to contact what brings you joy in your life and commit to increasing joy in your life this month. Kabbalah teaches that God did not create this world for suffering, but for love and joy. It is true that we need to learn many things while we are here and sometimes we have to suffer, but the main reason we have come into this world is to experience and teach joy. If we understand that this is what God wants and what we really want, we can be joyful even when we are challenged, because we are learning what we need to learn. It is also important to not be too serious or analytical. Seek to see the humor in life—it is always there.

Give yourself time to play, to enjoy nature, to dance, to sing, to meditate, to do whatever brings you joy. Within each of us is an inner child who absolutely loves to play and have fun. Let the inner child come out to play. Affirm that every moment can be an opportunity for you to connect with your inner child, your higher self, with God, and just remembering this will fill you with joy.

2. ELIMINATE OR REDUCE WHAT DOES NOT GENERATE JOY IN YOUR LIFE AND OPEN TO WHAT DOES.

Review the way you live your life on a daily basis, and see whether your time is filled with things that you do not want, but feel that you should do. If you find that you are the kind of person who spends more time listening to others talking about their problems or venting their anger than you would like to do, remember that you can diplomatically end conversations with such people without hurting them. Be mindful not to waste your time.

Sometimes people feel so obligated to do for others that they forget about their own needs and may even hurt themselves in the process. Being there for other people at your own expense usually generates resentment. Be honest about what your underlying motivations are when you do for other people at your own expense. For example, you may find that the real reason you did something for another was so he or she would think that you are a good person, and not because you really wanted to give to that person.

If you're honest, you will admit that most things you do, you do for yourself. If you know that, you should not resent other people, but ask yourself if you need to continue to prove that you are worthwhile to other people in ways that do not make you happy. If you find yourself spending time resenting other people, remember that you do not serve yourself, other people, and God by engaging in activities or relationships that drain you of your life force.

If you are at a job, in a relationship, or in anything else that does not bring you joy, take responsibility for creating this in your life, forgive yourself, and know that you can choose differently. It is not necessary for you to know why you allowed yourself to be unhappy or suffer in the way that you have. Sometimes this kind of exploration just keeps you stuck, feeling justified but discouraged. For example, I had a client who had a terribly abusive childhood. As he talked about his problems, he attempted to justify his unhappiness because of the kind of father and mother he had. I felt a lot of compassion for him, but at a certain point, I knew that I was not serving him or myself by continuing to listen to his justifications. I asked him if he wanted to be right or if he wanted to be happy. Would he be willing to allow himself to be happy? To be happy, you need to stop blaming other people, God, or yourself.

If you are willing to open to living a more joyful life, begin by saying yes to yourself, and inwardly agree to open to the kind of work and relationships that will allow you to express more of who you really are. When we can be authentic in our life, when our inner and outer lives are in accordance, we are happy.

I remember the day I left a very good job with the city government to do work that was more connected to my inner life. For the most part, I liked my job. I had a certain level of responsibility and influence, but I still worked in a bureaucracy. I could help other people, but it was not creative, and with each year it was becoming more of a routine. At the time, some people encouraged me to follow my inner guidance and others discouraged me, saying it was very foolish to leave a city position with a good salary, benefits, and pension. It is true that I am not making the same kind of money now that I was making even when I left fifteen years ago, but I am happy because I am doing the work I believe is my life purpose.

You may not be able to make the immediate changes you want, but affirm that you will do so at the right time. Affirm yourself, trust in God, and take steps in the direction you want to go. If you are unclear about the kind of work that best expresses your purpose, pray for divine guidance and assistance. You will be guided.

3. SERVE GOD WITH JOY.

Many psalms speak of the joy that comes from divine service. Our sages have said that the Divine Presence cannot rest upon us unless we are full of joy. It is said that Jacob lost the Divine Presence for many years because he was depressed over the loss of his son Joseph. Connecting with God brings joy and even ecstasy. Be conscious of your intention to sincerely connect with God whenever you pray or do a *mitzvah*. You will know that you have been brought close to God if you are filled with joy. Pray, meditate, and do *mitzvot* from a place of love and deep yearning to come close to God and you will easily be brought to joy. Reb Shlomo would compose the most beautiful melodies so we could sing and pray with joy. Sing and dance your prayers, make up your own melodies, and give yourself time to rejoice with God.

4. WIPE OUT YOUR PERSONAL AMALEK.

People search for happiness in many ways. We look toward a variety of experiences, possessions, relationships, or accomplishments for this happiness. When we arrive at our goals or obtain what we want, we may be happy momentarily, but the happiness does not last. In its place, we often feel a sense of loss or the fear of loss. It is frustrating not to be able to hold on to our happiness. It is not easy to be in a constant state of joy, as Reb Nachman asks. Yet when we experience joy, it feels so natural we wonder why we are not able to maintain it.

As we grow spiritually, we are in a state of joy more of the time. This is because we are better able to access the joy that is integral to who we are. Happiness has to be found within oneself. One can have everything that other people dream of and still be unhappy. One can have very little and be very happy. It is our own ego that often robs us of the joy that we are pursuing. It tells us that we are not enough, others are not enough, and we should or need to have more to be happy. This is the internal voice of Amalek. Be mindful of the voices within you that take you away from the experience of the absolute joy of being alive.

5. SEE GOD'S HAND IN YOUR LIFE.

Things do not happen randomly; nothing is an accident. God is communicating with you through everything that is happening in your life. Listen closely to what is being said to you; read between the lines. Remember that God does have a sense of humor, so you should too.

As we see from the Purim story, life is full of irony. Esther might have been criticized for living with a non-Jewish king, but through a turn of events she becomes the savior of the Jewish people. Like Esther, we never know when we will be called to do something absolutely amazing, and, like Esther, we all have opportunities in small or big ways to bring redemption to other people.

6. GIVE CHARITY.

According to Jewish law, people are to give to the poor on Purim or in the month of Adar. We are expected to give directly to at least two poor people. Even poor people are required to give charity to other poor people. Charity does not have to be money; it can be clothes, food, or other items. It can be small—even one penny or a piece of fruit—but everyone has to give.

Astrological Sign: Pisces

Pisces, according to astrology, is the twelfth month of the year, representing the final stage of human development. In Pisces, we complete what we have worked on all year; we let go and transcend physical boundaries to connect with the Divine and collective unconscious. In Aquarius, the previous month, we looked outward and conceived new projects; in Pisces we again look inward, visualizing a place of God consciousness in the human world. It is a time when the soul longs to bring heaven to earth, healing and completing on all planes.

Pisces was traditionally seen to be ruled by Jupiter, but acclaimed to embody more of its spiritual elements, such as faith, surrender of the ego, letting go of the illusion of separateness, and opening to unconditional love. Jupiter also rules over Sagittarius and Kislev, which hosts the holiday of Chanukah. Chanukah and Purim are connected. They are both rabbinical holidays in which evil was destroyed by the Jewish people in a miraculous way.

When Neptune was discovered, Pisces was assigned to Neptune. Neptune was the Roman god of the sea. The prophet Isaiah spoke of the time of the Messiah when "at that time the earth will be filled with the knowledge of God as the waters cover the sea" (Isa. 11:9). Torah is also compared to the sea. According to kabbalah, Pisces is the water sign that represents the messianic time when Godliness will be revealed on earth. The Vilna Gaon said Adar, the sixth of the winter months, corresponds to the sixth millennium, when Amalek will be destroyed.

As a water sign, Pisces operates in the realm of feelings. Like those born under the other water signs, Cancer and Scorpio, Pisceans connect through deep feelings. For the most part, Pisceans are deeply sensitive, intuitive, feeling-oriented people. Sometimes Pisceans try to absorb and transmute the negative energy around them and think of themselves as martyrs. Sometimes they become too sensitive for their own good and suffer. Pisceans are said to be the most compassionate and loving of people. These characteristics are also expressive of the loving, sensitive, and compassionate energy of this month.

Pisces, from the Latin word for "fish," is represented by two fish swimming in opposite directions. One fish is looking to Aquarius and the other to Aries. Fish are known to have spiritual properties. Other animals were said to be destroyed at the Flood; the fish were not. Fish swim with their eyes open at all times, and kabbalah likens fish to *tzaddikim,* who swim the waters of Torah with their eyes open, always alert. Kabbalah states that the two fish in Pisces represent Mordecai and Esther, who saved the Jewish people this month.

Hebrew Letter: Kuf

ק The kuf is the first letter of the word *kedusha,* which means "holiness." It also is the first letter of *korban,* which means "sacrifice," and of *kabbail,* which means "to receive." Of course there is a connection between these words and the energy of the month. The sacrifice of the ego allows for both receiving and holiness. Participating in the joy of this month is the easiest way to let go of the ego and open to the greatest holiness. Interestingly, the kuf is a letter that descends below the line, reflecting spirituality that enters into the material realm. It is this unification of the material and spiritual worlds that give this month a very special feeling of joy and holiness.

The word *kuf* means "monkey," which is the symbol of laughter for this month. We sometimes use the expression "to monkey around" to mean to play or joke. We see the play of the monkey in the celebration of the holiday of Purim. Monkeys are said to be the animal most like humans, and they are great imitators. Monkeys imitate humans, and humans imitate God. This letter representing the monkey also reminds us that reality is not what it appears to be. God and holiness are often hidden, but they are revealed naturally during this month.

Hebrew Tribe: Naftali

When Rachel lent her handmaid Bilhah to Jacob a second time, Bilhah bore a son whom Rachel named Naftali, saying, "With God wrestling, I wrestled with my sister and I have been able to do it" (Gen. 30:8). The Torah commentator Rashi explains that

Rachel did many things to be equal to her sister. She tried exceedingly hard, and Naftali represents her zeal. With the birth of Naftali, Rachel is happy and feels she has been successful in participating in the building of Israel by having more sons, even if they were through her handmaid. Rachel's accomplishment and joy are characteristic of this month.

When on his deathbed Jacob blesses Naftali, he says that Naftali is described as a deerlike messenger (Gen. 49:21) and as one who gives beautiful speeches. As a deerlike messenger, Naftali does things swiftly. Rabbi Samson Hirsch, in his commentary on Naftali, says that this blessing implies that Naftali may not be particularly productive or creative, but he knows how to express himself in beautiful words and carry out what needs to be done efficiently and quickly. The energy of Naftali reminds us to complete things as quickly as possible and to be mindful to speak good words as we do what we need to do. When we hesitate or procrastinate, we become vulnerable to depression and doubt. Naftali did everything quickly, so he was said to always be joyous. His good words also protected him and were reflected back to him.

Interestingly, Esther, the heroine of the story of Purim, which takes place this month, is called a feminine deer in the Talmud, as described in Psalm 22. The Talmud explains that as a deer is always attractive to its mate, so Esther was always appealing to Ahasuerus. It is said that Esther recited this psalm in preparation for her meeting with the king.

The blessing that Moses gives to Naftali sums up the highest potential of the energy for this month. Moses says, "Naftali is fully satisfied with what he wished for and is full of God's blessings. He shall occupy the sea and the south" (Deut. 33:23). Moses actually commands him to occupy the area around the Kinneret Sea. The sea in kabbalah refers to the Torah. In Koheleth (Ecclesiastes) it says, "All rivers lead to the sea" (Eccl. 1:7). The ancient kabbalistic text *Sefer Bahir* says that the sea is an allusion to

God. Because the sea is so vast, it is also a kabbalistic allusion to the world to come. The energy of Naftali represents the blessing of this world as well as the world to come, which comes through the inheritance of the Torah.

The *Ethics of the Fathers* provides an important teaching about happiness. It says, "Who is happy? He who rejoices in his portion." This is the energy of Naftali. Naftali was satisfied with the will of Hashem (God), and it was this that gave him the strength to do things quickly. The Sfat Emet, the Gerer Rebbe, said that when people are happy, they can be zealous because they remember that their actions can reach heaven. When we know we can make a difference, we are happy and we can work quickly.

Even though Naftali was the quickest of the tribes, Naftali was often listed last. When it came to the dedication of the Mishkon, the portable tabernacle constructed for the Divine Presence while in the desert, Naftali was last, which was a sign of humility. Naftali represents a kind of humility that believes that even though one is far away from God, one can come close to God, and this brings joy. Naftali represents Adar, which is the last month of the year according to the reckoning that begins the year with Nissan. As such, it is not an optimal time to create new projects, but a great time to complete them. What a blessing of abundance for this month, but we must also access the energy and zeal of Naftali.

Divine Name Permutation: HHYV

The hay (H) in the first two positions indicates a great flow from above from the worlds of Atzilut and Beriyah. The energy of the month is about an expansiveness of the mind or thinking. Often it is said that on Purim we should be in the "I don't know" consciousness. When we are privileged to recognize the awesomeness of life, not knowing is often a higher form of knowing. The vav (V) in the fourth placement indicates that the events in this physical world are the instruments, the channels, to express what is above. A hay in this position would indicate that the physical world is a vessel, but the vav informs us that it is a conduit. This tells us that everything in this world is a conduit for God's light.

Torah Portions

The Torah portions for Adar are about the building of the Mishkon, the special place where God could be most directly experienced (Exod. 36–40). The Mishkon was a physical testimony of the renewed relationship of the Jewish people with God after the sin of the Golden Calf. The Torah reports that the people gave from the heart with great joy and were so happy to have an opportunity to contribute in the building of the Mishkon (Exod. 35: 21–29). This reminds us of the joy of giving this month.

It is interesting to note that the Hebrew scriptures give just a few lines explaining the creation of the world, but the creation of the Mishkon is told in great detail and is repeated in varying versions seven times. Even though Jews were told to build the Mishkon, so God could dwell *within* them, much attention is given to the actual structure of the building. One might question why the Torah spends so much time on these details when the Mishkon only stood for forty years while the Jews were in the desert and then for a few hundred years before the first Holy Temple was built.

As we read all these details in varying accounts, it is natural to wonder what their relevance is to us today. Kabbalah teaches that the Mishkon was a miniature universe, a replication of our physical universe as well as that of the human being. Many kabbalistic secrets were encoded in all these details, the study of which goes beyond what we can do here. The details of the construction of the Mishkon, however, have important implications according to Jewish law today. On the most basic level, the thirty-nine categories of work prohibited according to the laws of Shabbat are derived from the definition of work on the Mishkon. The laws of Shabbat are given this month as well.

The Torah portions of this month as a whole reflect the energy of this month. As Adar is about the joy of experiencing Godliness in the physical world, the Torah directs attention to the construction of a physical building so as to reflect Godliness and reporting all the details relating to the service to be conducted in this building so as to remind one of Godliness. For example, in the chapter of Tetzaveh (Exod. 27:20–30:10), the Jews are commanded to bring pure olive oil to light the menorah so it will burn continually. It was not that God needed this service, but the people needed to be reminded of the light of God that was within them at all times. The clothes worn by the high priest also get much attention. The garments are important because they also reveal Godliness. Every article of clothing expressed a different spiritual attribute and provided atonement for a different character trait.

The Torah portion of Ki Tisa (Exod. 30:11) begins with the census and the requirement for every man to give a half shekel, no more and no less. Counting is an uplifting process communicating that each person is important. The fact that everyone gave the same half shekel equally brought a feeling of unity among the people. The fact that it was one-half of a shekel teaches that a person is incomplete in himself. This section is read before Purim. The Gemara says that because the Jewish people were so zealous in the giving of the half shekel, they were saved from Haman's decree— another connection between the Torah portions and the energy of the month. The giving of the half shekel expiated for the sin of the Golden Calf.

The main event reported in the Torah portion of Ki Tisa was the story of sin of the Golden Calf. Even though the Jewish people had witnessed so many miracles, a portion of the people, mainly the mixed multitudes, the Egyptians who joined the Jewish people departing from Egypt, were frightened when Moses did not return as expected. Being the magicians of Egypt, they used their magic to build a Golden Calf to act as a god for them in the absence of Moses, who had been their intermediary. They could not relate to an invisible, unknowable God and felt incapable of living life on a supernatural level. They needed something physical to relate to. God recognized this need and so commissioned the Mishkon as a physical place for the Divine Presence. A pillar of cloud stood by it by day and a column of fire at night.

In the next portion, Vayakhel (Exod. 35), the people are instructed to give what their heart inspires them to do. The Torah does not discuss exactly what was given, but is concerned with the intention in giving. Intention is what is important.

Holiday

Purim

HISTORY   The events that form the basis of Purim took place in Shushan, the capital city of Persia, in about the fourth century B.C.E. At this time, Jews lived in prosperity under the rule of King Ahasuerus. At a banquet King Ashasuerus orders his wife, Vasti, to dance naked before him and his guests, but she refuses. For this insubordination, Vasti is banished. In search of a new queen, the king stages a beauty contest. A Jewish girl named Esther wins and is selected as the next queen. She keeps her Jewish identity and her real name, Hadassah, hidden; Esther, in fact, means "hidden" in Hebrew.

At this time, the king appoints a new prime minister named Haman. Haman demands that people bow down to him and is incensed when Mordecai, Esther's uncle, refuses to do so. Haman convinces the king to destroy all the Jewish people in the land on a day chosen by the drawing of lots (Purim is the Hebrew word for "lots"). He says there is no unity, no brotherhood among the Jews, and makes plans for their extermination. Haman builds the gallows to hang Mordecai.

Mordecai persuades an initially reluctant Esther to plead for the lives of the Jews before the king. Esther realizes that it was Divine Providence that led her to the throne and that she has a certain responsibility to use this position now to save her people, even if it means risking her life. Esther undertakes a fast and asks the people to also fast for three days before she goes before the king. Through fasting, prayer, and unity with the Jewish people, Esther contacts a greater strength inside herself that enables her to carry out her mission. She appears before the king uninvited and invites him and Haman to a party. Esther decides that pleading before the king will not be effective. She will use her sexuality to arouse the king, she will flirt with him and even with Haman and through this, she will demonstrate to the King that Haman is not to be trusted.

After the first party, Esther invites them to another party for the next night. The king, not able to sleep that night, is reviewing his records and discovers that Mordecai has done him a great favor and was not rewarded. At the next party, he asks Haman what he should do to show favor to someone. Haman, thinking he is the one the king wants to show favor to, describes all kinds of wonderful honors. He is surprised when it is Mordecai that the king wants to honor. Mordecai is awarded the honors. Esther reveals her true identity as a Jew and informs the king that Haman wants to kill her and her people. The King is furious and orders that Haman hang on the very gallows prepared for Mordecai. The king issues an edict that Jews may defend themselves and there is a terrible war, but the Jews are victorious and celebrate their victory on the fourteenth of Adar. The fighting continued in the walled city of Shushan until the fifteenth, so that became the date of Shushan Purim.

The events of the story occurred over a nine-year period. God is hidden in this story. There is no voice from heaven speaking through a prophet telling the people what to do, as with the biblical holidays. In the Megillah (scroll) of Esther God's name is not mentioned once.

The heroine is a beautiful woman who, by winning a beauty contest and marrying a non-Jewish king, becomes the savior of the Jewish people. The story seems somewhat improbable, but the ways of God are not logical, as we discovered during Kislev with the holiday of Chanukah. In the Purim story, God's deliverance comes in the midst of feasting and drinking and sexual intrigue, revealing a most important teaching that God is everywhere and in everything. There is no split between the material and spiritual. The miracle of Purim demonstrates that God occupies all realms equally.

Kabbalah sees Haman as a reference to eating the fruit of the Tree of the Knowledge of Good and Evil. When God asked Adam, "Did you eat from the Tree of Knowledge?" he answered, *"Ha-meem ha etz."* The *Gemara* says *"ha-meem"* refers to Haman. It is the power of evil, the power of Amalek, that the original snake represented. Going beyond the knowledge of good and evil may be one reason for the recommendation to drink a great deal at Purim. Purim is about transcending the rational mind and being in the "I don't know" consciousness. This brings joy and a sense of wonderment to life.

The *Gemara* says that in the messianic time, all the holidays will be abolished except for Purim. I think that is because Purim embodies the consciousness of messianic time, when we will fully see God revealed in the physical world.

OBSERVANCE   On the thirteenth of Adar, the Fast of Esther is observed in memory of the fast called for by Esther. It is not observed with the same frequency as many other fasts, but still many people do observe this day as a fast day. Fasting was a traditional spiritual practice observed by the Jews when confronted with war or a pogrom. The Jews were instructed to fast before they battled Amalek in the desert.

On the fourteenth of Adar, the holiday of Purim commences with the reading, in its entirety, of the Megillah of Esther. In cities that are walled, the megillah is read on the fifteenth of Adar. Reb Shlomo insisted that the megillah be read very quickly. Many come to the synagogue dressed in costumes, and the megillah is read in an atmosphere of merriment amidst cheering at the mention of Mordecai, booing at the mention of Haman, and sometimes even whistling at the mention of Esther.

The holiday of Purim is a rabbinical holiday and does not have the restrictions according to Jewish law that biblical holidays do. For example, people may handle money, cook, and turn lights on and off. According to Jewish law, people are supposed to have a feast on Purim and drink so much alcohol that they do not know the difference between Haman and Mordecai. By the way, many people I know take this rabbinical recommendation very literally. The rabbis wanted people to become so intoxicated that they would experience everything as God. Good and evil are merely disguises of the one God. When we can see through the masks of reality and see God, we are happy. People dress up in costumes to demonstrate that life is full of masks, but it is fun because we know that God is behind them all.

Since the miracle of Purim took place through parties and alcohol, we reenact these scenes. Purim is a party time. There are concerts, spoofs, and a tremendous spirit of joy and open-heartedness that is enhanced through the widespread use of alcohol. Purim is not complete without eating *hamantashen,* those delicious three-cornered pastries filled with prunes or jelly, supposedly reminding us of the hat worn by Haman. It is somewhat silly, but it is in keeping with the fun spirit of the holiday.

People are also told to give *shalachmonis* (gifts) to at least two friends. Some make elaborate baskets with fruits, cakes, and wine; others make simple bags and pass out quite a few. It is fine to simply give two pieces of fruit. The great Rebbe Levi Yitzchok of Berditzov was said to kiss every banana, every apple, everything he gave for *shalachmonis*. It is definitely a heart-opening experience to prepare *shalachmonis*. Usually one doesn't give the gifts directly to friends but has them delivered through a third party.

Meditation

In keeping with the energy of the month, the following meditation is on the joy of oneness.

Sit for meditation and center yourself with the breath. Take deep breaths to release tension. As you inhale, become aware that you do not breathe by your own will, but by Divine Will. Open to receive the breath. Allow yourself to be breathed. Every part of the body, every cell within your body receives the breath. Now be aware that everything in creation is being breathed by the very same power that breathes you. Everything, everyone is breathed by God.

Actually our breaths are interconnected with nature. We breathe in what nature exhales and nature breathes in what we exhale. The breath that flows through us is the same breath of God. Sit in the awareness of the interconnection of all of life. Enjoy and relish each breath.

Practical Recommendations

1. MAKE TIME FOR YOURSELF.

Sometimes we are so busy fulfilling all our responsibilities, we do not take time to do things that bring joy in our lives. For example, Greg feels most connected to himself, to the world, and to God when he is in the world of nature. This makes him happy, but as a New Yorker he thinks that enjoying nature in the City is impossible on a regular basis. This is not true. Even in New York, there are beautiful parks. If one wants to get out of the City, it's not hard to do. One simply needs to make a commitment to do things that bring joy into one's life. Make a list of at least five activities and experiences that are joyful for you, make a plan, and commit to do at least two of these things this month and two additional things in the next two months.

2. DRESS UP IN A COSTUME FOR PURIM.

Dressing up in a costume will allow you to enjoy Purim even more. It is fun to get out of the usual roles you play in life, pretend to be someone else, and be seen in a different way. Choosing a costume that will keep people from recognizing you at all is great fun. You will be hidden like God, and people will be wondering the whole night who you are. Purim is a time when it is permissible to be absolutely outrageous. Men often dress up as women, and women dress up as Chassidic rebbes.

Get out of your mind and get into your inner child. Fulfill some of your fantasies. Purim is a wonderful holiday for play and fun.

3. TRY TO BE AS HAPPY AS YOU CAN.

One of Reb Nachman of Breslov's greatest teachings was that it was a great *mitzvah* to always be happy. It is perhaps an unattainable goal, but still we can strive to be happy regardless of what is happening around us. In order to be happy, Reb Nachman advised, we should think about all our good qualities and blessings. He said that the best way to be joyous is to pray, meditate, and do *mitzvot*. I agree that there is a joy to be experienced in prayer and meditation that is unparalleled.

Reb Nachman advises the depressed to read the passages in the prayer book that deal with the daily incense offering with great concentration. The incense in the Holy Temple had the power to remove the negative energy. Today, we can easily buy incense or essential oils to bring a feeling of joy into our space. Music is also very helpful for lifting the spirits. The prophets of old were always surrounded by music to keep them in a state of joy.

Make an effort to be happy. Even if you are sad, pour your heart out to God and you will be happy even in your sadness. When I was very ill, I told myself that if and when I recovered and regained my health, I would never be depressed again. If you have your health, nothing is so important that you should be unhappy about it. I can't say that I have always kept that promise, but remembering how I felt then helps me to lighten up. We need to keep things in the proper perspective.

4. TELL JOKES.

Telling jokes is a good way to increase joy for yourself and others. Reb Nachman spoke about the importance of jokes in healing as long as the jokes were not vulgar or denigrating. In recent years, Dr. Norman Cousins popularized the importance of humor when he checked himself out of a hospital and watched comedies as a way to heal himself. My uncle was a doctor and he had several joke books that he read and lent to his patients. As I write this, I am fondly reminded of a friend named Danny Mars; I don't see him too often, but when I do, he always has a few good jokes.

5. GIVE GIFTS TO FRIENDS AND THOSE LESS FORTUNATE.

Reb Shlomo used to say that on Purim you give to poor people in the same way you give to your friends. The poor who receive a gift may think you are giving it to them not because they are poor, but because they are your friends.

A wonderful service project for the holiday of Purim would be to make bags of *shalachmonis* and distribute them to the homeless, elderly, or homebound or those in hospitals or nursing homes. Also give *shalachmonis* to your friends, family, and people in your synagogue. Greet each person with a strong "Good Purim," in order to communicate strength, love, and hope. You will have much fun doing this.

A Tale to Live By

The energy of Purim can transform our lives, as demonstrated in this wonderful story that I heard from Reb Shlomo. When we are full with joy, gates open for us.

Pinchas was the poorest disciple of Kosnitzer Maggid, a great rebbe in Poland in the 1800s. On Purim, it was the custom in this community to line up and present a gift to the Holy Maggid, to receive a blessing.

Picture the scene in your mind. Pinchas, a holy *shlepper,* somewhat dejected, stooped over, and looking at the floor, is in line with everyone else to greet the shining light of that generation, the Holy Maggid. When it is finally his turn, he greets his rebbe in a soft, almost expressionless voice, says "Good Purim" softly, and prepares to leave quickly, embarrassed that he has no gift for the rebbe.

The Rebbe says to him, "Pinchas, why didn't you bring me a gift for Purim?"

Pinchas replies, "I have a wife and seven children. We have nothing to eat. I do not have money to buy you *shalachmonis.*"

"Pinchas, you know what your problem is? You do not know how to say 'Good Purim.'"

The rebbe demonstrates how one should say "Good Purim." He yells, "GOOD PURIM! GOOD PURIM, *heilige* [holy] Pinchas!"

He tells Pinchas to stand up tall, as tall as he can, and yell back to him, "GOOD PURIM." They yell "Good Purim" to each other several times. Each time the rebbe yells "Good Purim, *heilige* Pinchas," Pinchas feels as if he is receiving an injection of strength.

Finally, the rebbe tells him "Pinchas, go out and get me *shalachmonis.*"

Pinchas leaves and goes directly to the one neighborhood grocery store in the shetl. Usually, in the past, Pinchas would stand by the door of the store on Friday before the Sabbath, people would give him various foods as they left the store, and from this his family would live from week to week.

But now on Purim he actually walks into the store. He says, "Good Purim, Good Purim! Give me the biggest cake and the finest bottle of wine. I have to bring *shalachmonis* to my Holy Rebbe. I'll pay you tomorrow."

If he had said this before, he would have been thrown out of the store. But now the owner brings him the cake and wine he requested. Pinchas returns to the Holy Maggid and as soon as he approaches the rebbe, he yells to him, "GOOD PURIM, Holy Maggid." And the rebbe yells back, "Good Purim, *heilige* Pinchas." Pinchas gives the rebbe the *shalachmonis.*

The rebbe then says, "I want to give you *shalachmonis* back. I am giving you the gift that Purim should be with you all year long. The strength of Purim should be with you forever."

Pinchas walks away a new person. He goes back to the grocery store and says again to the owner, "Good Purim. My family has nothing to eat. Give me some food and I'll pay you tomorrow." The owner brings out the most extraordinary box of delicacies.

Pinchas goes to a clothing store and says "Good Purim, I need clothes for my children. I'll pay you after Purim." And they give him beautiful clothes for his seven children. He passes by a little women's boutique. He thinks of his wife, reflecting on how beautiful she used to be. He goes into the store. "Good Purim. Please give me some nice dresses for my wife." And soon he is carrying out bags filled with beautiful dresses for his wife.

Carrying all his bundles of goodies, he enters his home and yells, "Good Purim, Good Purim" to his children and his wife. In the past, so ashamed of not providing adequately for his children and wife, he could barely say hello to them when he entered the house. Now he looks them straight in the eye and says, "I have not been a good father or husband, but now I promise I will be better. The Holy Rebbe blessed me with the strength of Purim. Everything will change now. The first thing I want to do is to teach you to say, 'Good Purim.'" He tells his children to stand up straight, and he yells "Good Purim, wonderful children." And the children yell back, "Good Purim." He yells to his wife, "Good Purim, beautiful wife." She yells back to him, "Good Purim." They do this several times. There is such a feeling of love, blessing, and abundance in their home.

After Purim, Pinchas goes to the richest Jew in town and says to him, "The Holy Maggid blessed me with the strength of Purim. Would you lend me ten thousand rubles? I will give it back to you in four weeks." God was surely with Pinchas, for with this loan he started a business, and he soon became the richest Jew in Poland. Not only did he provide for his family and the poor, he supported all the Chassidic dynasties.

Nissan

MONTH: *March-April*

ENERGY: *Moving Toward Greater Freedom*

AREA OF HEALING: *Speech*

ASTROLOGICAL SIGN: *Aries*

HEBREW LETTER: *Hay*

HEBREW TRIBE: *Yehudah (Judah)*

DIVINE NAME PERMUTATION: *YHVH*

HOLIDAY: *Passover*

will never forget the first Passover seder I conducted for my students over fifteen years ago. I learned something very important and transformational that I want to share with you. Actually, every Passover I learn a variation of this very same lesson. I now understand that the reason I keep learning this lesson on increasingly deeper levels is because this is what the energy and the spiritual opportunity of this month are all about.

In the mid 1980s, I was planning to have about thirty-five students for first-night seder in my small Manhattan studio apartment. In those days, I did not know how to ask people to help me; even today, I am still not very good at it, but then I felt that I had to do everything myself. I was the rebbe, the rebbitzen, the cook, the shopper, the cleaner, the schlepper—everything. Even though the holiday was all about freedom, when I thought about this upcoming event, I did not feel very free. Actually, I initially felt quite overwhelmed, inadequate, and intimidated. There was little time to do all the preparations and the cooking, much less plan how to conduct the seder to make it unique and meditative. I had been blessed to have spent many Passover seders with Reb Shlomo, but this was the first one that I would be conducting. I wanted it to be even deeper than what I experienced. My students were also hoping for something extraordinary. Many were making great efforts or sacrifices to be with me, so I felt additional pressure.

At a certain point, I realized that I could not do this whole event myself, but I did not know anyone who could help me. I prayed that God would be my partner, and I actually gave it over to God. After all, it was for God that I was doing this, it was God's seder, and God would have to help. I put God in charge and appointed myself God's hardworking, humble assistant. This was more than a technique for coping with stress, because I experienced something absolutely wonderful. From that point on, I actually floated through the whole experience. I was amazed by all the miracles and support I received. For example, whenever I went shopping and was confronted with carrying big overloaded bags of groceries several blocks to my home, someone appeared out of nowhere to help me. Filled with awe by these coincidences, I paused and thanked God.

My small efficiency kitchen with little counter space and outdated appliances is not the optimal place for cooking. What made a challenging situation worse was that in the middle of my preparations, the very old stove broke down. Now this was a crisis. My landlord is a very nice man, but not one who responds to requests for repair in a timely manner. I always had to wait days or weeks for even a call back, much less a response. One time I even had to call the City when he failed to repair a leak in the ceiling and I had a flood in that very small kitchen.

I prayed to God and called the landlord about my predicament. The landlord is never at his office, so we always leave messages on the machine. That day, the landlord was there, and he actually answered the phone. I informed him that I was having people over for Passover dinner and I did not have a working stove. I could not believe that the very next day, early in the morning, I had a new stove. It wasn't exactly like crossing the Red Sea, but to me this was quite a substantial miracle as well as a concrete sign of God's involvement in this seder.

By the time it came to the evening of Passover I was exhausted. I had been cooking, peeling vegetables, chopping, and so on, up to the very last minute. Normally I would have been very upset to have people arrive for a dinner party at my house with the table unset, but now I figured that God wanted them to participate in the setting up of the tables and the setting of the table with plates and utensils, so it was all right. They seemed happy, almost grateful, to be able to contribute.

As the guests set up the tables, I wondered whether I would have the energy to speak at the table. I was beyond exhaustion. I prayed for God's help, and I then experienced another miracle. I took some deep breaths to relax, let go of my thoughts and sensations of being tired, opened my mouth, and was lifted up. When I lit candles, I received an influx of energy that ran through my body, invigorating me on all levels. It was as if I had been plugged into a powerful source of energy far different from what I was used to. It was a much higher voltage. It was something quite extraordinary. I again reminded myself that this was God's seder that I was conducting; that was why I was receiving such a blessing. That night I opened my mouth not knowing exactly what I would say, but the words that came out of my mouth were inspiring. I felt myself become a channel. I learned firsthand then that I do not do this work; God does this work through me, and I basically have to show up with an open heart and a sincere desire to serve.

That first Passover experience changed my life and the way I teach Jewish meditation. Before this experience, I used to prepare lesson plans for meditation classes, thinking about what I would say and even writing a script for myself. After this experience, I gave up preparing. I simply pray, focus on my intention to serve, let go, and allow the spirit of God to flow through me. As a result, my classes became much more powerful and exciting to the students as well as to me. Each class is always new, always unique, and very alive.

Energy: Moving Toward Greater Freedom

The month of Nissan is the headquarters for newness. Newness means that I am not bound to what was before. I am free to choose to do as I want. Someone enslaved in habits, limiting beliefs, and concepts cannot taste newness. Newness, like freedom, is a gift from God, a taste of transcendence. A sign that we are close to God is when everything feels new to us, full of wonder and possibilities.

This is the month to leave your personal restrictions and limitations and move to greater freedom. It is a time of miracles and redemption. This was the month when the Jewish people were redeemed from Egypt, it will be the month in the future when the final redemption will take place, and in every Nissan there is the hope and expectation that something new and wonderful will happen. Nissan is also called Chodesh Ha'Aviv, "the month of spring." The scent of

The scent of spring in the air makes us aware of the new life emerging in nature and reminds us to pay attention to the new energies stirring within us as well.

spring in the air makes us aware of the new life emerging in nature and reminds us to pay attention to the new energies stirring within us as well. There is a heavenly influx of grace and compassion this month that enables us to go forward in our lives.

The Torah says this about Nissan: "This month shall be for you the head of the months; it is the first for you of the months of the year" (Exod. 12:2). The sages of Israel proclaimed that on the Shabbat before Nissan or on Rosh Chodesh (the time of the new moon) itself if it occurs on Shabbat this passage from the Torah should be read. According to the prophet Jeremiah, whatever is called "first" for you means that it is for your benefit. This month of Nissan offers tremendous gifts on all levels of being.

There is a debate among religious scholars about when creation really began. Did it begin on Rosh Hashanah or Rosh Chodesh Nissan? Some kabbalists say that the external physical world was created on the twenty-fifth of Elul and humankind on the first of Tishrei, but the world of transcendental spirituality began in Nissan. It is for that reason that Rosh Hashanah is celebrated in Tishrei, but Nissan is an awesome time of inner divine revelation.

The epitome of the energy of the month is the holiday of Passover, the celebration of the miraculous departure of the Jewish people from Egypt. The Holy One could have redeemed the Jewish people through natural means, but the whole purpose of the exile and the redemption was for God to more openly reveal Himself. God wants to be known. The plagues were a revelation of different aspects of Godliness. With every plague, God revealed a different *sephira,* a different emanation. Even God says in the Torah about the plagues, "Now you will fully realize that I am God" (Exod. 10:2). The last plague was the most complete and intense revelation. It was not caused through an intermediary, as the previous plagues had been, but by God directly. "Around midnight, I will go out in the midst of Egypt and all the firstborn in the land of Egypt will die" (Exod. 11:4–5). The revelation of God's light was so intense that people died. The Angel of Death passed over the houses of the Jewish people and it is from that we derive the name Passover.

At the Passover seder, we are reminded that this Exodus was not just a one-time historical event. The Haggadah says, "In every generation one should regard himself as though he personally had gone out from Egypt" (Ex. 13:8). Metaphorically, we are all a little bit still in Egypt, as my rebbe would say. The Hebrew word Mitzraim, the name for Egypt, means "narrow straits" and represents all psychological, emotional, physical, and spiritual boundaries and constraints. Rabbi Yitzchok Luria, known as the Arizel, likened the descent of Jacob into Egypt to the soul entering the body. While we are in this physical world and in a body there will be varying degrees of bondage. We are all still in exile to the extent that we feel a sense of alienation from our true self. On every Passover and throughout Nissan, it is a propitious time to free oneself from one's internal and external constraints, to make a personal exodus from our personal Mitzraim.

Jews actually remember the Exodus many times each day. It is part of the liturgy of our daily, Shabbat, and holiday prayers. Its remembrance is contained within *tefillin,* those little black boxes strapped on the forehead and arm to tie oneself to the Divine Presence. Remembering the Exodus is part of the Kiddush recited every Shabbat. The Baal Shem Tov suggested that we think of the Exodus at all times, so as to always feel that we are leaving places of constraint and moving to greater freedom.

The power of speech is the healing dimension for this month. It is through our own speech that we redeem or enslave ourselves. Rabbi Yitzchok Luria said that *Pesach,* the Hebrew word for Passover, is a conjugation of the words *peh* ("the mouth") and *sach* ("speaks"), "the mouth speaks." This is evidenced in the Passover seder, where the main event is the telling of the story of the Exodus. The more questions we ask, either from the Haggadah or informally, the more the story can be told in greater depth. Kabbalah says that the highest form of speech is song. This level was reached on the seventh day of Passover, when the Jews crossed the Red Sea and sang in unison the very same words. Song has the capacity to bring people together by unifying their voices.

Words are very important in Judaism. The Torah states that God creates the world through speech. This is a metaphor, but what the Torah means is that creation is totally dependent for existence on God as speech is dependent on the speaker. It also implies that everything in creation is a divine communication. Not only did God create the world through speech, we create our reality through speech as well. Speaking is what distinguishes us from animals and is particularly important this month.

It is interesting to note that Moses, our redeemer, had a speech impediment. Even though Moses received clear prophecy of all that was going to happen, he initially refused the mission for he questioned how the Jewish people, much less Pharaoh, would hear him. Some say that he stuttered because the world was not ready to hear his words.

The Torah records the conversation Moses had with God. Moses pleaded with God: "'I beg you, I am not a man of words, not yesterday, not the day before, not from the very first time You spoke to me. I find it difficult to speak and find the right language.' 'Who gave man a mouth?' replied God. . . . 'I will be your mouth and teach you what to say'" (Exod. 4:10–12). Even though Aaron became a mouthpiece for Moses, Moses was the mouthpiece for God. And through the words of Moses reality changed. His words were powerful!

This month we need to tap into the energy of Moses and overcome the ways we hold ourselves back from speaking our truth, carrying out our life mission, and allow our voice to be heard by others and ourselves. And like Moses' words, our words can change reality.

General Guidelines and Goals

The following guidelines and goals enable us to direct our energies in the ways that are optimal for our growth and transformation in accordance with the energy of this month. It is recommended that you read and meditate upon them often in the course of the month. Reflect on their applicability to you, and allow them to direct and inspire you often this month.

I. CONNECT YOURSELF TO GOD.

To go forward in life, we have to attach ourselves to wholesomeness, purity, and God. We have to transcend limiting thoughts about who we are and who God is, which takes effort and grace. Meditation, prayer, and doing *mitzvot* are the most powerful tools to move forward to greater freedom. There is a tremendous heavenly influx of compassion that will lift us out of places of constraint this month, but we need to call out, make a place for God to enter our hearts and souls, and then listen to the quiet still voice inside each of us to guide and direct us.

As we grow and develop on the spiritual journey, we seek greater freedom from the limited and reactive ego states that keep us enslaved to negative behaviors and limited concepts of self. We want to be free to choose and express who we really are and not feel obliged to live up to a false image of who we think other people imagine or need us to be. People forfeit their freedom in a variety of ways. Besides the obvious addictions in varying degrees to food, sex, and drugs, many people experience some degree of compulsive negative thinking that keeps them reexperiencing the pain of early childhood wounding. There are many forms of slavery. Every addiction limits a person's capacity for free choice.

Just as the Jews called out to God when the slavery they experienced in Egypt became too intense, so we cry out when the personal existential pain we experience in our lives becomes hard to bear. It is often because of pain that people initially embark on the spiritual journey. We seek to go beyond our usual experience of ourselves, for we recognize that the ego mind that is causing the stress and negativity cannot offer the solution or healing from it. To become free, to become truly loving, we need to be attached to that which is free, that which is loving, and that Being is God.

To make this connection, meditate throughout the day and in various situations on the questions "What does God want? What does my soul want?" Then, begin to act and behave in ways that are in alignment to your inner knowing. You may become aware of choices between the higher knowing of the soul and the needs and desires of the ego mind. Make an effort to choose what your higher self, your soul, and God would want you to do and not what your limited ego mind wants. Also, take on a new *mitzvah,* a prescribed religious behavior, to help you make this divine connection.

Every *mitzvah,* every prayer, every meditation, if done with the right intention, can help to liberate you. In so doing, you can begin to gain the capacity to make choices.

Be careful to resist the attempts of the ego mind to co-opt this behavior for its own purposes. Needless to say, the ego may be threatened if it fears losing control. Struggle and conflict can ensue, sometimes on a very subtle level. It may be advisable to consult with a spiritual counselor or rabbi for guidance and objectivity. Sometimes people can be religiously observant, but their practice is actually driven by the needs of the ego, so that they are still quite enslaved by the evil inclination. My rebbe used to say the *yetzer hara* (evil inclination) wears a *strimmel,* the garb of the most religious. A sign of contamination by the ego is the tendency to compare oneself to others, to judge others, and to want to be honored. Be patient—life is often a battle between the *yetzer hara* and the *yetzer tov* (good inclination). Being able to observe this battle without judgment and with compassion is essential.

2. BE MINDFUL OF YOUR SPEECH.

As we learned, we create our reality through our words. King Solomon said in Proverbs, "A man's belly shall be filled with the fruit of his mouth. Death and life are in the power of the tongue" (18:20–21). The sages, in the *Gemara,* state: "Four categories of people will not receive the Divine Presence: flatterers, liars, slanderers, and scorners" *(Sota).* Slander is concerned the worst sin, even more grievous than idolatry. We should watch our speech carefully, for we create our reality through our own words. We even need to be careful when we praise others. When I say something nice about another, I always say that I do it not to flatter, but to speak the truth.

The Rambam (Maimonides) states that there are five categories of speech: (1) virtuous speech *(mitzvah),* the learning of Torah, prayers, and so forth; (2) forbidden speech *(nizhar), loshon hara,* gossip, lies, false testimony, cursing, and insults; (3) loathsome speech *(nim'as),* idle conversations about current happenings, political intrigues, and so forth; (4) desirable speech *(ahuv),* discussions on how to improve oneself and others; and (5) permissable speech *(mutar),* speech necessary for business and daily living. I would add negative criticism of self and others as part of *loshon hara.*

Make a strong effort to increase virtuous and desirable speech, eliminate loathsome and forbidden speech, and limit permissible speech this month. Remember that you also have the right to limit what you hear from others as well. You do not have to listen to *loshon hara* or loathsome conversation. You can simply inform the other person of this and direct the conversation to a higher plane. Note that your energy increases when you engage in virtuous and desirable speech and decreases when you engage in forbidden and loathsome speech.

The more mindful we are of our speech, the more powerful our words are when we speak. That is why it is said that when a *tzaddik* (righteous person) speaks, God fulfills his decree. Guard your tongue carefully. Don't waste your words and your words will be more powerful. You can actually heal people with your words.

3. AFFIRM THE PRESENCE, NOT THE ABSENCE, OF GOD.

The world is filled with the glory and presence of God, yet we are not always aware of God's presence. We too often affirm the absence, the distance and separation from God, rather than the connection and the passionate love relationship we can have with God. When we do this, we feel alienated from God and our true selves.

Believe in the oneness of God, the main tenet of Judaism. God surrounds creation and is within creation. Wherever you are, God is. You live in the midst of God, so God is always with you. Believe in miracles. Life itself is a miracle, and every day is filled with small miracles. This month make an effort to be conscious of the presence of God in daily life.

What would your life be like if you truly believed in the oneness of God, if you truly believed that God is immanent and transcendent? What might you do? How would the belief in the oneness and presence of God empower you to go forward? This month you can go forward in leaps and bounds, but going forward always takes faith. The obstacles may seem formidable, like the crossing of the Red Sea, but with faith, anything is possible. It is an auspicious time to take some risks.

4. FEED THE HUNGRY.

The Passover seder begins with the following words: "Whoever is hungry, let him come and eat." There are all kinds of hunger today. Probably the greatest hunger people in America face today is the hunger for family and community. Open your Passover seder to friends, and also to strangers. It will actually make your seder more powerful.

It is traditional to give charity during this month to enable poor people throughout the world to celebrate the Passover holiday. Many organizations take on the mission to distribute Passover food to homebound elderly people and poor families throughout the world.

The Torah tells us on numerous occasions this month that because we were strangers in Egypt, we shall be kind to the stranger. Find a way to demonstrate kindness to widows, the divorced, orphans, converts, the poor, and the vulnerable. In this way, you become God's hands and feet.

Astrological Sign: Aries

According to astrology, Aries is considered the first sign of the zodiac. It is a time of a new beginning. In its effort to evolve in a new way, the energy of Aries is willing to push past limitations and boundaries. The energy of Aries does not want to be defined by others, only by itself. This takes courage, passion, enthusiasm, and independence. Aries is a fire sign giving one energy and enthusiasm. Aries is a trailblazer and a leader.

The energy of Aries is about taking action in a very focused and direct way, but may be so focused on its own individuality that it may not understand or consider how its actions affect others. Aries is considered the most impulsive sign. People born under this sign of Aries like to start new projects, but often become impatient if these projects take too long to accomplish. Sometimes Aries takes action without thinking things through, and burns out, or hurts others.

Aries is ruled by the planet Mars. Mars was the Roman god of war. Aries comes from the Latin word for "ram," which is the symbol for Aries. The ram reminds us of the ram that the Jewish people were commanded to slaughter in Nissan prior to their departure from Egypt. The ram had been an Egyptian god, a symbol of riches and power. Slaughtering something held in the greatest respect by the Egyptians took a lot of courage.

Aries is considered a masculine sign, aggressive, competitive, and independent. The energy of Aries helps all of us to be self-confident, decisive, assertive, and courageous, empowering us to do new things this month.

Hebrew Letter: Hay

ה *Sefer Yetzirah* says that God crowned the letter hay for this month with the power over speech. The *Gemara* says that there is no true speech except prayer from the mouth. The hay of this month is the final hay in the Divine Name permutation YHVH. This hay corresponds to the *sephira* of *malchut,* the kingship of God. The Divine Name for this *sephira* is Adonai. Rabbi Tzaddik Ha Cohen said that it is in this month, the month of the tribe of Yehudah (Judah), that God's kingdom is established. It was in this month that Kinneset Yisrael, the Jewish people, were established. According to Tzaddik Ha Cohen, the letter hay corresponds to *emunah*, "faith." It takes faith to follow something that is not known, not visible. The Jewish people demonstrated that faith in leaving Egypt, crossing the Red Sea, and in wandering in the desert.

The letter hay is such a holy letter that it appears twice in the Divine Name YHVH. Kabbalah says that God created this world with the letter hay and the world to come with the letter yud. The vav is the connector between the worlds. The numerical value of the hay is five. It is no coincidence that we have five books of Moses, five fingers on each hand, five toes, and five levels of the soul. The Hebrew word for "light," *ohr,* appears five times in the creation story.

Hebrew Tribe: Yehudah (Judah)

After giving birth to three sons, hoping that with each son her husband would love her more, Leah gained an inner security and reached a higher state of consciousness. When she gives birth to Yehudah, her fourth son, she is no longer looking for her husband's love; she now stands strong, independent, and connected to God. The Torah reports that at Yehudah's birth, she says, " 'Now I will praise *[odeh]* the Lord.' Therefore she called his name Yehudah and she left off bearing" (Gen. 29:35). Yehudah was the only son of either Leah or Rachel who was not born out of pain, struggle, or competition.

The tribe of Yehudah is represented by the lion. The lion is the king of the animal world, and the descendents of Yehudah become the kings of the Jewish people. Jacob blesses him: "Yehudah, your brothers shall praise you. . . . The sons of your father shall bow down before you" (Gen. 49:8). Everyone, even Joseph, recognized that Yehudah was like the king of Jewish people in his time. As Judah was most prominent among the twelve tribes, so Nissan is the most prominent of months, beginning the year according to the Torah.

The name Yehudah contains within it the Divine Name YHVH plus a dalet. The Hebrew word *dalet* means "door." The name of this tribe is a doorway into God. This is why the kings and Messiah come from Yehudah. Furthermore the Jewish people are called Yehudim after Yehudah, indicating that all the tribes possess the attribute of thanksgiving that Yehudah personifies. All of this speaks to the majesty and importance of this month. More than other months, Nissan is a doorway to God.

The Torah records several incidents involving Yehudah that reveal the qualities and energy he represents. It was Yehudah along with Reuven who pleaded for the life of Joseph and finally convinced the brothers to sell Joseph rather than kill him. It was Yehudah who was strong enough to acknowledge publicly his sexual relations with a woman he thought was a prostitute but who turned out to be his daughter-in-law. It was Yehudah who was willing to offer his own life in place of Benjamin. The energy of Yehudah is forthright and courageous. Like the impulsive energy described by the astrological sign of Aries, Yehudah is impulsive and makes mistakes, but is strong enough to admit them, repent, and change himself. In this way, Yehudah demonstrates the kinds of qualities needed for the leadership of the Jewish people.

Reb Shlomo used to say that Yehudah was symbolic of the *baal teshuva,* the person who does wrong but repents, and Joseph represents the *tzaddik,* the righteous person who never does wrong. It says in the Talmud, that the *baal teshuva* is higher than the *tzaddik.* Transforming negativity is more redemptive than never doing anything wrong. This is another reason why the Jewish people follow Yehudah, rather than Joseph.

Divine Name Permutation: YHVH

God says to Moses "I am Yud-Hay-Vav-Hay. I appeared to Abraham, Isaac, and Jacob as El Shaddai, but I did not make myself known to them by My Name YHVH" (Exod. 6:2–3). YHVH is a wider and greater demonstration of divine power. El Shaddai is a revelation of God found in nature. People absorb this level of Godliness according to their worthiness. El Shaddai was the revelation of the Divine Name to individuals, according to their capacity to receive. YHVH is the name of the transcendent power of love and compassion, regardless of people's worthiness and independent of nature. It was this name that took the people out of Egypt and made them a holy nation.

The permutation for the Divine Name is in its proper and optimal placement for this month. It allows for the maximum flow of divine energy, the greatest divine revelation. The yud in the position of the world of Atzilut allows for a concentrated point of connection with Ain Sof. It expands in the letter hay in the world of Beriyah and is channeled through the vav in the world of Yetzerah and then expands in the world of Assiyah.

Torah Portions

The Torah portions read during Nissan speak in detail about the sacrifices that were given in the Mishkon, the portable tabernacle constructed for the Divine Presence while in the desert. There were thanksgiving offerings and sin offerings for intentional and unintentional sins. Some offerings were obligatory and others were voluntary. The sacrifices were a way for the people to draw close to God. When people sacrificed an animal, they were nullifying that animal part within themselves, letting go of the limiting parts of self in order to be better able to receive the holiness of God. Sacrifices were transformational when done with the proper intention. We are told repeatedly throughout the Hebrew Bible that the most important part of the sacrifice was intention.

In the Torah portion of Shemini (Lev. 9), on the eighth day, Aaron, the high priest and brother of Moses, is told to slaughter a ram along with other animals and pour the blood on the sides of the altar. This is reminiscent of the ram offering prior to the Passover holiday. The Passover holiday also lasts for eight days. Eight is symbolic of the supernatural, beyond the laws of nature. This is a month when there is a divine flow that enables one to transcend the laws of nature.

In this Torah portion is recorded the powerful story of Nadav and Avihu, who died in the act of performing sacrifices. From the simple reading of the text, it appears that their death was a punishment for performing the sacrifices in an incorrect manner. Kabbalah says that their death was a fulfillment, an act of grace. Their desire to be close to God was so great that the physicality that separated them from God was removed and their souls were liberated. The Torah then spends much time discussing animals that may and may not be eaten. If we eat animals that are not kosher, the Torah tells us there will be a blockage between the heart and the head, making it harder to access holiness.

The Torah portions give additional insight into the means of accessing freedom in life, the energy for this month. First, sacrifice is important. Sacrifices bring us close to God and enable us to release blocks. Whether they are actual or symbolic, sacrifices performed with the right intention rectify one's sins; as expressions of gratitude they open us to the divine flow of blessing in the most powerful way.

I remember when I was in college a very long time ago, I developed a ritual of my own that enabled me to quit smoking cigarettes. In my prayers, I mentally offered my addiction to cigarettes along with actual cigarettes on a makeshift altar for all the sins I had done in my life. I had tried to stop smoking unsuccessfully before, but this was the only way I was able to quit this terrible habit. It was hard, but I was successful.

Second, the Torah tells us that what you take into your body is also important. If you are feeling blocked and unable to go forward in life, the Torah says it might be because you are eating unkosher animals. The Passover holiday is also focused on food, on eating the foods associated with the holiday and avoiding others. As the saying goes, you are what you eat.

Holiday

Passover

HISTORY   The roots of the Passover holiday are found in the Torah story that begins with the brothers of Joseph entering Egypt in search of food during a time of great famine. Joseph, who was ruling Egypt at that time, distributing its food resources, eventually revealed himself to his brothers, who had sold him into slavery. He then invited his brothers and their families to settle in the land of Goshen, the best land in Egypt, during this challenging time. They were small in number initially, but they prospered for many years and became great in numbers and wealth in Goshen. Over time, Joseph died and the memory of his reign faded. A new pharaoh ruled Egypt, who, threatened by the power and proliferation of the Jewish people, instituted many measures to contain, limit, and oppress them. During this time, Moses, the redeemer, was born and through Divine Providence was raised in Pharaoh's house. Then, as the Torah says, "We cried out to God, the God of our forefathers. God heard our cries, and saw our affliction, our misery and our oppression. So God took us out of Egypt with a strong hand and an outstretched arm, with awesome power, with signs, and wonders" (Deut. 26:7–8).

Prior to the departure from Egypt, the Jewish people had to perform three *mitzvot:* circumcision, the slaughter of the ram, and the sanctification of the moon. It was these *mitzvot* that gave them the strength to leave Egypt and all the impurity there. They teach us about the process of accessing freedom. Circumcision gave the Jews the strength to overcome the compulsion of physical desires; a free person is free of compulsion. By summoning up the courage and fearlessness to slaughter the ram, the symbol of an Egyptian god, they freed themselves from idolatry, the belief in powers other than God. When the blood was placed on the doorposts of their homes, God passed over those houses in the tenth plague, the death of all firstborn, which became the basis of Passover.

The sanctification of the new moon made the Jews realize that everything changes and this gave them hope. The moon goes through its cycles, and from observing the moon, we learn that what is empty will be full and what is full will be empty. For the Jewish people, times of oppression would be followed by times of reemergence; soon they would be up and shining for the world to see like the full moon.

Also it was in Nissan, through the sanctification of the new moon, that the Jewish people demonstrated through speech their power over time. The time of the new moon was called out and that established the timing for the holidays, for they are all based on the moon. With this *mitzvah,* we gained the ability to call particular days holy.

Prior to the departure out of Egypt, the Egyptians and the Jewish people experienced in different ways the ten plagues that are described in the Bible and in the Haggadah (Exod. 6–12). After this, the Jewish people left Egypt quickly and then a few days later experienced another miracle at the crossing of the Red Sea (Exod. 14).

OBSERVANCE   The holiday of Passover lasts eight days. The first two days and the last two days have special restrictions. On those days, we light candles, have festive meals, and refrain from work. On the days in between, we can work, but many people like to extend the holiday to be with family.

The laws regarding the observance of Passover are more restrictive than those for any other holiday, which is somewhat paradoxical in that Passover is all about freedom. It is also paradoxical that Passover, which may be thought of as the most particularly Jewish of the holidays because it celebrates the historical deliverance of the Jewish people from Egypt, is the most universally observed of Jewish holidays. It has become a freedom seder for oppressed people. In New York City, many Jews marginally connected to the Jewish community and even many non-Jews make efforts to be at a Passover seder. More people attend a Passover seder than observe any other holiday. As my rebbe said, everything holy is full of paradoxes. It is also paradoxical that this holiday, which celebrates God's compassion and deliverance of the Jewish people, requires the greatest preparation and effort. People start preparing for Passover a month before.

Preparations for the holiday begin with the removal of *chometz* from one's possession. The Torah says, "During these seven days, no leaven should be found in your homes. . . . You must not eat anything leavened" (Exod. 12:19–20). *Chometz* refers to grains such as wheat, rye, spelt, barley, and oats that are mixed with water and allowed to ferment. Though Jewish law stipulates that one should not benefit from or even have possession of *chometz* during the holiday, the rabbis have devised a way for people to sell their *chometz* during the holiday so they do not have to throw everything out as was done in ancient times. Everything in the house is cleaned, *kashered* (made kosher), and prepared for Passover. Many people use this *mitzvah* as a time for intensive spring cleaning, getting rid of what is no longer used or needed.

Ideally, as we search and clean our physical house, we also do a similar process in our "inner house," within our heart and soul. Spiritually, *chometz* is associated with pride, negativity, and whatever does not allow one to be in the moment, all parts of the ego mind and subconscious that keep one limited and bound. Cleaning out the house of *chometz* is a spiritual purification process. As we remove and release our personal negativity symbolized by the *chometz,* we open to positive energy, creating greater possibility for newness in our lives.

On the fourteenth of Nissan, a powerful ritual known as *Bedikas Chometz,* the final look for *chometz,* takes place. Some pieces of *chometz* are placed throughout the house so the blessing ("Blessed are you, God, king of the universe who has made us holy with His mitzvot and commanded us to remove *chometz*") will not be said in vain. One searches every room by the light of a candle with a feather and a bag to collect the *chometz.* As one walks through one's home with a candle, without the benefit of electric light, it is easy to look into one's heart and soul for *chometz.* This ritual is one of those that one has to experience firsthand to understand its power.

A second ritual is the burning of *chometz.* This is also powerful, whether you do this by yourself or bring your *chometz* to a synagogue and watch it burn along with the *chometz* of others. To me, watching the fire burning the *chometz* is the final release, the burning away of the limited ego states symbolized by the *chometz.* There is a wonderful feeling of freedom afterward. After that, a powerful prayer, *Kol Chamira,* is said, through which people renounce all possession of *chometz* ("Any *chometz* in my possession which I did not see, remove, or know about shall be nullified and become ownerless as the dust of the earth"). Our words are important and complete this purification process. Though we may not have been successful in eliminating all possession of *chometz,* when we say these words, we wipe our hands of all *chometz.* It no longer exists for us.

The main food of Passover is *matzah*. *Matzah* was the unleavened bread that the Jewish people took with them as they fled Egypt. The Torah tells us, "Eat matzahs for seven days. By the first day you must have your homes cleared of all leaven" (Exod. 12:15). Made only of flour and water and baked within eighteen minutes so it does not rise or become leavened, it is called the bread of affliction and also the bread of freedom. *Matzah* is simple, humble, and in the moment. My rabbi used to call *matzah* medicine. The *Zohar* calls it the food of healing. At your seder, experiment with eating the *matzah* silently to increase the full impact of this experience. If you can get hand-made *matzah,* the experience will be stronger. As you eat the *matzah,* be aware that Jews all over the world are eating the same simple food, which Jews have eaten for thousands of years at this time.

There are many wonderful Haggadahs available today to guide your Passover seder, so I will not review the seder here. (There are also many books, including cookbooks, to guide you in preparing the special foods for the seder and for the entire Passover holiday.) It is great to have a variety of Haggadahs at your table, so people can share the unique insights into the rituals that compose the seder. To deepen your Seder experience, take time to question the structure and content of the Haggadah as you read through it. Explore why certain things are included in the way they are. These questions and the answers you find through commentaries or within yourself enable a greater sharing among participants and a deeper revelation of Godliness at the table.

The Passover table is a time for discussion and singing. In addition to the four cups of wine and the four questions, Hallel, songs of praise, are sung during the seder and throughout the holiday. As I said before, the seder is filled with words and song, and this reminds us of the healing of speech of this month.

Shir HaShirim (Song of Songs) is read on the second day of Passover. This mystical love poem expressing the passionate love between a man and a woman written by King Solomon is a metaphor for the love between the Jewish people and God. The seventh and eighth days of Passover commemorate the miracle of crossing the Red Sea. On the eighth day of Passover a final meal dedicated to the Messiah is eaten. At this time, we eat our last *matzah* and dream, talk, and sing about the final redemption. Passover was a taste of redemption, but the final and complete redemption will come in the future, God willing. This will be a time when there will be no war and no illness, and everyone will be aware of the oneness of God.

Meditation

The Divine Name permutation for this month is YHVH, with the letters in their proper placement. We are told that this powerful name of God was not given to Abraham, Isaac, or Jacob, but to Moses. Some translate this name to mean "I was, I am, and I will be"—God as Being itself. The following is a wonderful, powerful meditative practice on the Divine Name. (There are many different meditation practices on this name; please see my *New Age Judaism* and *Everyday Kabbalah* for some additional ones or contact me for audiotapes.)

Take a few minutes to center yourself with the breath. Take deep breaths. Inhale from deep in the belly, through the abdomen, the rib cage, all the way to the chest, hold the breath, and then exhale from the mouth. Do this several times. Now as you inhale, visualize the letter yud (Y) in the middle of the head. Meditate on the yud for several breaths. Then breathe in the letter yud and, on the exhalation, visualize the letter hay (H) in the shoulders and arms. Repeat this several times. Breathe in the yud and exhale the hay for several breaths.

Now visualize the vav (V) connecting the heart to the genitals and then place the final hay in the waist and the legs. Now coordinate the complete name of God with the breath. Breathe the yud into the head, exhale the hay in the shoulders, then breathe in the vav in the torso and exhale the final hay visualizing it in the waist and legs. Do this several times, optimally twenty-six times, which is the gematria for this name. As you visualize the letters, say their names silently to yourself. What color are they? If they are black, see if you can visualize them as white. You may find that the colors actually change and this is a good sign. Allow the letters to be placed deep inside of you, so you experience them at the core of your being.

Practical Recommendations

1. MEDITATE AND LEAVE YOUR BOX.

What does your Mitzraim, your Egypt, look like? In what areas in your life do you feel constrained? Where would you like to experience greater freedom and expansion in yourself and your life? Draw a picture of a box or visualize yourself in a box; then write or think about all the ways in which you are constrained in your life and all the feelings you experience being in this box of your life. The way out of Mitzraim is by being in it and going through it. Write down and meditate about what life out of this box would be like for you. Then take deep breaths and visualize that you can step out of the box. It is simple. Feel expanded and free out of the box. You are free.

2. IDENTIFY YOUR RESISTANCES AND FEARS.

Choose a spiritual, emotional, or material goal and select an image to symbolize this goal. Imagine that in front of you lies a long, straight, clear path directly to the top of the hill. Place your symbol on the top of the hill. Imagine that you at the bottom of the hill and you want to travel to the top. As you travel this path, you hear the voices of other people and within yourself telling you how difficult it will be for you to reach the top of the hill. Listen, and then visualize that you can take another step forward. This is an opportunity to recognize all the internal resistances, fears, and external opposition to your going forward in your life. Take time to journal and record what this experience was like for you.

3. IDENTIFY YOUR SUPPORTS.

Repeat the previous visualization, but this time, as you travel up the path, you see and hear people who are encouraging and supporting you to go forward and reach the top of the hill. See your symbol shining brightly on the top of the hill. Imagine people you know as well as people you do not know, even people from the Torah and Jewish history, cheering you onward and upward. Perhaps Moses, Abraham, Sarah, or Jacob are there rooting for you, applauding you with each step you take. See yourself climbing upward and visualize that you do reach the top of the hill. Take a moment to receive and absorb all the wonderful feelings of accomplishment and victory that you experience reaching the top of the hill. Take time to journal and record what this experience was like for you.

A Tale to Live By

The following favorite story is about faith, freedom, and crossing borders. It is one of the rabbinic miracle stories that compose Chassidic folklore, but it can also be interpreted on the lesser plane where we are all rebbes to each other.

Rabbi Yitzchok of Berditchev was a most beloved, awesome rebbe. One of his followers (*chassidim*) comes to him with the following request: "I have to go to Lublin. I need a passport. I am afraid to go to the police. Please give me a passport so I can travel safely." The rebbe walks into another room, and in a short time he comes out with a blank piece of paper. He hands it to his *chasid,* saying "Here is your passport."

It takes a lot of faith in your rebbe, to go to the border of your country and pull out a blank piece of paper as a passport. At the border, when he is asked to show his passport, he shows the blank piece of paper. When the officer sees the blank piece of paper, he salutes him and says, "I have never met such a person as you. Please let me provide a carriage for you, to make your journey more comfortable." This *chasid* was poor, but for this visit he was treated like royalty.

My teacher, Reb Shlomo Carlebach, heard the following story from a nephew of the person who was blessed to have had such a rebbe passport. In 1935, this man's uncle had to go to Germany from Poland. His uncle was a religious Jew with a long beard and long *peyis* (side hair curls by his ears). As Nazism was on the rise in Germany, traveling there might put him in physical danger. Because he knew the story of the Berditchever rebbe, he went to his rebbe, the Munkatcher Rebbe, and requested a holy passport: "I need to travel in Germany. I am afraid of what could happen to me there, looking as I do. Please give me a Munkatcher passport."

The rebbe said, "What makes you think that I am on such a level that I can give you such a passport?"

The *chasid* responds, "I know that you can. You are my rebbe. Please save my life."

The rebbe goes to another room and comes out three hours later. With eyes filled with tears, he hands him a blank piece of paper. The uncle goes to the border and is greeted by a Nazi soldier who asks, "Where is your passport?"

This man's uncle pulls out a blank piece of paper. The Nazi salutes him and proclaims, "Germany is honored to have such a person visit Germany. Let me give you a letter to the police to protect you, and have my people drive you around."

I can imagine this scene. This pious Jew, in complete religious garb, sits in a car and is chauffeured around quite royally by Nazis. It is hard to believe. When he returns from Germany, the rebbe asks him to swear never to tell anyone about the passport as long as he lives.

The rebbe passed away in 1936. On his deathbed, the rebbe said, "There is such a great darkness coming to the world. I cannot bear it. I do not want to live in such a world," and then he died. He died as *tzaddikim* (righteous people) often do, with full consciousness.

When this man's uncle became sick a few years later, he knew that he was dying. He gathered his family around him and told them the whole story of the Munkatcher passport. On his deathbed, he asked, "Please bury me with the Munkatcher passport in my hand. If the rebbe's passport opens gates in this world, who knows how many gates will it open to me in the world to come."

Even though we might not be on the level of these rebbes, we can give each other passports that enable us to go through borders and constraints that limit our freedom. There are all kinds of borders other than those between nations. There are borders between who I think I am and who I really am. There are borders between people, between husband and wife, between children and parents, between the human being and God. People live in different worlds, and sometimes it feels that the distance between them is insurmountable. We are stuck in our own ways and perspectives, and sometimes we can't enter each other's domains. We can't connect. During this month we have an opportunity to break through all kinds of borders, internal and external constraints, but we all need holy passports. We can give passports to each other. A passport could be a hug, it could be a look, and it could be a word, though it is often silent. In providing these we empower each other to go forward. And sometimes God gives us a passport directly.

Iyar

MONTH: *April-May*

ENERGY: *Healing of Body, Heart, and Soul*

AREA OF HEALING: *Thinking*

ASTROLOGICAL SIGN: *Taurus*

HEBREW LETTER: *Vav*

HEBREW TRIBE: *Issachar*

DIVINE NAME PERMUTATION: *YHHV*

HOLIDAYS: *Counting of the Omer, Pesach Sheni, Lag B'Omer, Yom Ha'Atzmaut* isa, a fifty-five-year-old homemaker, decided to begin therapy during Iyar, the month of healing. Like many people, Lisa was often obsessed about how she would be perceived by others and too often withdrew from interaction, fearing rejection. She was critical and judgmental with her family and very much wanted to improve her relationships with her husband and children. One of Lisa's goals was to be more loving and open-hearted. I told her that her relationships with others were a mirror of her relationship with herself and that if anything was going to change in her life, it had to begin with her. Though she claimed that she had worked on herself throughout her life, she doubted whether she could ever change.

"That seems to be a rather self-critical and limiting statement," I said, noting that in the past judging herself and others was a way for her ego to be in control. When she sat back and began to understand that this way would not help her to realize her goal of being open-hearted and loving, Lisa began trembling and crying.

"It's safe to feel your feelings," "It's safe to be vulnerable," I repeated to her many times. When she attempted to hold herself back and become analytical and judgmental, as was her way, her head ached. She confessed that she grew up afraid to speak up and viewing crying as a sign of weakness. I told her that it took strength and courage to feel feelings and that she was now able to do that.

"So what would have happened if as a child you were to speak your feelings," I asked.

"No one would listen," she cried. "No one was there."

With encouragement she went deeper. "There was no one to comfort me." Encouraged to give a voice to the feelings of little Lisa, she cried, "Notice me, give me some attention. I am important, I have a right to be loved."

This is the call of the inner child within each of us. This is the call of the soul. I told Lisa she needed to pay more attention to herself. She needed to honor and love herself. This is an important part of her healing. She questioned whether this would be self-centered and egotistical. I replied, "Imposing your projections and judgments on others is egotistical. It is not selfish to love yourself—it is your responsibility."

In Iyar, Lisa began to devote time to nourishing and affirming herself. Previously a Type A personality, constantly busy, she gave herself time to relax, meditate, and affirm herself. She placed herself in new social situations. She also learned to ask for clarification from others about her interactions with them; that eliminated a great deal of time and energy she had previously spent worrying. And most important, she began to express her wants, rather than blaming people for not reading her mind and meeting her needs.

And so Lisa began her recovery and personal change during the healing month of Iyar.

Energy: Healing of Body, Heart, and Soul

Iyar is the month of healing. The Hebrew letters for the name Iyar spell out the initials of the verse *"Ani Yud-Yud Rofecha,"* "I am God your Healer." Iyar is a time of detoxification, purification, and refinement of one's character traits. As spring begins to emerge more fully during Iyar, we also begin to bring ourselves to a new order, a new alignment. Iyar is a time of letting go of what does not support one's well-being—what is toxic, what is false—and a time for opening up to what does support one's well-being—what is true, what is real.

Lisa's story is a good example of the kind of spiritual work many clients go through particularly in this month. This kind of inquiry enables a person to gain new

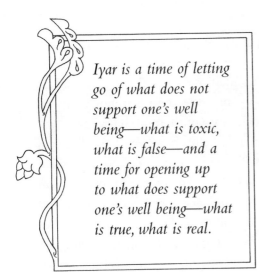

Iyar is a time of letting go of what does not support one's well being—what is toxic, what is false—and a time for opening up to what does support one's well being—what is true, what is real.

capacities of freedom and expression. As with Lisa, it may be necessary for many people to enter into some of the broken places deep inside themselves and contact the earlier wounds and scars that have previously limited them.

When I tell my therapy clients and meditation students that Iyar is a time for healing, they feel a combination of relief and gratitude for permission to bring forth their deeper issues. The number of people in my therapy practice increases in Iyar, and the work is deeper and more intense. The spiritual energy of this month enables this deep level of healing to occur in the easiest, most gentle, and life-affirming way.

Iyar is the connection between the previous month, Nissan, which hosts the holiday of Passover, and the following month, Sivan, which hosts the holiday of Shavuous. In Nissan, which marks the beginning of spring, there is a spiritual waking up to new possibilities, to new freedom within oneself. Passover marks the beginning of a new journey, a movement from internal or external constraint to greater freedom, expansiveness, and self- expression that culminates in the receiving of the Torah and divine revelation at Shavuous.

But before completing this journey, before this new freedom and expansiveness can be realized, we need to not only reflect upon the ways we have limited ourselves previously, but also to explore strategies through which greater freedom and self-expression may be actualized in very practical ways. This is the healing work during the month of Iyar. This healing work corresponds to the planting work done in Iyar.

Healing begins with a careful discernment between ego states masquerading as the self and the soul, which is our true essence and identity. Sometimes it's not so easy to tell the difference. As a guide, we are most likely identified with an ego state if we find ourselves spending a lot of time justifying our position, analyzing and judging the actions of others, or feeling frustrated when life does not always happen according to our desires or demands. When any of these occurs, know that you need to gain greater perspective. To the extent you are identified with this ego state, you will lack objectivity and not see the spiritual opportunity present in this life challenge.

To facilitate healing within yourself, you must choose to strengthen conscious contact with God and be willing to break through the blocks presented by the ego. Often the conflicts between the ego mind and soul of a person are reflected in the body. Many illnesses or conditions have a spiritual origin. Jealousy and anger take their greatest toll on us physically.

All healing requires a connection with God. The Talmud reminds us that those in prison cannot free themselves. By our attachment and connection to God, who is free and whole, we may experience these qualities ourselves. God is free as God is not limited by the laws of nature, cause and effect, time and space. God is whole, God is one. God cannot be divided into parts. God is within creation, but God is also beyond creation. When we make a connection with God or become aware of the Divine Presence, we gain access to greater freedom and become God-like. We become whole. Our consciousness is lifted upward, beyond ordinary modes of thinking and awareness. In the process of healing, through prayer, meditation, and doing good deeds, we tap into the part of ourselves that is divine, and we open ourselves to receive divine assistance and healing. As we heal, our body, mind, and soul are brought into alignment.

According to kabbalah, all healing is administered through angels. Angels are the conduits for the flow of divine energy into the physical world. The Talmud tells us that grass would not grow were it not for an angel that tells it to grow. Angels are messengers of God and, according to Judaism, we are surrounded by angels.

There are differing opinions in Judaism about who and what angels really are. Maimonides, the Rambam, says that angels are spiritual forces. Nachmanides, the Ramban, says that angels are objective beings. Probably both are true. Angels are spiritual forces since we are told that we even create angels by our good deeds. But we are also told that angels are objective beings who can assume a physical form when necessary, as did the three angels who visited Abraham. I know many people today who have sensed the presence of angels or have heard them and several people who claim to have seen them.

Kabbalah says if one is sick and must see a doctor, one should go to a doctor with a good reputation because he or she has greater angels working in conjunction with him or her. In Judaism, we generally do not believe that our healing comes from doctors, but from God through the ministry of angels. All healing involves a level of surrender, a letting go and allowing the divine healing and angelic energies to flow through us. This may be new, challenging, and possibly even scary for many people who are used to being in control and feel that they have to do everything themselves or it does not happen. True healing is a letting go.

General Guidelines and Goals

These guidelines and goals enable us to direct our energies in the ways that are optimal for our growth and transformation in accordance with the energy of this month.

It is recommended that you read and meditate upon them often in the course of the month. Reflect on their applicability to you, and allow them to direct and inspire you often this month.

1. PURIFY AND HEAL.

Purification and healing is the letting go of what does not support one's well-being, and the opening to what does. At the beginning of the month, take time to review your lifestyle, the quality of your life on physical, emotional, intellectual, and spiritual levels. Identify areas of your life that you would like to expand. Identify behaviors and activities that do not support your well-being. Make a plan to begin new life-affirming behaviors and activities that support you in the direction you want to go and reduce or eliminate destructive, negative ones.

For example, at the beginning of Iyar, I realized I wanted to be more physically fit and vital. I joined a gym and began an exercise regimen, something I had not done in over ten years. I noted that in Iyar clients and friends also made similar changes. My friend Stephanie realized that she wanted to be healthier and eat more healthy food, so she decided to become a vegetarian. Debra ended a relationship with a friend who drained her energy. Melvin realized that his marijuana smoking was a drug dependency and he needed to address the underlying causes of this negative behavior. Michael asked his employer for a raise that was commensurate with his increased responsibilities.

2. DEEPEN YOUR CONNECTION WITH GOD.

Iyar is an optimal time to undertake a routine of meditation, prayer, and doing good deeds as ways to welcome the power of divine healing. Be consistent in your practice. There is a tremendous blessing for healing this month. Remember, you cannot do it solely on your own. God is the true healer. Ask for God's help and open to being plugged in. Sometimes people pray for healing, but because they do not believe, inwardly, in the power of their words or in the power of God, they do not open to the experience of being healed. As you strengthen your contact with the Divine, you will open to greater angelic energies that will heal you on all levels of being.

According to kabbalah, there are five parts to our soul. Our soul is within the body, but it is also outside of the body. We become ill when there is a break between the soul energy that surrounds the body and the energy within. By doing *mitzvot,* opening one's heart to greater love, and reducing anger and jealousy, we actually strengthen the connection between the soul that surrounds the body with the soul that invigorates the physical body. This promotes healing.

3. BE WITH YOUR FEELINGS, WITHOUT BLAMING YOURSELF, OTHERS, OR GOD.

Generally speaking, what happens outside of you is a reflection of what is occurring within you. Many problems occur between people because each one thinks that the other should change. Who in your life do you think should change and in what way? Often, what we want to change in another person is a projection of what we want to change within ourselves. Seek to change yourself first before you consider trying to change others.

Become aware of the tendency to blame yourself, others, or God. The common tendency to judge and be overly critical of oneself weakens self-esteem and limits the flow of healing energy. Blaming keeps you stuck, feeling like a victim. Let go of blame, breathe it out with the breath, and take responsibility for your own healing.

As you take greater responsibility for your life, substitute compassion for yourself for blame. If you are in pain, feel your pain, without blame. Love the child within you who is hurting. Share your pain with others and especially with God. Ask and call out for mercy and healing. Always ask yourself, what am I learning and how can I grow from this challenging experience?

4. BE WILLING TO DISCOVER AND ACCEPT THE TRUTH.

Healing comes from being connected to what is true, what is real. It is as simple as that.

In situations where you feel pained or stressed, ask yourself if what you believe is absolutely true. Too often we become needlessly upset about something that is not relevant and not true. We regret the past, worry about the future, and are overly concerned about what we imagine other people think. We waste so much precious time and energy through this kind of faulty imagination.

When you are upset, ask yourself: Am I being objective? Can I be objective? If you are in a blaming or victim mode of thinking, know that you are not in touch with the whole truth. You are not being objective. If you cannot be objective, speak to someone who can help you be objective.

Healing requires a deep level of listening to oneself and being with oneself in the most honoring, respectful way. When we have the courage to be with the truth of our being, we contact God and experience peace and healing regardless of what is happening externally.

Be particularly mindful this month so you can make choices about where to direct your energy. Ask yourself often: Can I open and listen to the deep knowing inside myself that is coming from inner stillness, the voice of the soul, or do I listen and react to the chatter and hysteria of the ego mind, which is loud and clamoring for my attention? Breathe deeply and give yourself time to listen.

5. DEVELOP A WIDER RANGE OF EMOTIONAL CAPACITY.

Every person needs to be able to call forth different emotional energies in different situations. For example, at times we have to be strong and set definitive boundaries; at other times we have to be unconditionally loving and have no boundaries. Not having the capacity to express what is appropriate in any given situation is limiting and detrimental to ourselves as well as others. Though we may have a propensity toward one direction, for example, some of us are more kind than we are strong, we need to cultivate the whole spectrum of emotional capacities as presented in the kabbalistic Tree of Life (see page 203). In this way, we become complete.

For example, Abraham was known to embody the quality of *hesed,* loving-kindness, but in his life he was constantly challenged to demonstrate *gevurah,* strength. For example, it was not his nature or desire to send his son Ishmael away; he was challenged to do so. In this way, he gained the capacity to choose what is appropriate for every situation, rather than being limited by the feeling of "this is the way I am."

The spiritual practice of Counting of the Omer, which is discussed later in the holiday section of this chapter, invites a reflection, refinement, and balancing of the character traits within a person as represented by the *sefirot,* the divine emanations of the Tree.

6. GUARD AGAINST NEGATIVE BEHAVIORS, AND RELATIONSHIPS THAT ARE FAMILIAR BUT LIMITING.

Deep change is difficult, and it's easy to go back to old habits of thinking and behaving if we are not vigilant. Be mindful of the tendency to return to what is familiar but limiting. To keep going forward in our lives, we need to cultivate greater trust and faith. Fears of the unknown may surface, but you now have the courage to go forward.

Astrological Sign: Taurus

The astrological sign of this month is Taurus, ruled by the planet Venus. As an earth sign, Taurus informs us that the earthly plane is the arena for spiritual work now. The work of Iyar is to bring the spiritual illumination of Nissan into the earthly plane. In Nissan or Aries, we move forward, and in Iyar or Taurus, we stabilize and integrate. When the sun is in Taurus, we feel connected to the earth and we sense that nature is pregnant with new life that will soon emerge in all its glory.

The planet Venus, which rules Taurus, imparts beauty and love to this month. As the mythological goddess of love and beauty, Venus is an agent of harmony, integrating parts and bringing them into the whole. There is an underlying energy of love to tap into this month that brings everything together, along with beauty that enables us to appreciate the relationship and balance between the parts. As always, but particularly this month, it is love, even eros, that is a strong underlying motivator for change. It is love that heals.

Taurus is symbolized by the bull. The prophet Isaiah says, "The bull knows its master" (Isa. 1:3). The bull is said to have a level of discernment. Unlike the lamb (Nissan), which does not work, we need to be like the bull this month and plod along. Iyar is a time of spiritual effort, step by step, day by day, like a bull. If we keep our goals in mind, our efforts can also be joyful.

Hebrew Letter: Vav

ו Like the month of Iyar, the letter vav is a connector; it connects time, space, and people to each other. In English we would say the article "and" in place of the vav. As we learned earlier, Iyar connects the holiday of Passover, celebrating the Exodus from Egypt, to Shavuous, the holiday of receiving the Torah, which occurs next month.

The vav has a numerical value of six. The Torah tells us that God created the world in six days. This corresponds to the six days of the week in which we do our work and to the six directions in the physical world. Iyar is the month of healing work in practical ways. Interestingly, the first vav that appears in the Torah is the sixth word in Hebrew, "In the beginning, God created heaven *and* earth." The vav connects heaven and earth. Healing is also the connection between God and humankind.

In kabbalah, the vav, the third letter in the tetragrammaton, YHVH, is also a connector. The first two letters, yud (Y) and hay (H), refer to the spiritual light from above, and the last hay is the vessel of this world. The vav, then, connects heaven and earth. The vav represents the single line of light that connects the spiritual world to the physical world. Many kabbalistic meditation exercises involve the vav.

According to kabbalah, the vav is associated with *zer anpin,* which literally means "the small face" or "the son." This refers to the six *sephirot,* the divine attributes and channels by which we experience and connect with infinite Ain Sof. The name Ain Sof connotes the limitless unknowable God. These six attributes, meditated upon in Lag B'Omer, which occurs this month, are: *hesed,* loving-kindness (grace); *gevurah,* strength (restraint); *tiferet,* compassion (balance); *netzach,* victory (overcoming obstacles); *hod,* humility (splendor); *yesod,* foundation (bonding). The *sephirot* also form the basis for some kabbalistic meditation practices.

Hebrew Tribe: Issachar

The tribe associated with Iyar is Issachar. Issachar was Leah's fifth son. He was conceived on the night that Leah traded mandrakes (a fertility plant) her son Reuven found with her sister, Rachel, for a night with Jacob. At this time Jacob was living exclusively with Rachel, so Leah had to buy a night with him. That night Leah tells Jacob, "I have hired [sakar] you with my son's mandrakes" (Gen. 30:16). When she bears the son conceived that night, she names him Issachar.

Supported by the tribe of Zevulun, the tribe of Issachar contained the Torah scholars. Their work was to think and learn. They represent a kind of thinking that is rooted in divine wisdom, the higher self, and the heart. This is what needs to be cultivated in this month. We need to tap into the energy of Issachar. Iyar is devoted to the refinement and perfection of thought.

Divine Name Permutation: YHHV

If we compare the permutation of the Divine Name for Iyar to that of the previous month of Nissan, we find the third and fourth letters, the vav (V) and the hay (H), are reversed. This alerts us that there is a change in the flow of energy to the world of Yetzerah (the world of formation, the world of angels, the world of the heart) and the world of Assiyah (the world of action, our physical world, our physical body). Yetzerah is the heart of the person and Assiyah is the body, or the physical world. In particular, the hay in the position of Yetzerah shows that there is expansiveness in this world.

The energy this month supports the opening the heart. There is a greater flow of angelic energy this month. The hay in the position of Beriyah indicates that there is expansiveness in the mental dimension. The position of the vav in the world of Assiyah indicates an emphasis on bringing the light to the physical world, but the light is not fully manifested. As mentioned earlier, this month is a planting time rather than a reaping time.

Torah Portions

Purification is a major theme reflected in the Torah portions for this month. The entire book of Leviticus, in which this month's Torah portions are found, is devoted to acquiring purity and holiness. The Torah portions read for this month usually begin with a double reading of the chapters of Tarzria and Metzora (Lev. 12–16). These chapters are concerned primarily with purity. The word for "purity" in Hebrew is *tahor;* "impurity" is *tammeh*. Purity in Hebrew is about openness and being alive. When we are pure, we are healthy. Impurity is about being spiritually closed, connected with death. Illness is a form of impurity.

The Torah portions throughout this month reiterate the words "Be holy, for I, Your God, am Holy" and "I am God" (Lev. 19:2). The Torah reminds us numerous times in the Torah portion of this month that the human being has the capacity to be holy like God. Because our soul is a part of God, we can be holy as God is holy. The Hebrew word used for "holy," *kedusha,* means "separate." Holiness in Judaism is being separate from the world, while also being fully in the world. God is holy because God is separate from the world, yet the world is also filled with the glory of God. Our soul is holy because the soul is outside of the body, yet the soul is also within the body, invigorating the body.

Holiness in Judaism is not about being spiritually divorced from the physical world; rather, it is about experiencing God in the physical world. The body and soul are unified, each being made whole by the other. The goal of Judaism is not to separate the soul from the body, as in dualistic religions, but rather to experience God in our own bodies and in our relationships with others. In a surprisingly unique way the Torah tells us that what we eat, with whom we have sexual relations, and how we relate to other human beings makes a difference in our capacity to access the purity of our own soul.

The Torah instructs us through the portions for this month that it is in the sanctification of the basic physical things of life that we experience holiness and become holy people. It is not enough to just meditate to be holy. Through the mundane world and its myriad physical activities like food, sex, money, and business, we have the opportunity to experience God and holiness. In this way also, we purify ourselves and the world as well. Iyar is the grounding of Godliness in this world.

Holidays

Counting of the Omer

HISTORY   The Counting of the Omer is not a holiday in itself, but it is a spiritual and religious practice linking Passover to Shavuous in order to bring special awareness to the spiritual opportunity available during those days. The days in which the *omer,* or barley offering, is counted are the days in between these two holidays. Though the counting begins in the middle of Nissan and ends in the first week of Sivan, every day of Iyar is included. The energy of Iyar is very much represented by this practice.

The practice of counting the omer is cited in the Torah: "You shall count seven perfect Sabbaths from the day following the Passover holiday when you brought the omer as a wave offering until the day after the seventh Sabbath, when there will be fifty days. On the fiftieth day you may present new grain as a meal offering to God" (Lev. 23:15–16).

In ancient times, when the Holy Temple stood in Jerusalem, the omer was a daily ritual offering of barley. By offering barley, which represented simple animal food, one hoped to transform the simple unconscious instincts and behaviors into a higher, more refined spiritual awareness. Offering sacrifices in the Holy Temple was an ancient healing practice.

OBSERVANCE   The Counting of the Omer helps people to do the inner work of refining the character traits of the ego on a daily systematic basis, so the pure energies of the *sephirot,* the divine emanations, shine through. The counting also helps a person to be aware of the preciousness of each day. It is an ancient form of healing.

Each day, forty-nine days in all, from Passover to Shavuous, is counted, designated with a particular number, and assigned a special blessing. Many people today count the omer symbolically through prayer. Each week of the Counting of the Omer is devoted to reflection and meditation on a particular *sephira* (divine attribute) in relation to the other *sephirot* (see the Tree of Life).

For example, the first week is devoted to *hesed,* love. For that entire week we reflect upon the attribute of love and how we can open to its many faces. The second week is devoted to developing the quality of *gevurah,* strength, and we reflect on the ways we demonstrate strength, focus our energies, and set boundaries.

Interestingly, Iyar begins with the *sephira* of *tiferet,* which is attributed to compassion and healing. The Divine Name associated with this *sephira* of compassion and healing is YHVH, the primary permutation of the name of God. Compassion is the character trait that we most experience in our relationship to God. It is the energy most prominent in Nissan, the previous month. And it is the quality we most need to cultivate for our own healing in Iyar. It is our lack of compassion for ourselves that is our greatest block in being healed and connecting with God.

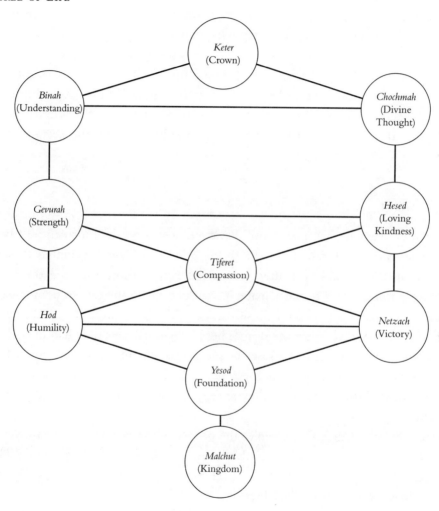

The second week in Iyar is devoted to the energy of the *sephira* of *netzach*. *Netzach* is the energy of endurance, of overcoming obstacles, and is associated with the right leg. This is the energy of bringing forth what you want in your life in a balanced way, through effort and trust. The third week of Iyar is devoted to the energy of the *sephira* of *hod,* known as "glory" and "splendor." *Hod* is the quality of humility, or submissiveness. You have to know how to let go of effort and allow God to work through you. The final week of Iyar is devoted to the *sephira* of *yesod*. *Yesod* is the foundation and is associated with the genitals. It is the energy of bonding. *Yesod* is the deepest core of a person.

Pesach Sheni

HISTORY   Pesach Sheni, or second Passover, occurs on the fourteenth of Iyar and has its origins in the Torah (Num. 9:10–11). When the Jews celebrated Passover in the desert in the second year after having left Egypt, those carrying the bones of Joseph were not allowed to participate. Joseph had made the Jewish people swear to take his body out of Egypt, and those carrying his bones were declared impure by virtue of having contact with the dead. These individuals felt they had missed a spiritual opportunity and went to Moses to see if this apparent injustice could be corrected. Even though they were doing a *mitzvah,* a good deed, by carrying Joseph's bones, because of the purity laws they felt separated from the rest of the people and punished.

Pesach Sheni was therefore given to the people who missed the first Passover either intentionally or unintentionally. It is also known as the second-chance seder. Though Pesach Sheni was not considered a festival day in ancient times comparable to the major holidays, it was a day of celebration.

OBSERVANCE   Pesach Sheni is observed today in some communities by eating matzah and bread together at a meal. Eating matzah brings a person back to the consciousness of Passover, but on Pesach Sheni it feels new and different to be eating matzah and bread together.

The first Passover has very stringent rules prohibiting the eating of bread and other forms of chometz (leavened food). Pesach Sheni is a time to revisit the Passover experience, in order to bring the newness and the sense of freedom of Passover more fully into your life once again. It stands as a reminder that we can change. If we missed the opportunity of the first Passover, or we did not experience Passover as fully as we might have liked, we are given another chance at Pesach Sheni.

Knowing that we have another chance, that we can always come back to the holiness of God, is an important teaching of Pesach Sheni. Pesach Sheni is a time of redemption, it is a time for teshuvah, returning to one's essence and returning to the Jewish people. There is no structural format for celebrating Pesach Sheni other than eating matzah again. It is a time to reflect and talk about the meaning of Passover, the value of being given a second chance in life, and the importance of opening to oneself to that second chance. Unlike many holidays, this holiday is not obligatory; it is a choice, as are the most precious and deepest things in life.

Lag B'Omer

HISTORY   Lag B'Omer is the thirty-third day of the Counting of the Omer, or the eighteenth of Iyar. The holiday of Lag B'Omer comes not from the Torah, but from kabbalah. Lag B'Omer commemorates the anniversary of the death, known as the *yahrzeit,* of the great kabbalist Rabbi Shimon Bar Yochai, acclaimed author of one of the principal texts of kabbalah, the *Zohar.*

Because of his spiritual radiance, Rabbi Shimon Bar Yochai was called the Holy Candle. Legend has it that during the time of the Roman occupation of Jerusalem in the second century, he lived in a cave with his son for twelve years surviving entirely off the fruit of a carob tree. It has been passed down through the centuries that there was a great and awesome spiritual light at the actual demise of Rabbi Shimon. As he was consciously leaving his body, he told people that he was happy, that now he would be unified with God. For him, dying was like going to the canopy of marriage.

Since ancient times, sages have celebrated the *yahrzeit* of Rabbi Shimon Bar Yochai. This custom was strengthened by kabbalists such as Rabbi Yitzchok Luria (the Arizel) and the Baal Shem Tov, the founder of the Chassidic movement. For those who honor this day and speak about Shimon Bar Yochai, it is a day of spiritual light. Because Rabbi Shimon Bar Yochai revealed the secrets of the kabbalah, the mystical secrets of the Torah, Lag B'Omer is a day of receiving the secrets of Torah.

Interestingly and not coincidentally, Lag B'Omer occurs in the Counting of the Omer on the day associated with the *sephira* of *hod* in the *sephira* of *hod*. *Hod* means "glory," "splendor," and has been associated with the quality of humility, because it allows what is to shine through. *Hod* in *hod* is the most auspicious day when spiritual light, the essence of reality, can optimally shine through.

Lag B'Omer also commemorates the end of a plague that had killed twenty-four thousand students of Rabbi Akiva, who was also a great kabbalist and commentator on the Talmud. Rabbi Akiva only began learning Torah at the age of forty, but in a few years he was recognized as one of the leading scholars and rabbis in the Jewish world. Also living during the second century in the period when Israel was occupied by Rome, he encouraged his students to fight against imperial power. Most of his students lost their lives in this battle or died of the plague. Though these students were considered the greatest Torah scholars in their day, oral tradition says they died because they did not give sufficient honor to each other. They were knowledgeable about Torah, but too competitive. They failed to perform the most important *mitzvah* of loving others as ourselves.

OBSERVANCE   Today, in Meron, a small city in Israel where Rabbi Shimon Bar Yochai is buried, hundreds of thousands of people gather each year on Lag B'Omer to celebrate the *yahrzeit* of this greatest saint with bonfires, music, and hair-cutting of little boys of three years of age. In Chassidic and Orthodox circles, many couples refrain from cutting their sons' hair until the boys are three. One of the sources for this custom is the superstition that because men perform more *mitzvot* than women, the lives of little boys are more physically vulnerable to Satan. By not cutting their hair, they trick Satan into viewing them as female rather than male. In the joy and celebration of Lag B'Omer, their hair is cut and their true selves are revealed. It is now safe for them to begin to learn Torah and look like Jewish boys, donning for the first time a *kippa,* the traditional skullcap, and *tzitzie,* the fringes on the inner garment.

In Israel, the United States, and Europe, Lag B'Omer is also a time for people to gather together, hear music, and speak of Rabbi Shimon Bar Yochai. It is a particularly auspicious time for meditation and making a connection with the soul of Rabbi Shimon Bar Yochai. When one is attached to a *tzaddik,* a righteous and holy person, one is elevated along with the *tzaddik* and filled with joy.

It is no coincidence that the *yahrzeit* of Rabbi Shimon Bar Yochai is in Iyar, the month of healing. In Judaism, the light and goodness of a *tzaddik* is said to become more powerful and accessible to people, especially for healing, after his death, when he is not in a physical body.

The *yahrzeit* of such a person is called Yom Hilula (Day of Memorial Rejoicing). It is taught that the soul of the departed is elevated to a higher level on the *yahrzeit*. Attend a Lag B'Omer celebration at a synagogue near you, or simply light a candle and give thanks that there are people like Shimon Bar Yochai who come into this world at times of darkness to heal and radiate God's light.

Because it was said that the students of Rabbi Akiva died because they didn't honor each other, today is a day to give honor to others, particularly those close to you. Take time to praise others, to reflect the goodness that you see within them. This kind of acknowledgment does not happen often enough. A wonderful treat is to set a special time for this kind of expression. In your family or in small groups, let one person be in the center while the other people speak of the good qualities that this person demonstrates in life.

Yom Ha'Atzmaut

HISTORY   Yom Ha'Atzmaut, Israeli Independence Day, celebrates the establishment of the modern State of Israel. For some, this was a miracle of biblical proportions. In 1948, after two thousand years of exile, hundreds of thousands of Jews from Germany, Austria, Poland, Russia, Yemen, Iraq, Iran, India, and other countries were brought to Israel. For many Jews and non-Jews, the establishment of the state of Israel is seen as the fulfillment of the biblical prophecy: "From the East, I will bring your children; from the West I will gather you. I will instruct the North 'Give back!' and tell Yemen (the South) 'Do not withhold.' Bring my sons from afar; my daughters from the ends of the Earth" (Isa. 43:5–6). It is considered the first step in the messianic redemption predicted by ancient prophecies.

From the time of the exile from the land of Israel in the first century until today, Jews have prayed to return to the land of Israel. Though the Jewish people were dispersed throughout the world for two thousand years, Israel was always the spiritual center, the Holy Land, for Jews, although there were always Jews who lived in Israel.

The Talmud speaks of the miraculous healing powers of the land of Israel. Along with many other claims, it tells us, "Anyone who walks a distance of six cubits in the land of Israel is guaranteed a share in the world to come." I'll never forget how Reb Nachman of Breslov made great efforts to travel to Israel. It took him many months of difficult travel, and he said that it was all worth it to just to stand in the land of Israel for a few minutes. In those few minutes, he had accomplished his mission. His soul was elevated by the sanctity of the land in a way that could not happen outside of the land of Israel, and he was spiritually fulfilled. A short time after his arrival in Israel, he was ready to leave.

Particularly in times of persecution, religious and nonreligious Jews looked to and fled to Israel as a refuge. During the Holocaust, Jews tried to escape to Israel, which was under British rule at the time. Sometimes Jews who tried to enter Israel were sent back to Germany to die at the hands of Nazis. After the war, Eastern European and German Jews were placed in deportation camps awaiting countries that would accept them. The majority of these Jews went to Israel, but many also fled to the United States. Upon the establishment of the State of Israel, Jews were expelled from Iraq. The doors of Israel were open to all Jews. When possible, Jews fled to Israel from other Arabic countries, where they had been persecuted, and the Jewish community from India fled en mass.

As soon as the United Nations voted to establish the State of Israel, the surrounding Arab states declared war on it. With little arms and with an army composed primarily of weary war refugees who were untrained as soldiers, it was quite a miracle that Israel was victorious against the large, wealthy Arab countries who sought to destroy it. After this military victory, known as the War of Independence, the independent State of Israel was declared by its own legal body, the Kenesset, on May 15, 1948, that is, the fifth of Iyar.

Interestingly, by divine guidance, and most likely unbeknownst to the secular leadership involved in the formation of the State of Israel at this time, Israel was inaugurated during the *sephira* week of *tiferet,* the week of compassion. Even with all its problems, the establishment of the State of Israel was truly an act of compassion. The hope in the establishment of Israel was that Israel would provide protection for the Jewish people, who had been persecuted and discriminated against throughout history.

The establishment of the State of Israel was an act of divine compassion, partially funneled through the compassion awakened in the hearts of Jews throughout the world, particularly in the affluent population of the United States, who made large financial and personal contributions to support the development and dream of Israel. Synagogues became campaign stations for the United Jewish Appeal, the main fundraising body for Israel, and raising funds for Israel became an integral part of American Jewish life in the 1950s and 1960s. Everyone gave to Israel and bought bonds for the State of Israel, with the hope and faith that the country would survive.

After the Holocaust, many were filled with doubt about the existence of God and questioned whether God had died along with the six million Jews. With the establishment of Israel, God became alive once again to many people. The establishment of the State of Israel harkened a revival in Judaism.

OBSERVANCE   How Yom Ha'Atzmaut should be celebrated is still debated in the Jewish community at large and in Israel itself. Should it be a secular or a religious holiday? Was it a full-fledged miracle like those that resulted in Chanukah or Purim? Should the psalms of praise known as the Hallel, which are said on Chanukah, be extended to this day of Yom Ha'Atzmaut? Some groups of Jews believe that Hallel should be said, but without the special blessing; others say that the establishment of Israel was a miracle comparable to the origin of Chanukah and that Hallel should be said with a full blessing. The debate goes on over whether this day should have the stature of a full rabbinic holiday. One of the reasons for its lack of acceptance as a full Jewish holiday in the religious camp is that the State of Israel was brought into being primarily by nonreligious Jews, who shaped its government not on Torah, but on Western ideals of democracy. Another reason is the fact that the establishment of Israel occurred through military victory. Israel paid a great price in loss of life during the War of Independence and in subsequent wars and continues to struggle for its existence. All the rabbis agree, however, that the establishment of the State of Israel has marked the beginning of the time of the Messiah.

As an aside, when Israel recaptured all of Jerusalem in the miraculous Six-Day War in 1967, the rabbis did not hesitate to declare the twenty-eighth day of Iyar as Yom Yerushalayim, Jerusalem Day, and give to it unequivocally all the sacraments of a rabbinical holiday, such as Hallel with a special blessing. As a result, Yom Yerushalayim redeemed another joyous day in the somber month of Iyar when musical celebrations and weddings could take place. At that time, to the Jewish people and to the world, the Israeli victory in the Six-Day War was an amazing miracle of biblical proportions. The tiny nation defeated the large surrounding Arab countries in six days, and with little bloodshed Israel recaptured Jerusalem, Sinai, the West Bank, and more, restoring

Israel to its biblical borders. For the first time, Jews had the opportunity to pray at the Holy Wall in Jerusalem. Unfortunately, however, all the captured territory did not bring peace, but more problems. Consequently, the celebration of Yom Yerushalayim on the twenty-seventh of Iyar has been muted.

In Israel itself and in New York, Yom Ha'Atzmaut is widely celebrated with street parades and special programs at synagogues. Hallel is sung, without a special blessing. There are no restrictions as to labor. And in Israel, it has become a day for weddings, along with Lag B'Omer and Yom Yerushalayim, in the time period of Iyar when weddings are normally prohibited.

Meditation

Deep relaxation promotes healing. Take slow deep breaths, breathing from the abdomen to the rib cage to the chest, and exhaling with a "Hah" sound that comes from deep in the belly. Pause in the space between the breaths and allow the mind to quiet. When the mind begins to chatter about the events of the day or engages in judging you or others, very slowly bring the focus back to the breath and back to being with yourself as you are in the present moment. Feel the breath move like a wave through the body. Give permission for the entire body to relax. Relaxation promotes healing.

Bring your attention to each part of the body, tighten the muscles associated with that body part and then relax them. Do this focusing, tightening, and relaxing with every part of your body from your feet, to your knees, to your buttocks and pelvic area, to your stomach, to your entire torso, to your shoulders, to your neck, to your face. Then tighten and then relax the entire body. Direct the breath to any places where there is pain, tension, or numbness and give your body permission to relax. If you are suffering from an ailment, ask God to heal you. Repeat to yourself several times with the breath, "God, please heal me now."

Repeat silently or in a low voice several times with the breath, "I am open to receiving God's healing, light, and love" or "Blessed are you God, the true healer." Stay in this deep state of relaxation as long as you want. Play soothing music as you relax deeply.

Practical Recommendations

1. BE PARTICULARLY CONSCIOUS OF YOUR DIET.

The Torah portions for this month give detailed attention to the foods one can and cannot eat. Kosher foods nourish the soul, and non-kosher foods do not. We may not necessarily understand why certain foods are permitted and others are forbidden, but the Torah does specify clearly the status of all food. Historically, Jews have occasionally been spared disease and plague by abstaining from foods prohibited by the Torah, while others eating those foods died.

Iyar, according to kabbalah, is the headquarters for the awareness of healing through food. The whole Jewish system of *kashrus* is designed to raise people's awareness of the spirituality and healing possible through the physical act of eating. The purely mundane biological act of eating can be raised to the level of a holy act. According to kabbalah, by eating, we redeem the Godly sparks in the foods we eat and raise them to a higher level by our consciousness and blessing.

It was in Iyar that manna came down for the Jews in the desert, and during the time the Jews ate manna, there was no illness and disease. At this time of the year, the temperature begins to change in many places, so it is particularly important to be sensitive to what the body needs and to adjust one's diet accordingly. Some undertake a cleansing diet at this time to help the body make the transition to another season. It is important in this month to drink a lot of water. It was in Iyar that Miriam's well was established. This miraculous water supply for the Jewish people, attributed to the merit of Miriam, traveled with them as they wandered through the desert until Miriam's death. Though we need water for our continued survival, water is an important natural cleansing and purifying agent particularly during this month.

2. CONSIDER BECOMING KOSHER OR VEGETARIAN.

Anyone who is spiritually sensitive and also eats meat, Jews and non-Jews alike, should consider buying kosher meat. By buying kosher meat, you are assured that the animal was healthy when slaughtered and that it did not suffer in its demise. This is important to your physical and spiritual well-being. It is said that animals slaughtered in a frightening, nonkosher manner secrete a toxic chemical at the time of their slaughter, which we then consume. Unfortunately, however, both kosher and non-kosher animals are fed antibiotics and growth hormones that may pose health risks to consumers.

Furthermore, the way the animals are treated in the animal factories is a violation of Torah law, which stipulates compassion toward animals. Unfortunately, animals are not treated better in the animal factories where they receive a kosher slaughtering. For these reasons and others, it is best to limit one's consumption of meat.

3. MAKE TIME TO PRAY AND MEDITATE EACH DAY.

Healing comes through your relationship with God and through your ability to let go of ego blocks. A regular meditation and prayer practice is a powerful tool for personal healing. If you do not have time for a separate or special period of regular meditation, here is a simple meditation practice you can do several times throughout the day.

Take deep breaths to relax and center yourself. With each inhalation, allow yourself to open, to expand. With each exhalation, allow yourself to let go, to empty. After several minutes of deep breathing, sit quietly, and listen to the chatter in the mind. Let the thoughts pass through the mind, and with each breath, turn your focus inward. Pausing in the space between the breaths, listen to the silence in the quiet spaces within your own being. Alternate between talking to God in your own words and listening to the responses, the subtle shifts in consciousness that occur within you in the silent spaces.

4. TAKE ON A NEW *MITZVAH,* A GOOD DEED PRESCRIBED BY JEWISH LAW.

The Hebrew word *mitzvah* means "to connect." When we do a *mitzvah,* we are connecting to God, the source of all healing. *Mitzvot* strengthen our relationship and communication with God. Those who are new to Jewish spiritual practice may want to consider taking on a *mitzvah* like saying blessings before and after eating, lighting Shabbos candles, or engaging in daily prayer or meditation. Additional basic *mitzvot* between people include giving charity, visiting the sick, refraining from malicious gossip (called *loshon hara* in Hebrew), and providing hospitality. If you do not know what to do, consult with a rabbi, mentor, or spiritual buddy. Start slowly and take on *mitzvot* at a pace that you can integrate into your life easily.

5. FIND SOMEONE YOU CAN RESPECT AND LOVE FOR A TEACHER OR SPIRITUAL GUIDE.

Becoming attached to a teacher or guide who can provide direction as well as objectivity for you is helpful on the spiritual journey. The ego mind is very clever and can easily deceive you. An objective person, someone who cares about your well-being, and someone who has traveled on the Jewish spiritual path farther and longer than you have, has invaluable experience and guidance to offer you. If you cannot find such a person, find a friend with whom you can be spiritual buddies. Check in with each other periodically for support and mirroring.

6. IF YOU ARE ILL, IT IS RECOMMENDED THAT YOU GIVE CHARITY.

According to kabbalah, charity opens gates of healing for people in the most powerful way. Reb Nachman recommended that a person in need of healing or experiencing difficult times give charity. You should not think you are "bribing" God in any way by giving charity. Rather, you should consider how you expand and purify yourself by giving charity and how this enables you to receive a greater flow of divine healing energy.

A Tale to Live By

Here is one of my favorite stories about Rabbi Shimon Bar Yochai in honor of his *yahrzeit,* which occurs during Iyar. We are frequently confronted with life situations that we do not appear to be able to change or resolve, but this story conveys a most important lesson about the power of love to heal and open gates that seem to be closed to us.

A couple came to Rabbi Shimon Bar Yochai for a blessing. They had been married for over twelve years and were heartbroken that they could not have a child.

"The house is too quiet," they both cried. "We do not want to stay married without children. Perhaps we will be able to have children if we are married to other people."

Rabbi Shimon agreed, "The gates of heaven are now closed to you." He told them to divorce, but to do so with great joy. He advised them to have a party, invite all their friends, and have everyone rejoice. Following the rebbe's instructions, the couple had a party with an abundance of food and drink, and everyone did rejoice.

During the party, the husband lovingly told his wife who was to return to her parents' house as soon as the festivities were over, "Before you leave our house for the last time, I want you to take the biggest treasure. Whatever you want, it is yours."

Later that evening, when the party had ended and everyone had left, she came into the bedroom that they had shared for twelve years and saw her husband sleeping. After watching him silently for several minutes, she decided, "He is my greatest treasure." So she called her friends and family to help her, and they took him and the bed together to her parents' house.

The next morning, the husband woke and was surprised to find that he was still with his wife at her parents' home. So they went again to Rabbi Shimon Bar Yochai for guidance about what they should do now. They realized that they loved each other so much, they really did not want to get divorced.

"Because you showed so much love and joy and closeness in beginning the process of divorce," Rabbi Shimon told them, "You now have achieved the necessary merit for having a child." And indeed they were blessed with a child later in that very year.

So we see from this story that love and joy can open the gates of heaven and bring the greatest healing and blessing. Reb Shlomo Carlebach of Blessed Memory would speak often about the power of love and joy to heal people, but it is particularly true during this month of healing. After the month of Nissan, it is our joy and love that will heal us the most powerfully and give us the strength to go forward in our lives.

Sivan

MONTH: *May-June*

ENERGY: *The Art of Receiving*

AREA OF HEALING: *The Subconscious Mind*

ASTROLOGICAL SIGN: *Gemini*

HEBREW LETTER: *Zayin*

HEBREW TRIBE: *Zevulun*

DIVINE NAME PERMUTATION: *YVHH*

HOLIDAY: *Shavuous*

illian, a therapist herself, had worked hard to overcome the panic attacks she suffered for many years. A rationalist and a pragmatist, she liked to be in control and confessed that she believed in what she could see, sense, or touch and questioned what was invisible. As she became more involved in Judaism, Jewish meditation, and spiritual counseling, she opened to a new way of being with herself. She intuited quite correctly that if she were to go deeper in Judaism and be open to the joys possible in a relationship with God, she would have to let go of her need to be in control and she was fearful that the panic attacks would resume. She realized, however, that her mind could not take her where her soul yearned to go.

Lillian described her dilemma in the following metaphor: She is at the entrance to a room of great spiritual riches, the door is not locked, but slightly ajar, light is shining through its crevices, yet she is afraid to enter. The door in Lillian's metaphor is the door of spiritual opportunity that we may all enter during this month of Sivan. Lillian recognized that this door represented freedom to her. Because of her fear of losing control, she held herself back from opening it. In this year, as she worked consciously with the energy of the months, she was ready to go forward in her life in a way that she could not do before.

As Lillian celebrated Passover during Nissan, she had begun to realize the deep desire to be in true relationship with God, who takes people out of bondage. She realized that she had placed herself in bondage by her excessive need to be in control. She did not want to remain in her circumscribed, limited box. She was ready to live more fully and authentically.

During Iyar, she had done considerable healing. She learned how to be with the feelings that were underneath her need to be in control. She expanded her repertoire of emotional expression in her relationships with others. Her heart opened with greater compassion for herself and others.

For many years, she had carried a grudge against her husband's family for their lack of support for her husband during his illness. Now, as she opened her heart during Sivan, she was becoming less judgmental and more giving. As a result, she was less emotionally reactive and genuinely more loving. Her relationships with family members improved. She was even willing to extend herself to help her husband's family.

During Sivan, Lillian's meditation and prayer life deepened in the way she had always wanted. Though she recognized that she could not control this God with whom she wanted to be in relationship, she was stronger in herself. She was now ready to let go of her need to be in control and not be afraid to lose herself. Like a newborn, she was beginning to trust God. During Sivan, she was able to receive not what she wanted, but what God wanted to give her, and this was more wonderful than she had imagined. The treasures she received were not quantifiable—they were priceless.

Energy: The Art of Receiving

Just as the trees and flowers begin to blossom during the spring month of Sivan, we blossom at this time as well. Sivan is a time of gaining clarity of vision, discovering one's life purpose, and receiving guidance and direction on actualizing our personal goals.

Sivan is a time of expressed creativity, of bringing forth and communicating what is deep inside of us. As we open to the greater expansiveness possible in this month, we

In Sivan, it becomes clearer to us where we are going, and we can radiate and share ourselves with others in a more direct and beautiful way.

become aware of depths within us that we were not conscious of before. This brings greater freedom, love, and joy.

This year, we began a new cycle of growth and transformation in Nissan. We worked on ourselves, healed, and purified ourselves in Iyar. Now in this month of Sivan we receive the fruits of our efforts, and more.

Sivan arrives in the late spring. Having done the planting work in Iyar, in Sivan we harvest our crop and enjoy the vibrancy of nature. Sivan is our time of fulfillment. We are now free to explore and to travel internally and externally. It is actually an auspicious time to travel. In Sivan, it becomes clearer to us where we are going, and we can radiate and share ourselves with others in a more direct and beautiful way.

The whole month of Sivan is about receiving. We celebrate the holiday of Shavuous, which is the Giving of the Torah (Matan Torah in Hebrew). Many people know how to give, and many more know how to take, but fewer know how to truly receive. Sivan is a time of learning how to receive on all levels of being. To truly receive is to be open without an agenda, to be present and accept every moment gratefully as a gift. The extent to which we are open determines what and how much we will receive. Life is so abundant, and there is such a flow of Godly energy, particularly this month.

To walk through the door to greater openness and expansiveness and avail ourselves of the spiritual opportunity of this month, as in Lillian's imagery, it is necessary to let go and empty oneself of limiting concepts of self, life, and God. The Torah was given in the desert, because we each have to become like a desert. We have to let go of our ego preferences and ego attachments, get out of the way, nullify ourselves, and receive what God wants to give us, which is much greater than anything we could imagine. It is we who limit ourselves, not God. This month we learn how to become the proper vessel to receive God's revelation.

Sivan is also a month for increased love, intimacy, and unity. This is demonstrated by the giving and accepting of the Torah, which could only occur during this month. A covenant between the Jewish people and God, the Torah is an expression of love, commitment, dedication, and intimacy. It is an everlasting partnership likened to a marriage. It is interesting and no coincidence that May–June, the month of Sivan, has always been a popular time for weddings.

It is said that when the Jews received the Torah, they were of one heart, so unified they were likened to one being. In the Torah passage that describes Israel's encampment at the foot of Mount Sinai at the time of the new moon of Sivan, the word "encamped" is in the singular rather than the plural form. It is this unity that enabled the Israelites to receive the Torah. This kind of unity is possible in Sivan.

Sivan is a wonderful time to deepen existing relationships and open ourselves to meeting new people whom we will draw closely to our heart. There is an open-heartedness in Sivan that makes it easy to communicate and bond with many different kinds of people.

General Guidelines and Goals

These guidelines and goals enable us to direct our energies in the ways that are optimal for our growth and transformation in accordance with the energy of this month.

It is recommended that you read and meditate upon them often in the course of the month. Reflect on their applicability to you, and allow them to direct and inspire you this month.

1. BE CREATIVE.

Sivan is a time of expressed creativity. Give yourself time to bring forth the creativity that is within you. Writing, music, art, dance, and so forth may provide a medium for expression. Enjoy the creativity of others. Go to plays, concerts, and art shows this month. In this time of such creativity, bring a new and creative consciousness to even the routine things in life. Cooking, making beds, and washing dishes can also be creative moments.

2. REALIZE YOUR PERSONAL RELATIONSHIP WITH GOD; NURTURE IT AND STRENGTHEN IT.

The complexity of the design of this world causes many people to deduce that creation is not random and that the world has a Creator. Fewer people, however, experience this Creator as involved in and caring about His creation. In the Ten Commandments, which were historically given in this month, God revealed Himself as the God who took the people out of Egypt. Judaism emphasizes that the Creator of the world is involved in and cares for His creation and responds to its requests and needs.

Take time this month to talk to God in your words. Say these words out loud, as if you were having a conversation with someone, like your best friend. This is actually a powerful meditation practice. Even if you are not sure whether you believe in God or in having a personal relationship with God, you can still talk to God about your confusion. And, most important, take time to listen to any shifts and insights that occur from this experience. God speaks to you through your Higher Self in the moments of silence.

3. STUDY AND LEARN TORAH.

We received the Torah in this month. The study of the Torah provides a powerful key to the depths within you. Study by yourself and study with someone who can open the doors of Torah to you. Many question the relevance of Five Books of Moses, known as the Torah or Pentateuch, to modern times, but that is because they have only superficial knowledge and no access to the holiness of Torah. They think that the Torah is merely literature and that the stories of people long ago are not relevant. If the Torah were only stories, it would not have captivated the hearts and souls of so many people for so long. People do not kiss a book of literature, but they kiss the Torah. People have even risked their lives to save a scroll of Torah. Why?

As a general rule, if your study of Torah does not fill you with greater love and devotion, you are not studying the true Torah. You must pray, and if necessary cry and beg, for the privilege of tasting the sweetness of the Torah. I love the metaphor of the Torah as a woman. She will not reveal her secrets until she is sure that she is truly loved. Pray for a teacher you can love and respect and who makes the Torah sweet and meaningful for you.

The Torah is much more than it initially appears to be. More than stories, it is a mirror of your own soul. Though translators have made great efforts to be accurate, the awesomeness of Torah becomes evident through understanding the commentaries from Mishnah, Talmud, Aggadah, and the oral tradition. The knowledge of Hebrew is essential to penetrate the Torah's depths, for each Hebrew word, each letter, is a divine revelation and message, according to kabbalah.

4. DEEPEN YOUR RELATIONSHIP WITH LOVED ONES.

As we have learned, there is a great opportunity during Sivan for increased love, unity, and intimacy. Add romance to your life. Buy flowers and gifts for loved ones.

Extend yourself by doing favors and showing your appreciation to your loved ones. And open yourself to meeting new and different people. Fully receive and appreciate all that you are given from others.

Most likely, you will meet people this month with whom you will feel immediately quite close, as if you knew them for a long time. Soul connections are not bound by time and space.

5. EXPERIENCE THE WORLD OF NATURE.

Nature is so beautiful in this month. Everything is blossoming and testifying directly in its own way that there is a Creator. Take time to experience the natural world. We are told that all of nature sings God's praises. Listen to the prayers of the trees, the grasses, and the flowers. You may be very surprised by what you hear. Let nature inspire you.

6. MEDITATE.

Meditation is the most powerful medium for getting the ego out of the way and bringing forth what is within you. This is a powerful month for meditation. Don't deprive yourself; give yourself time to meditate. Quiet the mind and be open to receive what is present for you.

7. OPEN YOUR HEART TO GREATER LOVE AND SERVICE.

The Jewish people received the Torah because they were united. In this month of receiving the Torah, open your heart to the unity of God and be mindful of your unity with all of God's creation. Whenever you learn Torah, pray, meditate, or do a *mitzvah* this month, take a moment to center yourself and formulate the intention that you dedicate its reward not for your own benefit, but for the benefit of the world. Your sole intention is to send God's light to the people and places that so much need to be blessed with God's light and peace. The Jewish people, along with many other peoples, have been praying and working for the healing and perfection of the world since the beginning of time. Take your rightful place in this chain.

Astrological Sign: Gemini

The astrological sign for this month is Gemini. An air sign, Gemini represents the energy that does not want to be contained. Air is ineffable. Mercury, the ruling planet of Gemini, was the Roman messenger of the gods who flew from the heavens to the earth, constantly going back and forth between the worlds. Similarly, the Torah, which is given in this month, is the messenger between heaven and earth.

People born under the sign of Gemini are free-spirited and always want their consciousness to be lifted up. Geminis want to leave the earth and fly to the heavens. Interested in ideas or any form of mental activity, Geminis are creative and skillful communicators. The planet of Mercury is associated with communication and intelligence.

Geminis are thought to be mercurial, quick to move from place to place, physically or mentally. Interestingly, this month the Torah documents the travel of the Jewish people in the desert. This is a great month to travel internally within oneself as well as externally.

Gemini is the perfect month for the Giving of the Torah for many reasons. The freedom-seeking energy of Gemini is best expressed in the Torah, which brings freedom and enables us to fly upward. Also appropriate to the theme of Torah is Gemini's symbol, the twins. Unlike most of the other months, which are represented by animals, Gemini has human twins as a symbol.

The significance of the twins has been explained by the great kabbalist Rabbi Tzaddik Ha Cohen, who said that the first three months of the year are associated with the three patriarchs. Nissan is the patriarch Abraham, who is associated with the energy of *hesed,* loving-kindness. It was an expression of divine *hesed* that took the Jews out of Egypt. Iyar is associated with the patriarch Isaac, who represents the energy of *gevurah,* judgment or strength. *Gevurah* is needed to do the healing work of Iyar. And Sivan is Jacob. Jacob and Esau were twins. The energy of Jacob is *tiferet,* beauty and balance. *Tiferet* is the perfect synthesis of *hesed* and *gevurah.*

Sivan is the most beautiful month. It is a time of fulfillment. Spring is in full bloom, and the Torah represents the flowering of God's wisdom. This month is the month of creativity. God is the Creator and source of all creative expression, the Torah is the manual, the blueprint for creation, and when we study it, our own powers of creativity are expanded.

Hebrew Letter: Zayin

The Hebrew letter associated with Sivan is the zayin. The zayin looks like the vav, the letter for the previous month, and builds upon what went before. As the vav represents the straight Godly light that descends from the spiritual world to the physical world, the zayin represents the light that returns or ascends to a higher state of consciousness and revelation.

The zayin resembles a crown. In this month, we receive the Torah, called the crown of creation. According to Rabbi Ginzberg in his book *Aleph Beit,* the zayin resembles the scepter of a king and conveys the royalty of this month. The king has the power to choose, and in this month God, the King, chooses to give the Torah to the Jewish people. This adds tremendous blessing to this month. The word *zayin* means "weapon." The Torah, given in this month, is considered a weapon that protects us from the trials of life within and without.

The zayin is the seventh letter of the Hebrew alphabet and also has the numerical value of seven. Seven is a beloved number in kabbalah. Seven refers to Shabbat, the Sabbath, also called the crown of creation. We work for six days in order to receive the Shabbat, the seventh day, which is God's gift to creation. Like the Torah, received in this month, Shabbat is the container of the mysteries and secrets of creation. The Shabbat is a revelation of God in the dimension of time.

Hebrew Tribe: Zevulun

According to the Arizel, Sivan is represented by the tribe of Zevulun. Zevulun was the sixth son of Leah. The Hebrew word *zevul,* "habitation," is the root of the name Zevulun. When Zevulun was born, Leah said, "Now my husband will dwell with me" (Gen. 30:20). Leah was hoping that Jacob would live in her tent and love her the way she so much wanted.

Kabbalistically, Leah's statement is a metaphor for the indwelling of the Divine Presence. In Judaism, the husband is always a metaphor for God, and the wife is either the Jewish people or the human soul. The passionate and animated energy of Zevulun reflects the abundance, the fulfillment of this month, epitomized by the Giving of the Torah, which is God's revelation in the world.

Zevulun was the tribe that engaged in commerce. Its members, blessed with great wealth, provided for the material needs of those of the tribe of Issachar, who studied Torah and did not work. Being connected to the expansiveness and openness of the seas inspired a passion and joy of life in the tribe of Zevulun. They experienced God in their involvement in the world.

We need to tap into the energy of Zevulun in this month. It is easy in this month to feel the passion, the vitality of life, and be empowered to enjoy the abundance of this world, the fruit of our efforts, and to share them with others and find Godliness in the world.

Divine Name Permutation: YVHH

In this month's permutation, YVHH, the hay (H) is in the third and fourth positions, the worlds of Yetzerah and Assiyah. The hay in the world of Yetzerah indicates expansiveness of Divine Light in the dimension of the heart and the world of angels; its position in the world of Assiyah indicates expansiveness in our physical world. This informs us that there is a greater flow of energy to the heart, more love energy this month, and also a greater possibility of manifesting Divine Light in the physical world.

This particular permutation of the Divine Name indicates abundance on the physical and emotional planes. This is what makes Sivan a month of love and intimacy and blossoming.

Torah Portions

Sivan introduces a new book of Torah, the book of Numbers. This book is known in Hebrew as B'Midbar, which is a word appearing in the first verse of the book that means "in the desert." The Torah was given in the desert, a place that cannot be claimed by anyone or anything, a no-man's-land. According to Jewish mysticism, the desert represents the nullification of the ego necessary to receive divine revelation.

This book of the Torah provides an account of the wanderings of the Jewish people in the desert, all the challenges, rebellions, and mistakes the people made on the spiritual journey during this time period. If we study these portions and allow them to enter us, we will see our own challenges reflected in their challenges.

The first chapter of the book is itself called B'Midbar, and this portion is devoted to a detailed explanation of the counting of the Jewish people, the flags and banners of each tribe, and the place each tribe occupied. The midrash, the oral tradition, tells us that it was an honor and a joy to be counted. Each person appeared in front of Moses and Aaron and gave his name. This chapter is always read right before Shavuous. Though the chapter may appear irrelevant today, it conveys an important and timeless message—people count. Knowing that you and others count brings self-esteem, which is a preparation for a relationship with God and receiving the Torah.

In the next portion, Nasso (Num. 4:21–7:89), is revealed the important formula for blessing people. "May Hashem bless and safeguard you. May Hashem illuminate His countenance for you and be gracious to you. May Hashem lift His countenance to you and establish peace for you" (Num. 6:24–26). This is an alignment of the energy of blessing of this month.

Toward the end of the month, however, the tone of the Torah portions begins to change in preparation for the next month. In Beha'aloscha Numbers 11:10 it says "The people took to complaining," reflecting the dynamic tension between the physical and the spiritual within the human being and spiritual challenges attendant upon our receiving of Torah and entering the land of Israel, the fulfillment or realization of our spirituality.

These Torah portions recount the complaining of the Jewish people. Many Jews complained about the manna, the heavenly food they were given to sustain them in the desert. Though the oral tradition tells us the manna could taste like anything people wanted it to taste like, yet, even so, many of the people cried for meat. The manna did not provide the physical satisfaction of regular food. The cry for meat represented the cry for physicality, for physical desires. In the desert, all their needs were taken care of and there was nothing to do but be close to God. As wonderful as that is, it is also not easy to maintain the sense of surrendered self necessary for such a state.

Many of the Jews in the desert did not want to live in such a supernatural realm, on the level of miracles; they wanted to return to a more ordinary reality where God is concealed and they experienced themselves as independent physical beings who do not receive what they need but participate in producing it.

"A wind went forth and blew quail from the sea and spread them over the camp" (Num. 11:31). The people were given meat, and when the meat was in their mouths, many were stricken with death. Though the Torah says that God slew them, I think that, because the people had been eating nothing but the pure food manna, when they ate the meat, their bodies could not handle it. It was not that God punished them; they died as a consequence of their act.

Also Miriam, the sister of Moses, was punished for complaining that Moses did not have sexual relations with his wife (Num. 12). She and her brother, Aaron, were also prophets, and they had sexual relations with their spouses. She was advocating for the marital right of Zipporah, the wife of Moses. She learned that Moses was on a much higher level of prophecy and it was not appropriate for him to have sexual relations. Moses pleaded for her healing.

Complaining is the preparation for the energy of the next month, Tammuz, a month of tests and judgment. As much as people want to receive, it is hard for people to stay with simply receiving, particularly true for this month. The ego asserts its own desires and its preferences, which is the root of all complaints.

Holiday

Shavuous

HISTORY   The holiday of Shavuous has four names that give us more information about it and Sivan. First, the Torah calls Shavuous the "Festival of Reaping." "And the festival of reaping, the firstlings of your works . . ." (Exod. 23:16). This refers to the reaping of wheat. Shavuous is an agricultural holiday, marking the end of the spring harvest. Second, the Torah calls Shavuous the "Day of First Fruits (Bikurim)." On this day the first fruits were offered in the Holy Temple.

Third, Shavuous is called "Festival of Weeks." The word *shavuous* means "weeks." The Torah instructs us to count seven weeks beginning on Passover and on the fiftieth day (seven weeks plus one day) offer a new grain offering to God (Lev. 23). The seven weeks refers to the Counting of the Omer; the fiftieth day after the Counting of the Omer is called Shavuous. The *Zohar* compares the seven weeks in which the omer is counted to the seven days a woman counts after her monthly menses. Just as the woman would immerse herself in the *mikvah,* a ritual purification bath, and be reunited with her beloved after the seventh day, so too is the community of Israel reunited with its beloved, God, on the fiftieth day, on Shavuous.

Finally, and Shavuous is mostly called Z'man Matan Toraetinu, the Giving of Our Torah. Interestingly, we are not told in the written Torah to commemorate the Giving of the Torah on a specific day, like the instructions for Passover or Succot. It says the Torah, specifically the Ten Commandments, was given in the third month, but it does not give the exact day.

The Torah says, "In the third month from the exodus of the Children of Israel from Egypt, on this day . . ." (Exod. 19:1). The rabbis concluded that it was the fiftieth day of the Counting of the Omer, the very same day as Shavuous, and therefore designated this holiday as the Giving of the Torah. The Torah reading selected for the day of Shavuous is from the Torah portion of Yitro in Exodus, recounting the giving of the Ten Commandments.

To better understand this holiday, take this little guided journey in your imagination (feel free to use the sets of Hollywood's *The Ten Commandments,* if you like). You are in the midst of the Jewish people, who have left Egypt in the most miraculous way on the fifteenth of Nissan, as recounted in the story of the Exodus. After a battle with the Amalekites, an ancient tribe who went out of their way to attack Israel, you arrive at the foot of the mountain on the first day of Sivan, the time of the new moon. On the first day, you rest. On the second day, Moses at God's instruction, begins to prepare everyone for the upcoming big event. Moses tells you and all those around you that you would be given the privilege of becoming a holy nation, a kingdom of priests, by following *mitzvot,* commandments, that you would be given connecting you directly to God, the Being who brought Israel out of Egypt.

You express your willingness to enter into this relationship and be a part of this nation. On the third day, Moses tells you not to ascend or touch the mountain, lest you come too close and die. On the fourth day, Moses instructs you to abstain from marital relations and cleanse your clothing and says, "On the third day the Lord will descend before the eyes of all the people upon Mount Sinai."

In any case, Moses is summoned to the top of Mount Sinai, and you are with the people who are at the bottom of the mountain. You, along with everyone else, are once again told that you should not ascend the mountain. It sounds from the Torah description that there was volcanic activity on Mount Sinai. The mountain was smoking and shuddering, and there was lightning and thunder. Yet Moses ascends to receive the Ten Commandments.

There is an ongoing debate about exactly what the people heard, what they experienced, on that day. Some say they fainted upon hearing God's voice and had to be revived ten times, once after the recitation of each commandment. The fainting represents the realization that God is the true power, the true existence of the world, and that people do not have any real existence on their own. People cannot stand and do not in truth ever stand on their own.

The *Gemara,* the commentary on the Torah, says that God actually placed the mountain upon the Jewish people, forcing them to accept the Torah. Though many take this quite literally as an actual concrete occurrence, I think it is best understood as a metaphor. This image conveyed a most important message. Reb Shlomo would ask, "Do I have a choice whether I keep Shabbos? Do I have a choice whether I love my child?" On one level, we always have choice, but on another level, the deeper things are beyond choice. They are an expression of who we are, and we would not be ourselves without them. The image of a mountain hanging above us was to impress upon us that life is possible with Torah and without Torah we might as well be dead. Because it is so integral to who we are, it is beyond choice.

Other commentaries, like those of the Ramban and Rashi, say that the Ten Commandments were given instantaneously, but the people could not comprehend them. After the first two commandments were repeated to them, they asked Moses to be intermediary because they were not able to bear the intense holiness and power of the transmission. The people, upon seeing the flame and the smoke and hearing the thunder around the mountain, said, "We will do, and we will hear. Let God not speak to us and we will die." This became the trademark for the Jewish path. The people had faith in Moses to instruct them in what God wanted from them.

The Rambam concurs that the people heard the first two commandments, but they only heard the sound of the voice; they could not comprehend it. Moses had to teach them. I remember Reb Shlomo saying in the name of some Chassidic rebbe that the Jews actually did not hear anything. It was pure silence, the silence of the aleph, the first letter in the Ten Commandments, and even this was too much for most people.

The *Gemara* says that the Torah was given to the Jewish people, but the whole world was invited; the souls of many belonging to other nations were also present and also received the Torah at Sinai. Many of these people feel a strong attachment to the Jewish people and the principles of Judaism, and some of them choose to convert and become Jews.

It is important to know that much of Judaism, much of what we call Torah, is not simply the Ten Commandments or what is written in the Five Books of Moses. Much comes from the oral Torah, a body of knowledge that was also received by Moses but was not written down and was orally transmitted through the generations until the time of the Temple. But then it was said that it never was written down in its entirety. Torah is still very much an oral transmission that a student receives from a teacher. For thousands of years, Torah has been developed, intuited, and interpreted by the rabbis to respond to the needs of the time.

OBSERVANCE   The holiday of Shavuous is awarded the honor and holiness of the other major holidays with certain restrictions for its celebration to preserve and heighten its sanctity. Candles are lit, a festive meal is given in which Kiddush is recited, and Hallel, the special psalms of praise, are recited, as in the holidays of Passover and Succot. I find that the first few moments when the holiday is ushered in to be the most powerful. There is quite a heavenly and powerful transmission of grace to be experienced if one is open to receive it.

Beautiful, unique customs accompany Shavuous. Many synagogues decorate their prayer space with greens and flowers. At least on the first night and day of Shavuous, people traditionally eat dairy products with honey because the Torah is nourishing like milk and sweet like honey. Blintzes, cheesecake, and lasagna are popular foods during Shavuous.

The book of Ruth is read during Shavuous. This book recounts the journey of childless Ruth as she accompanies her mother-in-law, Naomi, back to Israel after the death of her husband. By declaring her devotion and commitment to her mother-in-law, Ruth converts to Judaism. In a fantastic story, Ruth becomes not only a Jew, but a foremother of the House of David. Upon her arrival into Israel, Ruth is introduced to the king, Boaz, who is related to her mother-in-law, Naomi. In a short time Ruth conceives a son with Boaz, who is an old man and who dies the next day. From this humble non-Jew comes the Messiah. Ruth, the perfect convert, demonstrates the same qualities of faith and selflessness that the Jewish people displayed when they received the Ten Commandments. The recitation of the book of Ruth inspires each Jew to be like Ruth, to demonstrate selflessness and make a choice to be Jewish.

The custom of staying up all night studying on the first night of Shavuous is called Tikkun Leil Shavuot, which means "the fixing of the night of Shavuous." It is said that the Jews slept late the morning that the Torah was given because they did not feel worthy of being present. Self-esteem seemed to be a problem even in those days. By staying up on the first night, we hope to correct this error and demonstrate our eagerness to learn and be connected to Torah. Though this custom is only four hundred years old, it is so popular and well observed, at least in the New York City area and in Israel, that it seems to be thousands of years old.

Kabbalists prescribed that study for the night include the written Torah, the oral Torah, the *Zohar,* and halacha, Jewish law. This was based on a passage from the *Zohar* written thousands of years ago commending those who stayed up all night learning.

Many people think that Torah is only the study of the past, the Five Books of Moses, or the commentaries. Torah also includes our personal commentary on what we study. Torah is a living, evolving, and dynamic transmission. Through the study of Torah, we hear God's voice.

Meditation

This month is all about receiving. Meditation is the ultimate act of receiving, and through meditation we learn how to better receive our lives. Meditation is not just an act that we do when we sit for meditation. We can also meditate when we walk down the street, do our errands, pray in synagogue, eat, and interact with people. It is consciousness, it is presence, and it is awareness. Through meditation, one gets out of the way so to speak and becomes an empty vessel in order to truly receive the essence of what one is meditating upon.

Prepare for meditation by bringing your attention to the breath. As you inhale, the abdomen expands, and as you exhale, the abdomen contracts. Do this for several minutes until this form of breathing becomes natural for you. Now take deep breaths from deep in the belly, below the abdomen and through the rib cage and to the top of the chest, and then exhale through the mouth, making any sound that enables you to let go even more deeply. Let go of stress, let go of negativity, let go. Pause between the breaths. From the place of deep letting go, begin the inhalation. Feel that you are opening up at the place you have let go. With each exhalation, there is the letting go and with each inhalation, there is the opening. Feel that you breathe with your whole body. The whole body opens with the inhalation and relaxes with the exhalation. With each breath, you allow yourself to open and relax a little more deeply. The chatter of the ego mind quiets. As you breathe, be aware that you do not breathe by your own will, but by Divine Will. Receive the breath. Open to the experience of being breathed.

As you inhale, imagine that you can breathe or are being breathed from the soles of the feet all the way to the top of the head. Imagine that the top of the head opens, and you exhale through the whole body. Do this for several breaths. Then imagine that you are a vessel. With each inhalation, you open, and with each exhalation, you let go and empty. What do you want to fill your vessel with? You can breathe in what you want. If you want peace, breathe it in. If you want love, breathe it in. Or simply remain open and empty. Receive this moment, or God, not as an object of your own ego projection, but as this moment truly is, or as God is being God. You can extend this to meditating on others. Open to the experience of seeing them as they are, and not as you want them to be or not be.

Practical Recommendations

1. SET A SCHEDULE FOR THE STUDY OF TORAH.

Because the Torah was received in this month, it is a wonderful time to increase your Torah study. People are very busy, and it is easy to postpone spiritual study. If you are busy, it is fine to spend even a few minutes each day reading and studying spiritual books. All this is a part of Torah. It is wonderful to learn a little bit before you go to work, during a break in the course of the day, or before bed.

You will also receive the love and beauty of Torah even more if you learn with someone else as well. Learn with people who know more than you and people who know less. Learning Torah with others increases love in the world.

2. ASK YOUR SPOUSE AND FRIENDS TO LET YOU KNOW WHAT THEY WOULD LIKE TO RECEIVE FROM YOU.

Tell them that you want to demonstrate your love for them by giving them something that they would like to receive. This makes them feel that they are important to you.

3. GIVE BLESSINGS TO PEOPLE YOU KNOW.

In one of the Torah portions for this month, we receive the formula for blessing other people. Blessing is a powerful spiritual practice. A little-known secret is that the best way to receive blessing is to bless others. In the course of the month, make a point to bless five different people. You can throw a blessing in casual conversation, such as "God bless you," or you can give a full blessing. Take time to center yourself, quiet your own mind as much as possible as you breathe, and allow yourself to open to divine blessing and light. Feel your deep yearning to be a channel for blessing with each breath. Reflect on the needs of the person in front of you and allow the words of blessing to flow through you. If you like, you may raise your hands above the top of the person's head.

You may begin the blessing with the following words, "May God bless you" or "May you be blessed." Or if you like, you can say the traditional priestly blessing: "May Hashem (God) bless you and safeguard you. May Hashem illuminate His countenance for you and be gracious to you. May Hashem turn His countenance to you and establish peace for you."

4. BE HOSPITABLE.

Invite someone to your house for a Sabbath or other meal. If you do not keep the Sabbath, this will be a good way to start. If you do, you already know about this *mitzvah*. Sharing bread together is an important way to unite with Jews and with other peoples of the world. There is such divisiveness within the Jewish people. We do not have to agree with each other to love each other, but we do need to love each other. Some of this disunity could be alleviated by simply sharing a Shabbat meal together.

5. ENGAGE IN A PROJECT THAT BRINGS UNITY INTO THE WORLD.

It could be something as simple as arranging a date between people (a *shidduch*) or engaging in dialogue and really listening to people who are different from you.

A Tale to Live By

The following story, a favorite of mine, occurred to me at the end of a private meditation session with one of my clients. Though I guided him in an initial meditation that is usually a springboard for deep feeling-release work, he asked to remain silent for most of the session. As we meditated silently together, there was a powerful presence of love and grace in the room. I commented afterwards that what we can open to and receive in silence is sometimes greater than what can be accomplished in words. I then told this story to my client.

The following story reveals an important teaching about receiving, which is the energy of this month. The greatest things that we give to and receive from others are spiritual. The true beauty and power of the spiritual cannot be expressed in words; nor is it limited to space or time. Only one who is able to be an empty vessel can receive such treasures.

There were two great and holy rebbes who had been the best of friends since childhood. Though they lived a few hours journey from each other, they would write each other every week. One would send a letter with a messenger on Friday morning. The messenger would travel, rain or shine, through the forest and along all the back roads for several hours and then wait for a reply from the other rebbe. Often he would see the rebbe's face light up with great delight as he opened the envelope and looked at the letter he had carried. Sometimes the reply would be a short time in coming. Other times, the rebbe would excuse himself for several hours before he would return to him with a reply.

"How awesome must be the Torah exchanged between them," he reflected to himself. "What a privilege to be a messenger of such holiness."

Upon receiving the reply, he would immediately return with it to his rebbe before the Sabbath. This practice went on every Friday for years.

After years of transporting these letters, the messenger could not contain his curiosity. He yearned to read of the holy thoughts contained in the letters he was transporting.

"How do such great rebbes talk to each other?" he wondered. "I have such a deep desire to know," he confessed to himself and God. "I'm sure it will help me with my own service to God," he rationalized to himself.

He struggled with this desire and it became stronger and stronger. He knew that this correspondence was private, too holy for the eyes of a commoner like himself, yet he was so tempted to just take a peek. His evil inclination got the better of him one day and he opened the envelope.

He could not believe what he saw. He was fully expecting to find written the deepest words of Torah, words expounding the secrets of the universe on the page. Instead, he was surprised to find only a blank piece of paper. He felt like a fool, transporting a blank piece of paper back and forth all these years.

He soon became angry. He had made considerable effort to transport these letters, traveling hours through rain or shine, through cold winters and hot summers, and now to find out that he was carrying only blank pieces of paper infuriated him.

"I should have looked earlier," he admonished himself.

He schemed and said to himself, "Maybe in the future, I'll save myself some time. I'll just take the day off, and at the end of the day I'll return with the empty piece of paper, like before. My rebbe will not know the difference."

When he returned with the blank piece of paper to his rebbe, the rebbe did note a difference in him and confronted him. He could not lie to his rebbe and confessed that his evil inclination had gotten the better of him. He had opened the letter and was amazed, confused, and angry to discover that he had been transporting blank pieces of paper all these years.

The rebbe explained, "Because of the closeness of our souls, there are no words that can express our love for each other. The Torahs we have to exchange with each other are also beyond words. Only a blank piece of paper can hold such love and such knowing."

Tammuz

MONTH: *June-July*

ENERGY: *Seeing Life as It Is*

AREA OF HEALING: *Seeing*

ASTROLOGICAL SIGN: *Cancer*

HEBREW LETTER: *Chet*

HEBREW TRIBE: *Reuven*

DIVINE NAME PERMUTATION: *HVHY*

HOLIDAY: *The Seventeenth of Tammuz*

In February, Mark had made plans with his friend Stuart to travel for a month in Europe during the summer. But now, in the beginning of Tammuz, Stuart informed Mark that he could not take the trip with him. Mark was shocked and angry, because he had assumed that they were both committed to this summer trip.

As a reason for bailing out of the trip, Stuart explained that he was buying a house, and he did not want to be away for so long. Nevertheless, Mark was surprised and dismayed, because, even though Stuart had not responded to his calls to discuss the trip several times earlier that spring, Mark assumed that the trip was still going to happen. He did not see the signs of reluctance in Stuart's failure to respond, because he trusted him and considered him a good friend. Stuart apologized and, as penance, offered Mark a free plane ticket anywhere in the United States. Stuart told him that he had new plans to travel for a week with another friend in the United States and invited Mark to come along. It seemed to Mark, however, that this last-minute invitation was pouring salt in his wounds.

Mark was getting angrier and angrier about the whole thing when he heard about the energy of the month of Tammuz at a New Moon gathering. Tammuz, he learned, was a time that called for clear seeing, for extra sensitivity to the reality of our self-deception and the truth of our existence. Mark immediately made the connection of his anger at what he perceived to be Stuart's betrayal and the need for the clear-seeing energy of Tammuz. He began to put aside his anger, accept his own responsibility for what had happened, and attempt to grow through this reversal.

The story of Mark exhibits many components typical of the energy of Tammuz. According to kabbalah, for the month of Tammuz the area of healing is seeing. In accordance with this practice, Mark began to see through his anger and understand his role in this incident. He had failed to see the signs of reluctance shown by Stuart in not responding to his calls. He had misunderstood the way Stuart had felt about their relationship.

This is also the month of tests and judgment. Mark had assumed that Stuart was a good friend, but in fact the friendship was casual and had never been tested. After Mark's anger subsided, he began to reevaluate his friendship with Stuart and reflect upon what it means to be a good friend. Tammuz is also a time of reversals and this was also demonstrated in this example.

The story of Mark and Stuart's broken plans is a typical Tammuz occurrence. You plan to do one thing, and something else happens. Then the opportunity for new understanding, growth, and change occurs.

Energy: Seeing Life as It Is

Summer is fully upon us in Tammuz. The sun is shining brightly, the days are their longest, and the heat of the summer is at its strongest. Without the benefit of air-conditioning, the heat of Tammuz can be intense and even brutal, especially in Israel.

From a secular perspective, many think of the summer as a carefree time, a time to relax, travel, and have fun, but according to kabbalah, Tammuz is a heavy and challenging month. The heat one experiences this month is not just physical; it is also emotional and spiritual. That's why we need to be mindful of the emotional intensity, and why we must be particularly sensitive to ourselves and others this month.

Tammuz is still ultimately a good and wonderful month, but only if we know how to use its particular intense energy constructively. When we do this, we are able to grow through challenges in ways that may not be possible at any other period of the year. Through self-examination, we can come to see that even the negative experiences we have had in life have deepened us and have been a positive part of our growth.

During the three months prior to Tammuz much blessing flowed from the Divine. Historically, the Jews were taken out of Egypt during Nissan, so we too opened to divine compassion to take us out of places of constraint during that month. During Iyar, the Jewish people received the manna in the wilderness and prepared to receive the Torah in Sivan. So too did we heal in Iyar and open to receive in Sivan. But for the next three months, beginning with Tammuz, the blessing of the Divine Presence is more hidden. The heavenly flow is not the same as before.

Kabbalah says that the months of the year are divided between Esau and Jacob. The first three months, Nissan, Iyar, and Sivan, are given to Jacob. There we find so many joyous Jewish holidays. The next three months, Tammuz, Av, and Elul, are given to Esau. After many battles, Jacob reclaimed part of Av and all of Elul, but Tammuz is still totally in the domain of Esau, so the energy of this month is characteristic of the qualities attributed to Esau. Esau was said to be in the physical world, engaging in physical pleasures and warlike behavior. Like the nature of Esau, Tammuz is a time when people engage in worldly and physical pleasures. Tammuz is also traditionally a time of challenge to the Jewish people, and is generally not an auspicious time to begin new business ventures or projects.

Tammuz is a month of being tested. We receive the Torah in Sivan, a time of receiving on all levels, but the blessing is not really ours unless we have earned it. So in Tammuz we must earn our blessings so they become our own. Now is the time to reach deep inside ourselves, to muster our own resources and see if we have the inner strength and discernment to stay focused and connected on the spiritual path. Because God's presence is not as obvious in this month as in other months, it is easier for us to see our negative traits. This is not easy, but necessary. The blessing of this month is that when we become aware of our negative traits, we begin to heal and transform them. Awareness is the first step.

Tammuz is a time of judgment. During this month, we may be confronted with things from the past and find that we now have the opportunity to choose differently than we did before, to heal and clear negative behavior patterns in our relationships with others, with ourselves, and God. Though challenges and tests take many forms and occur on many different fronts of our life, if we grow through them, we merit the divine blessing inherent in them and are able to see and appreciate what is really essential and true.

Now is the time to reach deep inside ourselves, to muster our own resources and see if we have the inner strength and discernment to stay focused and connected on the spiritual path.

This may be hard, for what we held dear and true may be now seen as false and unnecessary. During this month, we will be tested to see through appearances, and if it is necessary, internal and external structures will begin to break down to allow the true seeing to occur. This breakdown may not always occur by our conscious choice.

This is also the month of reversals, as the Divine Name permutation is reversed this month. What we held as true may now be seen as false, and what is false may masquerade as the truth. We may think that one thing is happening, but in actuality it is the opposite. It is confusing, but all will become clear to us if we are open to see things as they are and not as we want them to be.

Kabbalah teaches us that this month the area of healing is seeing. The difficulty we have in seeing life clearly causes many problems and unnecessary pain for us at all times, but particularly this month. The healing of seeing of this month will enable us to see through appearance and deception. We may feel hurt or betrayed, but if we recognize that we have been given the gift of seeing things more clearly, we will be happy and uplifted.

General Guidelines and Goals

These guidelines and goals enable us to direct our energies in the ways that are optimal for our growth and transformation in accordance with the energy of this month. It is recommended that you read and meditate upon them often in the course of the month. Reflect on their applicability to you, and allow them to direct and inspire you often this month.

I. OPEN TO SEE THINGS AS THEY ARE AND NOT AS YOU WANT THEM TO BE.

This is the month of the healing of seeing, for improving the clarity of our vision. What we see reflects our thinking. We see our own projections and often do not see things as they really are. We may be comfortable or uncomfortable with what we see. Ask yourself often this month, "Am I seeing things as they are, or am I simply projecting my own needs and desires onto this person or situation?"

This month, open up to seeing things more clearly, as they are and not as you want them to be. Don't be afraid to question your assumptions. Trust that what is, as painful as it may seem to you and as deceptive as it once was, will lead you to greater freedom. God is truth, and what is true brings freedom.

Everything is inverted during this period. What we held to be true, we find out is not true. Steve is only one of so many real-life examples from friends and clients that demonstrates the healing of seeing this month. Steve had gone to several different doctors hoping to find some relief for the discomfort of dry eyes. A few months earlier, a highly esteemed doctor who was the head of the hospital performed an operation to help him. Though he experienced some relief initially, his condition actually worsened. By the time it was Tammuz, he was beside himself with pain.

Steve had been looking forward to a summer of dating and fun, but soon found that he was barely able to work. At the end of the day, he could do nothing but go home and hope that he would soon be able to go to sleep. Steve's "looking forward" had turned into his not wanting to look at much of anything—an example of the kind of reversal so typical of Tammuz. Gradually, he became anxious, fearing that his discomfort might incapacitate him and leave him unable to work. He had trusted his doctor, since the doctor had so many impressive credentials. Steve wanted to believe in him and went back to him time and time again as the pain in his eyes increased.

Eventually, during Tammuz, Steve saw the situation clearly and realized that this great doctor had actually harmed him terribly. He now realized that he needed to find another doctor. So he found another doctor who performed yet another operation, and by the following month the pain in his eyes had gradually subsided.

2. BE FLEXIBLE.

Tammuz can be, as we have seen, a month of reversals. We expect one thing to happen, but something totally different occurs. As much as we may like to think we are in control, we need to realize our limitations, let go, and invite God into our lives. This is one of the deep teachings for this month.

As hard as it may be, we must realize that whatever happens to us can be an opportunity for growth and healing. We grow the most when confronting our greatest challenges. Tammuz is also a month of judgment, and we need to accept that nothing happens by chance and nothing is coincidental. Though we have free will, everything occurs by Divine Providence. This is the ultimate paradox. We reap the results of a lot of past karma this month. If we can accept what occurs to us with equanimity, we will be happy, even in hard times.

3. BECOME AWARE OF YOUR NEGATIVE TRAITS.

During this month it is easier to become aware of the ways in which you have limited yourself and others. As you become aware of your negative traits, do not judge yourself harshly. Right now, simply take note of the areas in yourself you want to work on. Most important, have compassion for yourself. Always remember and believe that you can change and become the person you want to be.

Awareness is the first step in transformation. This is the beginning of a process of repentance known in Judaism as *teshuvah,* which grows in intensity in the following months.

4. FEEL YOUR FEELINGS RATHER THAN BLAMING OTHERS FOR THEM.

This month is a time when emotions are strong and passionate. Though passion adds vitality to life, it can also be destructive if not channeled and expressed appropriately. Too often, people react to what they are feeling and are quick to blame others for not giving them what they want, rather than communicate clearly and directly what they would like to receive. This expression of anger, moreover, may make it impossible for their underlying needs to be met by the person with whom they are angry.

For example, during Tammuz, Sharon became angry with Paul for not calling her when she was sick. In an emotional frenzy, she told him that she was very disappointed by his lack of caring. She wanted to terminate their relationship and told him to not call her ever again. Paul did not realize how important his calling was to her, but in her anger, she closed the door to him. Now he felt there was nothing he could do, so he did not call her. This sort of thing is a common Tammuz experience if we are not mindful.

If Sharon could have been more aware of the vulnerable and yearning feelings underlying her anger, she would have called Paul herself rather than waiting for him to call. Paul is a sensitive, loving man and would have welcomed being there for Sharon if she had asked him. Instead, she chose to test and judge him. If she could have shared her vulnerability with Paul and let him know how important the relationship was to her, she might have been able to strengthen it rather than lose it. But sometimes things happen as they were supposed to happen. Everything is Divine Providence. Perhaps Sharon and Paul had to separate, so each of them could be more open to meet their true soul mate.

In this month, be mindful to feel your feelings without blaming others. Make "I" statements about your feelings, rather than accusatory "you" ones. Feelings are simply feelings. If you allow yourself time to process your negative feelings rather than dumping the onto others, they will dissipate and transform.

Astrological Sign: Cancer

The astrological sign of Tammuz is Cancer, a term that in English has negative connotations, reminding us of the disease and reflecting the serious challenges of this month. The Hebrew word for Cancer is *sartan,* which means "Satan," a name that also reveals the difficulty of the tests of this month.

The sign of Cancer is the crab, an unkosher, unattractive, insectlike crustacean. Like the crab, the energy of this month and people born this month often have a hard outer shell and a soft center. The crab moves sideways, rarely forward to its goals. I have heard it said that for every step forward the crab takes, it takes two steps backwards.

Tammuz is not a great time to go forward in one's life. It is not a good time to start new projects. The crab, however, is tenacious, and a certain tenacity is necessary in this month. Tammuz is a good time to work on existing projects.

The ruling body of Cancer is the moon. The moon is always changing, making Tammuz an emotional time with many ups and downs in moods and feeling states. One has to learn to ride the emotional roller coaster of Tammuz. The moon affects the waters of the earth, and Cancer is a water sign. Water takes many shapes and forms and is associated with feelings and desires. This month is a time of deep, intense, and varying feelings accompanying all kinds of desires. All this contributes to the emotional volatility of this month.

The qualities associated with people born under this sign provide additional information about the energy of this month. People born under the sign of Cancer are known to be highly emotional and sensitive souls, albeit sometimes moody. Understanding life through the domain of feelings, they are also known to be intuitive, compassionate, and nurturing. They are also said to be strongly connected to the home, which is what offers them some stability and protection from this month's energy. However, people born this month may also bear negative traits. They tend to be worriers and, like the crab, they may retreat into their shells, often hiding their sensitive feelings. Also, like the crab, which has difficulty going forward in a direct way, Cancerians make their desires known in subtle ways and may feel that they have to resort to deviousness, as they are unable to approach or resolve a matter directly.

Hebrew Letter: Chet

Rabbi Yitzchok Ginzberg, in his wonderful book *Aleph Beit,* provides much information about each of the letters. He informs us that the form of the chet is the combination of the two letters preceding it: the vav on the right, which is the letter of Iyar, and the zayin on the left, which is the letter of Sivan; a little line called a *chatoteret* connects them. The *chatoteret,* which also begins with a chet, means a "bridge." From this, we learn that what we accomplished in Iyar and Sivan prepares us for what we will do in Tammuz. When we put the vav and the zayin together, it forms the letter chet, which resembles a gateway.

Tammuz is a gateway into summer. Tammuz represents another kind of gateway, a passageway to a portion of the yearly cycle that the soul must enter alone. The Divine Presence is said to be somewhat more distant than in previous months. God works in more concealed ways this month, and we are left alone with ourselves more than during any other month except Tevet. Though the sun is shining brightly during this summer month, Tammuz can be a dark night of the soul that one must pass through before entering into the light of day.

The Hebrew word chet, which is the eighth letter of the alphabet, means "transgression." The word chet ends with the Hebrew letter aleph. The aleph is silent. Aleph, as the first letter of the alphabet, always represents the one God. The Baal Shem Tov teaches that from this we learn that even when we sin, God is with us. This is always important to remember. The Talmud says that the sight is the source of most transgressions. We see, we lust, we become heated in passion, and we transgress. This month is the healing of seeing.

The letter chet is also the first letter of the word *chayim,* which means "life," and also of *chuppa,* which means "canopy" as in the covering used in weddings. Kabbalah tells us that there is a connection between words that share the same letters or have the same numerical value. What might the connection be between life, sin, and the wedding canopy?

Here is my theory. Sometimes through transgressions, people are brought deeper into the essence of life. When people do wrong, they eventually suffer, and when the suffering is strong enough, they have to face themselves and what they have done. In this way, many people become deeper and better people. When they are able to rectify their transgressions and grow from the experience, they are made more whole than before. They are more connected with the truth of who they really are.

The Hebrew word *teshuvah* refers to that rectification process. *Teshuvah* literally means "returning." Returning, *teshuvah,* is like getting married, for on the deepest level, *teshuvah* is a return to the soul's initial and intimate connection with the Divine. The *chuppa,* the wedding canopy, represents the Divine Presence and protection that helps make the connection between the two people who stand under it. The *chuppa* brings wholeness.

Hebrew Tribe: Reuven

Reuven was the firstborn son of Leah and Jacob. As you may recall, Jacob wanted to marry Rachel, but he was tricked into marrying her older sister, Leah, first. On the wedding, Jacob had sexual relations with Leah thinking she was Rachel. Out of this union, Reuven was conceived.

When Reuven was born Leah said, "Surely the Lord has looked upon my affliction and now my husband will love me" (Gen. 29:32). The name Reuven comes from the

Hebrew word *re'eh,* which means "to see." Though Reuven was born out of deception, his name implies that a higher vision, God's seeing, was present. Leah tricked Jacob, but still their marriage was supposed to be. The birth of Reuven was a sign validating this marriage. A general guideline for this month as expressed by the birth of Reuven is that what appears to be is not what is, but still it is supposed to be. Leah was not Rachel, but her marriage to Jacob was still supposed to take place.

Leah and Rachel exemplify Tammuz's energy of reversals. Leah, the woman who tricked Jacob into marriage, bears him six sons and ends up buried next to him for eternity; Rachel, the one he truly loved, is buried on the road. Be mindful of reversals this month. Remember, what appears to be happening may not be what is actually happening.

As the firstborn of Jacob, Reuven had a claim to leadership of the Jewish people, but he saw that Joseph, the firstborn of Rachel and Jacob, was more gifted and qualified for that position. For that reason his brothers conspired to murder Joseph. Even though it meant losing his birthright as the firstborn, Reuven defended Joseph to his brothers by suggesting that they place Joseph in a pit rather than murder him. Reuven intended to return later to rescue him. In this incident, Reuven modeled to some extent the capacity of letting go of self-interest for the sake of the truth.

Reuven was also a strong protector of his mother, Leah. As we saw in Iyar, he gathered mandrakes to increase fertility, and Leah ended up trading them with childless Rachel for a night with Jacob. Most children as young as Reuven may not want more siblings to share with their parents, but Reuven knew that his mother so much wanted more children and he did what he could to help that. As a result of the mandrakes he gathered, Issachar was born.

After Rachel's death, Jacob had moved his bed into the tent of Bilhah, the handmaid of Rachel. As Leah's protector, Reuven was angry and offended by this move, so he moved his father's bed into his mother's tent. And to top it off, some midrashim say, he even slept with Bilhah; others say he did not. At any rate, he was criticized for overstepping his boundaries as Jacob's son.

On his deathbed Jacob gave Reuven a blessing characteristic of the energy of this month. He says that Reuven expresses Jacob's power and his dignity, but he is also "unstable like water" (Gen. 49:4). Reuven too often acted upon his emotions, however well intended they were, and this made him unfitting for the leadership of the Jewish people. Later on, the tribe of Reuven also participated in the Korach rebellion against Moses. This is reflected in the destructive energy of this month.

Before Moses died however, he healed the blessing that Jacob had given to Reuven by saying, "Reuven shall live and not die and let his men be numbered" (Deut. 33:6). Reuven had repented and it was accepted. Though he did not assume the leadership of the Jewish people as the firstborn, his tribe was blessed with strength and joy and dignity. This blessing brings redemption to this month.

Divine Name Permutation: HVHY

The position of the letters in the permutation of the Divine Name for this month tell us much about the energy of this month. First, the letters are in the reverse order. Instead of YHVH, which would indicate the optimal flow of divine energy, the order of the letters is HVHY. This reversed order tells us that this month is a month of judgment and that everything is reversed. Things will appear to be one way, but in actuality they are the opposite.

We note that the yud (Y) occupies the world of Assiyah, our physical world, the world of action. The placement of the yud in this world lets us know that not much is happening on this plane. Things are hidden. It is not a time to expend too much energy in doing. It is not a time to start new projects. Lie back; Tammuz is a more internal time. The hay (H) in the world of Yetzerah informs us that the world of the heart, the world of emotions, is very active. This is where one should focus. Expanding the heart and doing *mitzvot* that open the heart and help make a connection between the heart and the higher spiritual worlds is indicated. The vav (V) in the world of Beriyah indicates that there is a flow from the world of Atzilut and Yetzerah. One does not process much with the mind, but rather allows the mind to be a vehicle to transmit the heavenly flow from above. It is not a time for critical analysis, which only inhibits the flow of heavenly energy. There is a great flow from above as indicated by the hay in the world of Atzilut, but one must know how to get one's mind out of the way, so it can be received by the heart. Meditation will be particularly helpful this month.

Torah Portions

The Torah portion for beginning the month of Tammuz relates the story of the spies sent to survey the land of Israel before entering it (Num. 13). Upon seeing the inhabitants of the land, the spies, with the exception of two of them, report that "we were like grasshoppers in our eyes and so we were in the eyes of their eyes" (Num. 13:33). They murmured against Moses and Aaron saying, "If only we had died in the land of Egypt and if only we had died in the wilderness" (Num. 14:2). They only saw their own fear projected. They did not see things as they really were and, most important, they forgot that the land had been promised to them by God. They were afraid of entering into the land, and ultimately their fears and desires were fulfilled.

Most of the Jewish people who were alive at that time did not enter the land of Israel, only those two spies who saw that the land was good were alive to enter the land. The incident of the spies is an example of the mistake of "seeing" as it relates to the energy of this month. One has to be mindful this month and consider whether what we see is true or whether it is our own fear projected.

The next Torah portion recounts the rebellion of Korach (Num. 16). Two hundred and fifty men, leaders of the Jewish people who were followers of Korach and certain Reuvenites, claimed that Moses had concentrated too much power in the hands of his family and tribe, the Levites, who served in the Mishkon, the holy tabernacle hosting the Divine Presence. But though they were jealous of Moses and Aaron and felt that they had the right to the priesthood, they did not express this directly. They couched their argument in idealistic terms, claiming that "the entire assembly, all of them are holy."

At Moses' request, the ground opened and swallowed up those participating in this rebellion. Others carrying incense also perished in a flame. Many people were then angry and criticized Moses for the death of Korach and his supporters, and fourteen thousand of this group were punished and died in a plague. Though this was a small percentage of the Jewish people at this time, it still was devastating. Such is the energy of this month.

Also in this month are reported the deaths of Miriam and Aaron, the brother and sister of Moses (Num. 20). The Jews continued to complain to Moses about living in the desert. Even Moses became emotionally reactive this month when he hit the rock to bring forth water rather than just speaking to it, as God commanded. Moses was also punished for this and could not enter the land of Israel. Moses dies alone in the desert. We have no idea where he is buried, or even if he was buried.

The events of rebellion, punishment, death, and loss portrayed in the Torah portions read during Tammuz reflect the emotional intensity of the energy of this month.

Tempers run high at this time, and people do not see the blessings that are present for them. Instead, there is constant complaining and lack of gratitude, and even Moses, our greatest prophet, overreacts.

Holiday

The Seventeenth of Tammuz

HISTORY   Unlike most Jewish holidays, which commemorate happy, redemptive events for the Jewish people, the seventeenth of Tammuz is a day of fasting and repentance in keeping with the energy of this month. The practice of fasting redeems and transforms this negative energy.

Many destructive events said to have occurred on the seventeenth of Tammuz are commemorated on this day. Descending from Mount Sinai with the two tablets on the seventeenth of Tammuz, Moses broke the tablets upon seeing so many Jews worshiping the Golden Calf. The Golden Calf was built that day, and many Jews who had participated in the sin of the Golden Calf died on it.

At the time of the First Temple, the daily offerings in the Temple ceased on the seventeenth of Tammuz due to a shortage of sheep. Some also say that an idol was placed in the Temple on that date. Furthermore, it is said that on the seventeenth of Tammuz Noah sent a dove out of the ark to see whether the water had receded sufficiently, but the dove could not find a dry place to rest and returned.

But the seventeenth of Tammuz is a significant day for the following reason. Each time the breaching of the walls of Jerusalem that resulted in the destruction of the First and Second Temples later in that year on the ninth of Av occurred on the seventeenth of Tammuz. Jerusalem was under siege from the seventeenth of Tammuz until Tisha B'Av, the ninth of Av, three weeks later. This was a time of waiting for the inevitable, a time of going inside oneself to find the spiritual resources to cope with what was unimaginable. It must have been a terribly emotional heartbreaking time. The Three Weeks became a special period of time to commemorate this terrible waiting. Tammuz, the month of Cancer, is the only month that could contain that kind of brokenness.

OBSERVANCE   The seventeenth of Tammuz is traditionally observed with a fast day that extends from the break of dawn until sunset. It is permissible to eat and drink the preceding night and even until dawn. This day of fasting does not have the same restrictions as the fasts of Yom Kippur and Tisha B'Av. Washing and the wearing of leather shoes are permitted. Nor is it as mandatory as these other fasts. People who do not fast well or who would be made ill from a fast are not required to fast on the seventeenth of Tammuz. However, people who do not fast are advised to eat simple foods and refrain from indulging in food and drink. In addition to fasting, people are advised to engage in introspection, to review their actions, and repent of anything bad that they have done.

The seventeenth of Tammuz begins a three-week period of restrictions called the "Three Weeks." This commemorates the siege of Jerusalem before the destruction of the Holy Temple. During this time, many religious Jews refrain from music, dancing, the cutting of hair, and marriages until after Tisha B'Av, the ninth day of the next month.

During the Three Weeks, one is advised to be careful and avoid situations of danger, more so than at other times during the year. Though travel is permitted, one should exercise more care when traveling. Some choose not to fly in airplanes during this time, but that is a choice; it is not prohibited by religious law.

Meditation

In view of the fact that the beginning of the destruction of the Temple occurred during this month, the meditation practice is devoted to the building and strengthening of the inner Temple, enabling us to experience God's presence within us. When we are able to do this, we will see God's presence reflected in the world. This will be a true healing of seeing, for we will see the true essence of everyone, and everything.

Light a candle, sit in a comfortable position for meditation, and take deep breaths to center and relax. As you take deep breaths, pause in the space between the breaths. It is an empty, peaceful place.

Now imagine yourself entering your private sanctuary. This is a miniature Holy Temple where the Divine Presence resides in you. This is a place of safety, refuge, simplicity, and beauty. What does it look like? What does it feel like? What is in your sanctuary? Imagine you have in your sanctuary all that brings you consolation and comfort. What do you bring in to comfort you? Who is there with you?

Within your sanctuary is a candle burning brightly. Its flames flicker upward. If you like, gaze at the candle with your eyes open or keep your eyes closed and visualize the candle in your sanctuary. The light of the candle radiates a message of hope, eternity, and holiness. The light is God's light; it is the light of your own soul. Be with the light.

Light has the power to transmute darkness, negativity, and sadness. Let your sadness and hurt merge into the light. The more sadness and hurt you release, the brighter the flame.

Now close your eyes and imagine that you are the light. Your body is a candle and your soul is the flame. Feel the brightness of your own light. See it shine brightly.

How can you support or nurture your own light to shine even more brightly?

Practical Recommendations

1. BE DELIBERATE THIS MONTH.

Do not make rash judgments. Make an effort to calm yourself and refrain from acting out of an emotionally heated place within yourself, which is easy to do this month. This month is a time of feeling a range of deep, intense, and varying feelings and desires. Give yourself time to be with your feelings.

2. TAKE TIME TO BE QUIET AND MEDITATE EACH DAY.

This month is a time to be internal. There is a great heavenly flow, but as it is more hidden this month, we need to meditate to be able to receive it.

3. SPEND TIME AT HOME.

This is not the month to do great traveling around the world; rather, it is a time to be at home. Make your home more beautiful physically and spiritually. It is a time to become closer to the people you live with, to make your home a miniature Holy Temple.

A Tale to Live By

This month the area of healing is seeing. We often make judgments about people and life situations based on externalities. As we purify our seeing through prayer, we have the privilege of seeing more of the truth of what is.

There was much opposition to Chassidism in its formative years. An opponent of Chassidism had heard many amazing claims about the Chernobyl rebbe and wanted to meet this rebbe himself to see if there was any validity to what his followers said about him. He understood that followers see their rebbe as a wondrous being, an angel, an intermediary, but he assumed this was just wishful thinking on the part of simple people.

He traveled to see the rebbe and had the privilege of sitting at the table with the rebbe for a meal. As he watched the rebbe eat, he didn't see anything extraordinary; he simply saw a man eating. But the food falling out of the rebbe's mouth onto his beard gave the impression that the rebbe did not have the manners of a cultured person. He was ready to dismiss the rebbe and all the claims he had heard about him, yet he stopped himself.

He excused himself from the table, went into a corner, and prayed to God. "Master of the Universe, please let my eyes be open to see the truth of what is. Please let me see the essence of the rebbe, and not just the externalities."

When he returned to the table, he now saw that the rebbe was shining from one corner of the world to another. The rebbe was indeed a great light. His eyes had been purified through prayer so he could see the hidden truth.

Av

    Month: *July-August*

    Energy: *The Wholeness of Brokenness*

    Area of Healing: *Hearing*

    Astrological Sign: *Leo*

    Hebrew Letter: *Tet*

    Hebrew Tribe: *Shimon*

    Divine Name Permutation: *HVYH*

    Holidays: *Tisha B'Av, Tu B'Av*

he month of Av is about tears of loss and tears of joy. Sometimes we don't want to cry. Sometimes, we cry in spite of ourselves. Some of us will not cry in the presence of other people. Others will cry only to other people. Sometimes we may feel like crying, but we hold back and feel that our tears are pointless. How would we cry if we knew that our tears were not in vain, that they make a difference, and that our crying opens gates to heal not only ourselves, but the world? This is the question to be mindful of during this month.

Even though Larry came to see me many years ago and he came only a few times, I will always remember him. In the first fifteen minutes of the session, I felt intuitively that I was in the presence of an exceptional young man. He was about nineteen years old. He told me he had been a rebellious teenager, so bored with school he often played hooky and did not even show up for months at a time. He was eventually expelled from high school in his senior year. Though he was quite brilliant, he did not have a high school diploma and did not know what to do with his life. As a teenager, he did not feel understood by his parents. They were intolerant of his free-spirited lifestyle and were disappointed and angry that he did not want to go to college and become a doctor or lawyer.

He came to me to receive guidance and a better understanding about a mystical experience that had transformed his life. Several months ago he had fallen in love with a young woman. It was his first real infatuation and he was intoxicated by it. After a few months, the young woman rejected him and he was totally devastated. Extremely depressed and unable to leave his room, he cried continually. He had never experienced this kind of pain before and even thought of committing suicide.

At a certain point, he passed through a gateway into the depths of his soul. He cried for God, who created this world for love and joy and wants people to love each other; but people fail to do so and there is so much pain and suffering in the world.

A few days later, "out of the blue" he received a phone call from a friend in California who invited him out for a visit. He went the next day. Once there, he felt instantly better. One day while he was alone, he had a spontaneous meditation experience in which he was filled with the realization of the oneness of all of creation. He was filled with the love of God. It was an ecstatic experience that lasted for a few days, yet it transformed his life. Because of this experience, he now wanted to become immersed in Judaism and dedicate his life to helping people. I directed him to various books and places of Jewish learning. I imagined that sitting in front of me was a future rabbi who would truly inspire many people.

Energy: The Wholeness of Brokenness

Av is considered the most emotionally intense month of the year, a roller coaster of feelings; however, much of the potential downside, the negative energy of this month, can be diminished if we are careful to really listen to ourselves and others. Misunderstanding what is heard and jumping to conclusions are the source of many problems in this challenging month. In the land of Israel and in many places in the world, Av is the hottest month. This heat is reflected on the emotional and spiritual planes of our lives as well.

Av means "Father" in Hebrew. The father is a symbol of love and giving in Judaism. By this name, we know that whatever happens in this month, even bad things, will ultimately be for good. The analogy of a child learning to walk illustrates this underlying principle and the process of growth for this month. At first, the child is supported by the parent. At a certain point, the parent lets go so the child will learn to walk on his or her own. Sometimes the child falls, which may be painful, but the parent is still nearby. Eventually, through various attempts and trials, the child learns to walk. The falls taken are all part of the learning process.

The goodness of this month is further indicated by the fact that the letter associated with this month, tet, is the first letter of the word *tov,* which means "good." The Talmud tells us that, in the future, even the sorrowful days of Av will be transformed into days of joy.

The *Gemara,* however, states explicitly that the luck of Jews is bad in Av and Jews should avoid going to court even if they have a good case and are favored to win. The month is not an optimal time to negotiate new business contracts either. During one period of the Nine Days, I was happy when my brother's appointment to negotiate a business contract with his most important client was postponed.

Av hosts the saddest day of the year, Tisha B'Av, which commemorates the destruction of the First and Second Temples in Jerusalem thousands of years ago. But this month is also host to what the Talmud tells us is the most joyous day of the year, Tu B'Av, which was historically the time when there was such love and joy in the air that women would dance before the men and marriages took place on the basis of just one glance.

It's no coincidence that these two polar events take place during the same month, because in fact they are related and interconnected. These holidays reveal the dual character of the energy of this month and model for us a very important spiritual principle: out of destruction comes rebirth and newness. And though these historical events occurred thousands of years ago, both occurred in this month and both reflect the kind of emotional intensity present this month even today.

What does the destruction of the Holy Temple mean? How is it characteristic of the energy of this month? In ancient times, the Jewish people believed that the Holy Temple in Jerusalem was the meeting place between humankind and God. In the past, God was alive in the world and lived in Jerusalem in the Temple. Several times a year, the people would journey to the Temple in Jerusalem, offer sacrifices, and receive blessings and atonement for their sins.

It was a glorious time in Jewish history. But what is its relevance to us today? Why is it considered the saddest day in the Jewish calendar? We will explore these questions in greater detail in the section related to the holiday itself, but for now it is important to understand how the day reflects the overall energy and spiritual opportunity of the month.

In the hearts and souls of the Jewish people, the Temple remains the symbolic representation of God's presence in the physical world. Jewish prophets inform us that the Temple was not the property of the Jewish people alone, but through the service of the Jewish people in the Temple, all nations of the world are blessed. Its destruction is a loss to the world, not just to the Jews. For many religious people, the Temple was a microcosm of the universe. When the Temple stood, the spiritual and physical worlds were connected. The destruction of the Temple resulted in an exiled Divine Presence, termed now the Shechinah. All of the personal and communal losses we experience in our lives are represented by the loss of the Temple.

From a kabbalistic perspective, all pain, alienation, and suffering result from the perceived schism between God and the world. This separation results in blockages of the flow of divine energy between the spiritual and physical worlds, which are reflected in our personal lives and communities. As a result, we do not experience our inherent oneness with all people. If we did, how could there be war or famine?

Consequently, we all exist with a widespread sense of alienation. What we do and who we are are not connected, and the divine soul within the human body is pained by this disharmony. It is not just the soul that suffers. From a kabbalistic perspective, the source of all physical disease and illness is a lack of flow between the Godly soul and the body.

The first days of the month are known as the "Nine Days" and culminate in Tisha B'Av, the Ninth of Av. During this first week particularly, we may feel a sense of loss and alienation we cannot attribute to anything specific. Rather than attempt to distract ourselves, we should simply be with ourselves. It is a time to meditate on the disconnectedness in our personal and communal lives.

During this time, one needs to guard against an exaggerated sense of self and pride that may lead to quarrels and strife. Though these quarrels are petty in origin, they can be divisive and devastating in their consequences. Passions run high at this time, so be mindful and careful not to be emotionally reactive. Listen carefully to what is said and what is not said. Take time to reflect and deliberate upon what you heard before you take any action or make any response.

The first week in Av is an optimal time to slow down and reflect upon your personal losses and the lack of inner or outer harmony in your life. Allow yourself to feel the range of feelings that are present for you as you open this gate of brokenness within yourself. Each human being is potentially a miniature Holy Temple, and, like the ancient Temple, we all are a little broken. Too often people run away from feelings of brokenness, distracting themselves with food, sex, television, shopping, partying, working too hard, and so on. Allow yourself to feel your feelings without blaming yourself, others, or God. You are supported and entitled. It is a great privilege and spiritual gift for you to do so now.

The first nine days of Av are the time to weep and feel one's brokenness. Weep for yourself, for others, and for God, who created the whole world for love. But who is ready to receive this love? Are you ready to receive and share this love?

There are many kinds of crying and tears. There is a crying that comes from the mind, from thinking negative thoughts. This crying often leaves one drained, exhausted, and sorry for oneself. There is, however, also a crying that comes from deep in the soul. These are holy tears, and when they flow

> *The first week in Av is an optimal time to slow down and reflect upon your personal losses and the lack of inner or outer harmony in your life.*

through us, they purify, heal, and strengthen us. The soul has such deep feelings, and too often people are afraid to feel their own depths until they are forced to do so by challenging and painful life events.

Our tears can open gates in heaven and within us. When we go deep inside to the depths of our personal pain, we often see that it is not personal at all. We discover that the real reason we are crying is because God's presence is not realized in this world. What was true for Larry is true for all of us who plunge into the depths of our pain. When we allow ourselves to feel the deep feelings within our own soul, to feel its grief, its sadness, its brokenness, paradoxically our pain is lifted from us and we are made whole.

Spiritual crying is an important practice this month. When we cry for God, we are healed and we can heal others as well. We feel our pain, and it hurts, but by feeling our brokenness and that of the world, we actually become more whole. The Talmud tells us, "There is nothing more complete than a broken heart." It is a paradox. Out of the feeling of brokenness, we receive solace and redemption. Through our tears, we see what is essential and true. We gain clarity and vision. We are more vulnerable, open, and accessible to others.

The world is filled with needless suffering and hatred. We can blame politicians for world conditions, but if we are really honest with ourselves, we will begin to acknowledge our personal responsibility for God's exile and concealment in our lives. Power struggles and game playing between people are rampant on the micro or macro levels. God created a world with ample resources for everyone, but because of our greed and selfishness we do not share them or ourselves freely with others.

God instructs us in the Torah, "Make Me a sanctuary and I will dwell within you" (Exod. 25:8). The verse does not say "in it," but "within, or among, you." The Hebrew is clear, telling us that the purpose of the outer Temple is to experience the presence of God within. It is not the physical structure that is important; it is only a vehicle for the interior experience. Too often we become so trapped in externalities, in form and structure, that we forget the real purpose of everything we do.

When we imbue our own physical creations with life and meaning, they become idols to us. We forget that their purpose is to facilitate the internal experience of God's presence within us. This is what we each must learn this month. And sometimes we learn this best through loss. If there is loss in your life, particularly during this month, accept it as a growth opportunity. Through loss, we learn what is essential.

The Talmud tells us that in every generation, when the Temple is not rebuilt, it is as if we have destroyed it. This refers not merely to the physical structure of the Temple, but rather to the embodiment of the spiritual essence, what the Temple represents in our life. We can each, in our own bodies, homes, and communities, build holy sanctuaries for the indwelling of the Shechinah, the Divine Presence. We can each experience ourselves as a Holy Temple. Every home can be a Holy Temple.

Toward the middle and end of the month, there is greater clarity and openness. The first Sabbath after Tisha B'Av is called Shabbos Nachamu, the Sabbath of Consolation. The energy of the month shifts dramatically. Having entered into the depths of our own souls earlier in the month, we now have access to the souls of others in a new way. Hope and love are rekindled. It is a good time to travel and connect with others, to open to the joy of God's love and presence in your life and in the world.

General Guidelines and Goals

These guidelines and goals enable us to direct our energies in the ways that are optimal for our growth and transformation in accordance with the energy of this month. It is recommended that you read and meditate upon them often in the course of the month. Reflect on their applicability to you, and allow them to direct and inspire you often this month.

1. LISTEN TO WHAT IS SAID AND WHAT IS NOT SAID.

This month is for the healing of hearing. It is important to truly listen to others this month. We do not always hear correctly what is said in words, nor do we always hear what is not said and implied in silence. Always ask for clarification when necessary. Do not make assumptions. Be careful not to react without thinking to what you hear this month.

2. CREATE OPPORTUNITIES FOR DEEP LISTENING AND SHARING WITH OTHERS.

Now is the time to share your pain with others and to be open to hearing their pain as well. Sharing our vulnerability with others allows us to bond. In the sharing of our pain and our humanness, we become close to each other and to God. This brings rectification and healing.

3. GUARD AGAINST JUDGING YOURSELF AND OTHERS.

One of the reasons for the destruction of the Temple was because people did not love each other. It is called *sinas chinam,* "causeless hatred." We have to guard against our tendencies to produce causeless hatred.

The cause of *sinas chinam* is egotism. Watch for the tendency to judge others, to see yourself better than another, and when it comes up in the course of the month, let it go. Watch for the tendency to be jealous of other's accomplishments, and also let it go. When we let go of our judging mind and allow our hearts to open, we will be filled with love.

4. BE CAREFUL OF YOUR SPEECH.

Refrain from gossip or speaking negatively about others or yourself. Judaism recognizes the power of words and has many laws about what should and should not be said. If we need to say something to another that may in any way be perceived as criticism, we should do it directly and respectfully, and only if we feel that that person will be able to hear what we have said. Otherwise, we need to be silent. So much unnecessary pain, particularly in this month, is caused by speaking without considering the effects our words will have on others.

5. BECOME A MORE GIVING PERSON. LOVE UNCONDITIONALLY AND WITHOUT REASON.

The antidote to *sinas chinam* is love, unconditional love. All true love is unconditional. If love is conditional, it is more like business than love. Unfortunately, the business mentality has entered into the realm of personal relationships. People often give to others with the specific intention of receiving something in return. If they don't get what they want, they withdraw their love. So they may call it love, but it's really business, and in spite of all their "giving," they continue to feel isolated and lonely.

Giving for the joy of giving is pure and healing. It builds true relationships. Find opportunities to give without considering what you will receive. Reb Dessler, in his book *Strive for Truth,* reveals an important insight about the nature of love. We don't really first love people and then give to them. Rather, we give to people and then we come to love them. If you want to have a lot of friends, give to many people.

6. MEDITATE AND OPEN TO GOD'S PRESENCE IN YOUR DAILY LIFE.

Though the Temple was destroyed this month, God is still and always present. Particularly in this month, we need to create opportunities to experience the presence of God in our lives. By studying Torah, praying, doing *mitzvot,* and meditating, we experience the Divine Presence, the Shechinah. This provides comfort and consolation for this time. Take time to open your consciousness to God's presence even when you are not engaged in a prescribed spiritual activity. It is a *mitzvah* to be aware that God is one and God is everywhere.

Astrological Sign: Leo

This month of Leo is ruled by the sun. The sun is a metaphor for spiritual energy. Kabbalah teaches us, however, that the greater the positive energy, the greater potential for negative energy, a range especially evident this month.

The sun is a fire sign, and Leo exhibits the two qualities of the fire sign, its ability to impassion or enliven and its ability to destroy. In Tisha B'Av and Tu B'Av, the two holidays in this month, we see both aspects of fire revealed. Fire is purifying, illuminating, and transformational if it is properly channeled and contained. God is compared to fire, but a fire that burns and does not consume; God is holy fire.

Without fire, there is no passion. Without passion, nothing happens in the world. But fire is also destructive and dangerous if it is uncontrollable. What can take a long time to build, fire can quickly destroy.

The energy of Leo, of Av, is passion. Av is fire. While the previous month, Tammuz, is represented by the crab, which is introverted, Av is represented by the lion, which is extroverted. When necessary, he roars to let everyone know that he is the king and that he will do everything he can to protect his territory. He wants and demands to be the focus of our attention. We must take note of him as he struts around the jungle in his dignified and majestic way.

People born under the sign of Leo are known to resemble the lion. They like to be the center of attention. They are known to be generous, somewhat flamboyant, and courageous. But Leos are also known to be vain and ostentatious. Many world leaders are born under the sun sign of Leo. Interestingly, the Messiah, according to Judaism, will come from the tribe of Judah, which is associated with the lion. And the Talmud tells us that the Messiah is to be born on Tisha B'Av, which occurs during this month.

Like the lion, all of us feel during this month a passionate desire to be heard and noticed. If this desire is channeled appropriately, there will be great creativity and generosity will be displayed. If not, there may be pretentiousness and egoism that lead to needless strife. If we can be sensitive to this energy and give each other the needed acknowledgment and validation, much conflict may be avoided.

Hebrew Letter: Tet

 Tet is the first letter in the word *tov,* which means "good." The letter tet indicates that Av is ultimately a good month. The *Gemara* says that if one sees a tet in a dream, it is sign that something good will happen.

If we examine the form of the letter tet, it looks like a vessel with an inverted rim. It does not pour out, but contains within it. Moreover, it is likened to a womb. As such, the tet represents what is hidden, the potential contained within creation and within each person.

This idea is further supported by tet's numerical value, nine. The number nine reminds one of the nine months of pregnancy. Tet connotes the power of pregnancy, the power to conceal and contain within oneself all that is good. Recall that the chet, the letter of the previous month, resembled a wedding canopy. This month is the impregnation. The birthing process begins in the next month, Elul.

As an aside, the number nine is the numerical value of the word *emet,* which means "truth" (aleph is one, mem is forty but it is counted as four, and tet is four hundred but is counted as four). Truth is tremendously healing, yet it sometimes forces one to relinquish comfortable illusions, which can be difficult to do. Some of the loss we experience this month may be about the discovery of truth. As hard as the process is, the truth is good and it is good that we seek the truth.

After each phrase in the six-day creation of the world, God pronounced it "good." By saying "good," *tov,* God told us that all of creation is a vessel to contain within it the goodness of God. Interestingly, the word *tov* is the thirty-third word in the Torah, which reminds us of Lag B'Omer in the month of Iyar, the thirty-third day of the counting of the Omer. Though the word *tov* appears many times in the creation story presented in Genesis, it only appears one more time in the entire Torah. The other time it is used is to describe Moses at the time of his birth, because of the light that shone within him.

Meditating on the letter tet this month will open you to the experience of what is intrinsically good, even though it may be concealed. In your meditation, visualize the tet. Trace it on your inner screen. Be with the tet. Merge with the tet. And if you like, project yourself and your life inside the tet.

Hebrew Tribe: Shimon

The tribe of Shimon, the second son of Leah, represents the energy of Av. The name Shimon is derived from the Hebrew word *shimo'a,* which means "to hear." The whole month of Av is devoted to the healing of hearing. Looking at incidents recorded in the Torah about Shimon—his mistakes, passion, and emotional intensity—provides us with clues about the energy of this month and directs us to be mindful of our own human tendencies and passions.

When Leah named her son Shimon, she said, "Because the Lord has heard that I was hated, he has therefore given me this son also" (Gen. 29:33). Because these are such strong words for a mother to use at the time of a child's birth, it is easy to see how this child might have been emotionally scarred from birth. Like his older brother Reuven, he carried the legacy of being a child of a woman who felt less than appreciated and even hated, because Jacob favored her sister, Rachel. Leah's sentiments in naming Shimon may have predisposed him to be somewhat volatile, with a chip on his shoulder, so to speak. Much of Shimon's actions might be seen as an effort of a son to defend and rectify the perceived lower status of his mother.

Shimon was most known as the passionate defender of his sister, Dinah. Dinah had wandered independently into town and been kidnapped and sexually violated by the prince of the region, Shechem. He, however, fell in love with her, and his father, the ruler of the region, went to ask Jacob for her hand in marriage to his son. Jacob's sons were infuriated and devised a plan requiring the men of the region, including the prince, to be circumcised as a condition for marriage to Jewish women. The ruler and prince believed them, and all the men in the region circumcised themselves. On the third day after their circumcision, when they were the most weak, Shimon organized an attack that resulted in their deaths. The Torah tells us, "And it came to pass when they were in pain that two of the sons of Jacob, Shimon and Levi, Dinah's brothers, took each man his sword and came upon the city and slew all the males" (Gen. 34:25). Fearing the consequences of such violence, Jacob confronted them about what they did, saying, "You have brought trouble on me, making me odious among the inhabitants of the land" (v. 30), but Shimon and Levi responded without remorse, "Should he have been allowed to treat our sister as a prostitute?" (v. 31).

The events of the story are as troubling to many readers today as they were to Jacob and to later rabbinic sages. Was it right that all the men of the city were killed because of the actions of the prince? Torah commentaries justify it by saying that the men were lewd and immoral and rape was a common everyday occurrence there. But was it really a rape? Kabbalah tells us that Dinah and Shechem were actually soul mates. Shimon, however, *hears* that his sister has been raped, and he acts to defend her. Shimon reacts emotionally. He does not talk to his sister about what happened. He and Levi do not even discuss their plans with their father or their other brothers. As a passionate defender of purity, Shimon is a zealot. He is passionate and principled, but he is at times out of balance, and the Jewish people reap the karma of his actions.

Shimon's zealotry and passionate emotions also made him a leader in the plan to kill his brother Joseph, the first son of the beloved wife, Rachel. Instead of being killed, due to the persuasion of Reuven, his older brother, Joseph was sold into slavery. As terrible as all this was, it is considered part of a divine plan to bring Joseph and then the Jewish people to Egypt, as had been prophesied to Abraham years before.

At the time of his death, Jacob assembled all his sons to bless them. But instead of blessing Shimon and Levi, Jacob tells them that he disapproves of the evil actions they did in their lives and that his soul will not shield them from responsibility. He lets Shimon know that his tribe will lose its separate identity and be dispersed within Israel. The tribe of Shimon was absorbed into the tribe of Judah and became the teachers, for this profession enabled them to do the learning they needed to do.

One more incident concerning the tribe of Shimon is recorded in the Torah (Num. 25:6–15). Zimri, an elder and a prince in the tribe of Shimon, fell in love with Cosbi, a princess of Midian, a non-Jew. The Torah tells us that they were having sexual relations in front of Moses' tent, as a challenge to the authority of Moses, and they were slain by Pinchas, known as a young zealot. Did Pinchas act correctly in killing this couple? Kabbalah deepens the question by telling us that Zimri and Cosbi were soul mates and a reincarnation of Dinah and Shechem. They thought they acted with pure intentions to bring in a new order. The Jewish people initially were very upset by their deaths, but God approves of Pinchas's actions because he had pure intentions. Pinchas is rewarded the covenant of peace, which is God's way of saying that he now needed to learn the ways of peace.

Shimon is the perfect representative of the energy of Av because he is the passionate zealot. We see that, throughout history, it was passionate zealotry that led to the divisiveness and destructiveness characteristic of this month. But in the time of Messiah, the passionate energy of this month will be transformed.

Divine Name Permutation: HVYH

In examining the permutation for this month, we see a reversal of the letters. The hay (H) and vav (V) are usually in the order of vav and hay and they now occupy the first and second positions rather than the optimal third and forth positions. This reversal indicates judgment and this judgment applies to the first two weeks of the month. The yud (Y) and the hay are in the proper order, and though they are now in the third and fourth positions, it indicates that it is also a time of mercy and compassion that we find in the last two weeks of the month.

The permutation for this month is like the one for Tammuz except that the last two letters are reversed. The yud is now in the world of Yetzerah and the hay is in the world of Assiyah. This month the emphasis is not on the heart, but on the world of Assiyah, this physical world. The Godly Light enters into the world of Assiyah, our physical world, more easily and we experience this in the last weeks of the month. The heart must be quieted, become small like the yud, so the Light can flow into this world.

Torah Portions

With this month, we enter into a new book of Torah entitled Devarim, or Deuteronomy. Devarim literally means "words," and this book is the words of Moses as he recounts the high points of Israel's journey from Mount Sinai and tries to prepare the Jewish people for the challenges they will face in the next phase of their journey. It is distinguished from the earlier books in which Moses functions as a scribe for God's words; here Moses talks to the people as a human being. He even shares his very human feelings, his deep grief and disappointment about not being able to go into the land of Israel with the rest of the Jewish people.

In addition to recounting events, this book includes basic teachings and spiritual practices of Judaism. The Shema, the basic declaration of faith used in the Jewish prayer book, is taken from this book, as is the practice of saying blessings after eating. The Ten Commandments are repeated, in the Torah portion of Va'eschanan, read on Shabbos Nachamu, the Sabbath after Tisha B'Av. The reading of the Ten Commandments is once again a sign of forgiveness. It hints at the forgiveness of Yom Kippur, when Moses obtained forgiveness for the sin of the Golden Calf and returned with a second set of tablets.

But mostly this book is an instruction manual for the future. It even includes predictions of all the catastrophes that the Jewish people will experience in the years to come. And if we look at history, we see that these predictions were fulfilled. Moses tells the Jewish people that they will enter the land but not follow God's ways, so they'll be scattered. He tells them that they'll yearn for God, however, and eventually be brought back to the land. God will not abandon the Jewish people—an important message for this month of Av.

Moses speaks here in both theoretical and practical ways. He tells the people that God is not beyond them, but available to them. He reviews the laws of *kashrus,* tithing, the observance of the holidays, and many other practices designed to preserve the holiness of the people.

In Deuteronomy Moses prepares the people for the tests and challenges they will have to face in entering Israel. Some of these teachings seem particularly relevant today.

Several times he reminds the people that Israel is God's gift to them, not because they are better than other people, but only because of God's love and covenant with them.

But what is most important is that, beginning on the Sabbath after Tisha B'Av, we read each week for seven weeks a Haftorah that is a special portion from the prophets selected to offer consolation to the people. This represents the healing and compassionate energy of the latter part of the month, which extends into the next month of Elul.

Holidays

Tisha B'Av

HISTORY   Tisha B'Av, the Ninth of Av, has historically been a painful day for the Jewish people. Though it primarily commemorates the destruction of the First and Second Temples in Jerusalem, throughout history many other terrible persecutions and destructive events are recorded to have occurred on Tisha B'Av.

The first recorded event was that it was on Tisha B'Av that the Jewish people heard and believed the reports of the spies who scouted the land of Israel and advised them not to enter it. For this, the Jewish people were condemned to wander in the desert for forty years until the whole first generation of Jews who fled during the Exodus had died. Legend has it that the Jews did not die of natural causes during the time they were in the desert. What happened was that a certain percentage of them, approximately fifteen thousand people, would die each Tisha B'Av. According to the legend, people would build graves for themselves. On Tisha B'Av, they would lie in these graves, go to asleep, and not awake in the morning.

Jews endured discrimination and persecution in almost every country they resided in, and Tisha B'Av was often the time when the worst incidents occurred. The Jews were expelled from England in 1290, from France in 1306, and from Spain in 1492—all on Tisha B'Av. Communities were destroyed during the Crusades on Tisha B'Av beginning in 1096. The Talmud was burned in Paris in 1244 on Tisha B'Av. The deportation from the Warsaw ghetto to Treblinka in 1942 began on Tisha B'Av.

Tisha B'Av is best known as the commemoration of the destruction of the First and Second Temples in Jerusalem. Although the First Temple remained standing for hundreds of years, prophets had predicted its downfall because of the widespread idolatry in the Temple itself and throughout the country. One of the prophets, Zechariah, was beheaded on Yom Kippur by Jews who did not want to listen to these prophecies. With such internal divisiveness, the Jewish people were vulnerable. The Babylonians destroyed the First Temple on Tisha B'Av in 586 B.C.E.

When the Babylonians were conquered by the Persians, the Jewish people were allowed to return to Israel and rebuild the Temple. Soon Persia was conquered by Greece. Israel, now under the domain of Greece, was greatly influenced by Hellenism, which threatened the purity of the Temple and of Judaism. After the Maccabeans defeated the Greek Syrian Empire, the Jewish people formed an alliance with Rome, the emerging world power, to protect Jerusalem.

It took a bit of juggling to appease the Roman Empire, but Israel was relatively stable for a long time. Though the Second Temple was destroyed by Rome, the real problem cited by the rabbis for its destruction was the internal divisiveness within the Jewish people. Jews did not love each other.

The few stories in the Talmud used to justify the destruction of the Temple point to the root of the destruction as the causeless hatred between Jews. We do not know if these reports are factually true, but their message is what is important and particularly relevant today in a time of great Jewish divisiveness. It is the lack of unity of the Jewish people that made Jews then, and also makes them now, vulnerable to the aspirations of other nations.

The principal incident given in the Talmud is between Bar Kamtza and Kamtza. Though no reason was given, Bar Kamtza and Kamtza were enemies, but inadvertently Bar Kamtza was invited to a party of Kamtza's. When he arrived at the party, he was asked to leave by the host. Bar Kamtza wanted to stay and offered to compensate his host financially for what he would eat and drink during the party. His offer was refused. He offered to pay for half and then for all the expenses of the party if he was allowed to stay. His offer was rejected and he was physically ejected from the banquet in an embarrassing and public way.

Bar Kamtza then said to himself, "Since the rabbis seated at the banquet did not rebuke him for the way he treated me, it is evident that what he did was acceptable to them. I will go and spread slander against the rabbis in the royal palace." And he did just that. He went to Caesar and told him, "The Jews have rebelled against you."

To verify this claim, he suggested, "Send them an animal sacrifice and see whether they offer it in their Temple." Caesar sent a fine calf with Bar Kamtza. On his return trip to Jerusalem, Bar Kamtza caused a blemish in the calf's upper lip that he knew would make the animal unacceptable for offering according to strict orthodox standards. The rabbis considered offering it anyway because they did not want to ruin their relations with Rome. But they were overruled by a group of zealots who did not want to compromise the standards regarding animal sacrifices and allow people to think they could offer blemished animals in the future. The rabbis considered killing Bar Kamtza so that he would not be able to tell Caesar that the offering had been refused, but ultimately they didn't do that either. So eventually this simple incident, Jew against Jew, was the start of the Roman war against the Jews.

Another painful incident occurs later on after the war had already started. There were those who wanted to negotiate peace with the Romans, knowing that any military effort would be devastating and unsuccessful, and those who wanted war, believing that God would make them victorious. The wealthy people of Jerusalem offered to sustain the Jewish people with food and wood that was estimated to last for twenty-one years. The *baryoni*, the zealots who advocated the overthrow of Roman rule through war alone, burned the storehouses of wheat and barley and wood, so the Jewish people would have no option but to fight. Along with the Romans, they did not allow anyone to leave the besieged city.

The Second Temple was destroyed on Tisha B'Av in 70 C.E. Over a million Jews died fighting for independence. Many others died of starvation and crucifixion. There were many ancient biblical curses demonstrating what would happen if Jews did not fulfill God's will. Many of them were fulfilled during this time. In addition to the death and degrading behaviors of war, there was a great religious crisis.

Could Judaism continue to exist if there were no Temple? Many people doubted that Judaism could or should survive without the Holy Temple. Rabbi Yochanan Ben Zakkai escaped from Jerusalem and negotiated with the Roman authorities for Jewish control of a city called Yavneh. There he rebuilt a Judaism that is most known today. In so doing he made Judaism more accessible than it had been before. Under Roman rule, the Temple had become corrupt. This new rabbinical Judaism advocated by Rabbi Yochanan was radical and more democratic than the previous system. The rabbis, rather than the priests or prophets of the Temple, became the principal keepers of the faith. By following rabbinic law, every Jew could be a high priest, every home and synagogue could be a Holy Temple.

At the time of the Second Temple, Christianity was one sect among many within Judaism. Christian Jews prayed in synagogues and kept all the Jewish holidays. After the destruction of the Temple, they separated from Judaism. Though Christian Jews were initially persecuted by the Romans, they sought to differentiate themselves from the Jews and appease the Romans.

OBSERVANCE   Tisha B'Av is a day of abstinence. Next to Yom Kippur, it is the most widely observed fast day. The fast begins on sundown and ends on sundown of the next day. During this time, no food or drink is taken and sexual relations are prohibited. The synagogues are dimly lit, sometimes just with candles, and in many places people sit on the floor or on low benches as they would if they were mourning the loss of a loved one. People wear sneakers rather than leather shoes. There is little social greeting or socializing. The smiles, warm greetings, and embraces prevalent during other holidays are absent. If you knew nothing of this holiday beforehand, you might think that people were either unfriendly or depressed. The atmosphere is very subdued, and everyone is encouraged to be inwardly directed and self-reflective.

In my orthodox synagogue, the *mechitza,* or divider that separates men and women during prayer services, is removed and women participate in the service along with men. This dramatizes the important message that we are all together in loss and grief. The book of Lamentations, Eicha, written by the prophet Jeremiah is chanted.

On Tisha B'Av morning, the *tallis* (prayer shawl) and *tefillin* (phylactenes) are not worn. There is none of the usual singing during prayer services. The Torah reading is from Deuteronomy when Moses forecasts the exile and destruction of the Jewish people for not keeping God's will and encourages them to return to God when this occurs.

The book of Kinot is chanted. The *kinot* are the assembled poems recounting destruction and pain of the Jewish people throughout history. In New York, there are many activities for Tisha B'Av. Lectures and movies about suffering abound. At one synagogue, the film *Schindler's List* was shown in the afternoon.

Every year, I find it awesome to witness the solemn observance of Tisha B'Av. Reflecting that this practice has continued for thousands of years is quite humbling. Grieving for the loss of the Holy Temple for thousands of years on the holiday of Tisha B'Av is a powerful testimony of the claim of the Jewish people to Jerusalem and the Temple Mount. This claim becomes more important today than ever.

When Napoleon witnessed Jewish people fasting and weeping on Tisha B'Av, he inquired as to the reason. Amazed to learn that they were weeping over an event that occurred thousands of years before, he remarked that this people would be victorious in the end.

Tu B'Av

HISTORY   Tu B'Av is the fifteenth day of Av. The moon is full, as bright as it will be. On the sixteenth day of the month, the moon already begins to diminish. On Tu B'Av the days begin to get shorter. The weather begins to shift and the scent of fall is in the air, even though there may be some more hot days ahead.

The oral tradition records this day as the day when the death of Jewish people in the desert ceased. As mentioned before, a certain percentage of wandering Jews died on Tisha B'Av. In the last year prior to entering the land of Israel, Jews entered their graves as in years past and were surprised to find that they did not die. They thought they had miscalculated the day, but when the full moon appeared, they knew that the curse was over and they would live and enter the land. So Tu B'Av was regarded as a sign that the sin of the spies was forgiven. It was established as a day of general forgiveness and purification.

Tu B'Av is known as the most joyous day of the year. On this day in the time of the Holy Temple the young maidens would all dress in white dresses and dance before the men. This was most unusual, for generally men and women were separated in public gatherings. They would flirt and with their eyes say, "Look at me." And in one look, marriages would be made. It was on this day that the people from the various tribes would meet for the purpose of marriage. Each marriage brought joy not just to the couple, but also to the community and to God.

Kabbalistically, the full moon marks the high point of the energy of the month. The major holidays such as Succot and Passover occur at the time of the full moon. The fifteenth of Av is an even more special full moon, because it immediately follows the Three Weeks and the Nine Days. Because the descent into darkness and sadness is the greatest during the Nine Days, the ascent into light and healing is also the greatest at the time of this full moon.

Tu B'Av is forty days before the twenty-fifth of Elul, which marks the beginning of creation. Forty days is a mystical number in Judaism. The oral teachings say that the soul mates are called to each other forty days before their birth. Humankind was created on the first of Tishrei, six days later.

OBSERVANCE   This Jewish Sadie Hawkins day has been resurrected, at least in New York City, but it is not quite the same as in ancient times. I doubt that there are many engagements occurring between people who have just met on this day, as in former days, but there are numerous singles events and the women often dress in white, as is the custom for this day. The women dance in front of the men in the hope that sparks are ignited that will lead to marriages.

For people who are married, Tu B'Av is a time to be with your beloved. Take time to look together at the full moon, gaze at your beloved and see your own soul reflected back to you.

The Torah portion read on Shabbos Nachamu is called Va'eschanan. During this portion, Moses recounts the giving of the Ten Commandments. This is a hint at the forgiveness for the sin of the Golden Calf.

Meditation

We have so many feelings stuffed inside that have never been given the space or time to be heard or processed. This month is an auspicious time to feel and release them.

Do not be afraid to feel your feelings. Feelings are simply feelings. They are not bad or good. Often people make judgments about themselves and others and do not allow themselves or others to feel what is present for them. Sometimes people are afraid of being overwhelmed by their feelings, so they close down and numb themselves. This is most unfortunate because it keeps them blocked up and unable to open to receive all the goodness of life. It is safe to feel your feelings. Repeat this to yourself many times until you really know it deep inside yourself.

Take deep breaths to center yourself. Observe where you are right now. Take note of the physical body and any sensations, tensions, or any particular awareness in any part of the body. Then, using the breath, relax the body as you learned to do in the meditation given for Iyar. Let the entire body relax.

After the physical body is more relaxed, become aware of the emotional body without judgment, and allow yourself to be with any feelings that may arise within you. Be with the breath and allow yourself to experience your feelings without having to explain, judge, or rationalize. Just take note of what you are feeling, what is true for you right now, and allow yourself to be with the feeling. Give yourself space to be with your feelings. Give yourself permission to be vulnerable. You may notice as you open to your feelings that you meet a place of your own resistance.

You hear the voice inside you that says, "This is too painful, too overwhelming." Take deep breaths, and relax. And as you open, be compassionate and gentle with yourself.

If you are in touch with a loss during this meditation, give yourself time to feel your loss. If this loss involves another, you may want to visualize the person and talk to him or her about your loss. You may note other feelings present for you such as guilt, hurt, betrayal, and anger all mixed in the sadness. Give yourself the opportunity to feel all the feelings present for you. For example, you may notice first the feeling of anger. Be with that as fully as possible. Then as you go deeper inside, you may find under that feeling of anger a feeling of sadness or hurt. After being with that feeling for a while, you may discover the need to be loved. Underneath that one you may find that there is longing to love. And as you stay with this feeling, you may find that there is a great love inside wanting to be felt and expressed.

At a certain point, there will be silence and a deep peaceful feeling. When you come to silence, simply be aware of the breath and sit there. Then deepen the breath, and let each breath take you deeper inside to the most private and intimate place within your own being. In this most quiet place inside yourself listen to your soul. What does your soul say in the silence? Sit for as long as you like, and perhaps record the voice of your soul in your journal.

Practical Recommendations

1. DELAY INTERACTIONS THAT MAY BE DIFFICULT, PARTICULARLY DURING THE FIRST PART OF THE MONTH.

As we have learned earlier, tempers are easily ignited during the Nine Days. I mentioned the above recommendation to a few friends who said they wished they had known. They had unnecessary skirmishes with people that were quite stressful in the beginning of the month.

So be extra sensitive this month. If we take time before we react to a negative situation, we will most likely respond in a way that will be much calmer and constructive than if we reacted immediately. Let's learn from the mistakes of Shimon and others.

2. REVIEW RELATIONSHIPS WITH PEOPLE YOU DO NOT LIKE.

We all have people in our lives we don't like. We avoid them and have as little to do with them as possible. These are often people who are close to us, either a member of our family or a person at work or synagogue. Most likely, they have hurt us numerous times. We have not forgiven them, and we continue to carry resentment and anger toward them. During this month, simply make a list of these people and consider working on letting go of your anger, so you can move on.

3. DO NOT SPEAK OR LISTEN TO *LOSHON HARA*.

Loshon hara means evil speech—malicious gossip, saying bad things about other people, putting people down. Since the area of healing this month is hearing, pay careful attention to both what you speak and what you hear. The Jewish laws regarding speech are very detailed and profound. Set barriers around what you will allow yourself to hear. For example, according to Jewish law, it is only permissible to hear derogatory words about another if this information is important because you are planning to do business with or marry this person.

For example, if you knew two people who were planning to enter into a business together, it would be permissible for you to warn one about the other if you knew that one of them would not be an honorable, responsible partner. Otherwise, it is not necessary to talk badly about other people. Take note how you feel when you curtail *loshon hara*.

Just today, one of my clients wanted to ask me about some *loshon hara* he heard about someone else who is no longer living. I asked what difference it would make in his life if he knew whether this *loshon hara* were true. He agreed that it would not make any difference in his life, and we both felt better for not discussing it.

4. GIVE TO PEOPLE YOU KNOW AND ALSO TO PEOPLE YOU DO NOT KNOW VERY WELL.

Because historically this was a time shaped by petty conflict between people, it requires proactive steps to heal conflict. Give of your time, your attention, your love, or your resources. Stretch yourself in giving. If you like, keep a record of your giving. Be careful that you do not give to the point that you feel resentful, but give out of a generous and loving spirit. Give to experience your own personal joy of giving.

Giving brings healing and unity to the world. Paradoxically, the greatest benefits from giving are to the giver. It is quite liberating to give without thinking of your personal gain. If you are feeling broken-hearted this month, give to someone else.

5. EXPAND YOUR AWARENESS OF GOD IN YOUR LIFE.

Because the external Temple was destroyed in this month, it is very important that you make efforts to experience God's presence inside you. Here is a recommended practice that you can do wherever you are. Repeat to yourself with the breath, "Wherever I am, God is" or "God is with me now." Or repeat a verse from Psalms that speaks to you. As you go about your errands and chores, repeat this phrase as many times as you want. In the middle of your work, whatever you do, take a break for two minutes and repeat this phrase. If you are doing manual work or chores like dishwashing, repeat this phrase and witness how even the most mundane activities become transformed.

A Tale to Live By

I heard the following story more than fifteen years ago from Reb Shlomo Carlebach. This story made a deep impression on me, conveying an important message about loss and transformation. It's also representative of the energy of this month since it is about loss and rebirth.

Two men had been the best of friends since childhood. They were committed to sharing everything with each other. Having assembled a sufficient amount of money, they decided to travel to make some business deals in the big city to expand their fortunes. Though the journey to the big city took a few days, it seemed like a short time because it was such a great joy for them to be together.

At night they placed the bag containing their money by their heads as they slept. One morning they actually forgot to take it with them when they left. They realized their omission toward the end of that day. They were quite upset because this was all the money they had in the world. As they retraced their steps back to where they had spent the night, they could barely hope that the money would still be there. They had slept near a widely traveled road, and surely one of the many people passing by would have seen it and taken it.

When they returned to the very place where they had spent the night, they were astonished to find the money still there. Upon this discovery, one of the men started crying. He told the other man that they must now quickly divide the money and go their separate ways. In a state of shock, they did this and almost immediately parted company with each other with hardly a good-bye.

Years went by, and the man who decided to part from the other became a beggar, while the other man became a millionaire. The beggar wasn't a great beggar and had to travel constantly from town to town, barely surviving.

One day the beggar came into a new town and tried to get acquainted with the other beggars to find out who the rich people were, who the givers and the misers were. The other beggars resented his coming into their territory, but when the beggars named his best friend as the wealthiest man in town, he was astonished and blurted out, "He is my best friend."

The beggars thought he was playing a joke on them and they decided to play one on him. The beggars told him, "Go there before Shabbat. He gives the most wonderful food to the beggars." They knew that this rich man was the biggest miser and would kick him out as he did all the other beggars.

The poor man arrived at his door before Shabbat as he was advised to do, but the rich man saw only a poor man at the door and told his servant throw him out with nasty words.

With nowhere to go, the beggar went to the *mikvah,* to immerse and purify himself in the holy water and come close to God. He reflected, "I do not have anything much in the world, but still I can come close to God."

When he was in the *mikvah,* the group of beggars decided to play another joke on him. They took away all his clothes and snickered to themselves, "This will show him. He will truly have nothing, and be unable to get an invitation to anyone's home."

When the man emerged out of the *mikvah* and discovered that his clothes, his only possession, had been taken, he began to dance. The beggar group went to synagogue and stood in the back, laughing about the prank they had just played on this man who claimed to know the richest man in town. Somehow the rich man found out about it, and on his way home from synagogue, he passed by the *mikvah* to get a look.

He was astonished to recognize his best friend dancing with no clothes on but in great joy. He embraced him warmly and asked, "I have a question for you. When we found the money against all odds, you started crying. It was you who decided that we separate from each other. Now I see you, a beggar, with nothing, not even with clothes to wear on your back, and you are happy and dancing. I do not understand this behavior."

His friend explained, "Life is a wheel. When we discovered the money, I knew that we were at the high point and I saw that if we stayed together, we would both go down. Though I was so sad to leave you, I knew that if I did, you would be protected.

"When I came into this town and learned that you were here, I was happy. When you refused to see me, I accepted it. When my clothes were taken and I had nothing in the world left, I knew that I was truly at the lowest point. I rejoiced because I knew the wheel would turn again and everything would be restored to me. So I am happy."

The rich man divided his fortune and gave half of it to his best friend.

Elul

MONTH: *August-September*

ENERGY: *Returning to the Inner Stillness Within Change*

AREA OF HEALING: *Action*

ASTROLOGICAL SIGN: *Virgo*

HEBREW LETTER: *Yud*

HEBREW TRIBE: *Gad*

DIVINE NAME PERMUTATION: *HHVY*

HOLIDAY: *Selichot*

orgiveness is a major theme of the energy of this month. It is not always easy to forgive when we have been hurt, but it is easier when we realize that an attack against us is not personal. If we can see God's hand in what has occurred, and appreciate how the challenges we are facing are taking us forward, it is easier to forgive the person who hurt us because we see that they played a significant role in our growth. This month is dedicated to this kind of review.

In Elul, Michelle's daughter was invited to a few bar mitzvah celebrations at the synagogue where Michelle used to belong, and Michelle dreaded returning, even to drop off her daughter. Months earlier, Michelle had terminated her membership at this synagogue after several unpleasant experiences with the rabbi, the cantor, and a few women friends. She was afraid to return and face them. She felt they had betrayed her trust and her friendship and she felt like a victim.

Through therapy, Michelle realized that the greater truth was that she had spiritually outgrown her former synagogue. She was not a victim; rather, she exercised her powerful freedom of free choice an had chosen another place to worship. She felt betrayed by the rabbi and cantor, but she saw that what they did was not exactly betrayal. She realized, with the true seeing eyes of Tammuz, that what they did to her was not personal. Actually, in Tammuz she was given an opportunity to see clearly their all too human self-serving side and she no longer could hold them in the esteem that she had previously. As a true spiritual seeker, she realized that she could no longer in good conscience confine herself to the back-stabbing politics and spiritual narrow-mindedness characteristic of this synagogue. She needed to be true to herself.

In many ways this realization was a gift, because it enabled her to go to another synagogue where her spiritual needs would be better met. She was welcomed and appreciated in this new synagogue. Once out of her former synagogue, she could breathe more deeply. She felt liberated. She was asked to teach in the upcoming year and even read from the Torah, as she so much loved to do. She felt that it was a gift and a pleasure to be there.

When she realized the deeper truth about what had really happened in her former synagogue during this month of Elul, it was easy to let go of the feeling of being a victim. She understood that the circumstances with the rabbi and the cantor that had hurt her were the forces that propelled her to change synagogues. She was grateful on many levels that she had left. She saw God's hand in what happened. She could forgive the rabbi and the cantor for their human frailty, and yet still choose to move on. Having forgiven the rabbi and the cantor, she could enter into her former synagogue briefly as needed. She felt whole and good about herself.

Energy: Returning to the Inner Stillness Within Change

Elul is known in Judaism as the headquarters for *teshuvah,* which literally means "to return." *Teshuvah* has many facets to it. In its most common usage, it often connotes a return to or an acceptance of a greater level of Jewish observance. It also refers to the acknowledgment of an error, the resultant feelings of regret, and the commitment to correct a situation and behave differently in the future. On the deepest and most mystical level, *teshuvah* is the return to inner wholeness, beauty, and potential, a return to the soul and its innate connection with the Divine. *Teshuvah* is the healing and letting go of what keeps us separate from others and God and from being who we really are. Beginning with the second day of Elul, the shofar is sounded four times daily after morning services to highlight and intensify this inner turning and powerful awakening of the soul present in this month.

Elul begins somewhere toward the middle to end of August and continues to the middle of September. Even though the heat may still be strong, there is a subtle change in the quality of light upon the arrival of Elul, and we sense that fall will soon be upon us. In many places in the world, the days will become shorter, the air cooler, and the leaves will once again turn into beautiful colors before they fall to the ground. We will see before our very eyes the cyclical dance of nature. Some of us will greet these changes with joy and some with regret; nevertheless, the natural changes will occur. Nature will turn inward once again.

As we both witness and experience the inevitable cycles of life, we are drawn inward to the consciousness within us that does not change. Through the spiritual grace of this month it is easy to get in touch with what is pure and constant within us. It is interesting to note that the astrological sign of this month is Virgo, which is symbolized by a virgin. This is the only astrological sign that is feminine. According to Kabbalah, the feminine refers to the capacity to receive. There is a unique goodness that an inward-turning person can receive during this month. Kabbalah says that this is hinted to in Proverbs 18:22: "Who finds a wife [virgin] finds great good." Elul sweetens the judgment energy of the two previous months, Tammuz and Av, and brings a hidden goodness.

As our consciousness turns inward this month, we are able to access a certain detachment that enables us to become aware of the ways in which we strayed from actualizing our potential. We see the good and not so good within us. As the last month of the year, we naturally find ourselves reviewing, assessing, and evaluating the accomplishments, challenges, and short-comings of the entire year. It is the time to get in touch with the essence of what is important in life. We find ourselves reflecting on the dominant themes of the last year, what soul qualities we were encouraged to develop and express during the year, what lessons we needed to learn. Many of us will be brought to new levels of appreciation for the personal relationships that have nourished us in this last year and the accomplishments we were able to achieve. Others of us will be more aware of unfinished business and the work needed to heal relationships so we can truly open to newness in the coming year.

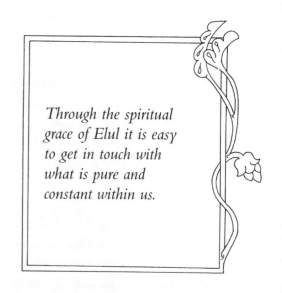

Through the spiritual grace of Elul it is easy to get in touch with what is pure and constant within us.

Elul is a time of spiritual accounting. For those who have had a relatively easy year, it may be easier to come to terms. Those who have had difficult year may become discouraged, feel burdened by sins, and question the capacity for real change. Know that this despair is natural at this time and temporary and it can be a launching pad for the *teshuvah* experience. We are not really stuck. As we feel our regrets for the mistakes we have made in our lives this last year and we allow ourselves to feel our own brokenness, it becomes clear that we want something so pure and so deep and that we cannot do this on our own. If we call out to God from this place of brokenness, there is a heavenly grace that we can draw upon in this month that is unique. The gates of heaven are open during this month.

The first letters of the Hebrew verse *"Ani ledodi vidodi li,"* "I am my beloved's and my beloved is mine" (Song of Songs 6:3), spell out Elul. This signifies that there is an intimate and loving closeness between God and people this month. It is said that in Elul God wanders in the fields, while on Rosh Hashanah, God sits on His throne like a king. The metaphor of God sitting on His throne as King expresses the awe inspired by our awareness of God as the creator and ruler of everything. The perceived distance between us and God is reduced in Elul, God is very close to us, and the experience of God's unconditional love is more accessible. Nevertheless, we must want it, and we must work for it.

Elul directly precedes Rosh Hashanah, the Jewish New Year. Elul is the time of spiritual preparation for the high holiday. The *teshuvah,* the inner work of returning to one's true essence, done during this month will affect our capacity to stand before God on Rosh Hashanah and draw down the blessings for the coming new year.

Kabbalah talks about two kinds of awakenings: from above to below and from below to above. In Nissan, which hosts Passover, there is an awakening from above, a flow of heavenly grace from the spiritual world to this physical world. In Elul, there is also a flow from above, but we must initiate it by our actions and spiritual yearning. Because we have to work for this heavenly grace, we earn the blessings, and this enables us to integrate them into our lives in a way we would not do if they were just given to us.

Take note of the kinds of conversations you have during this month. The quality of *teshuvah* is in the air, whether people are consciously undertaking the process of self-evaluation or not. I have noticed that *teshuvah* is the theme of many plays and television programs, even situation comedies.

During this month, you may also find that you are brought into contact with people you have not seen for a while and are now given an opportunity to heal and complete the relationship in a way that was not possible before. For example, Gladys ran into her ex-husband unexpectedly and had a chance to talk to him in a more sympathetic and communicative manner than had been possible during their separation and divorce. You too may have unexpected meetings or calls out of the blue. On the other hand, if you feel a desire to connect with someone you haven't had contact with in a while, listen to your inner voice and follow your heart. It generally is a good time to reach out to people you want to be close to and wish them a happy and healthy new year.

During this month, you may find yourself revisiting places and situations that on a conscious level you would choose not to, but nevertheless, opportunities are being provided for you to let go of the residual negativity imprinted on your soul, so you can truly go forward in your life. For example, we saw how Michelle had to return to the synagogue she left due to unpleasant experiences with a variety of people. Another person I know, Jennifer had to visit family members whom she had not seen in a long time and for whom she harbored negative feelings. In both these cases, an important exchange occurred that helped heal and liberate each woman from continuing limiting patterns of behavior. In all your encounters this month, look to bring forth the healing and the forgiveness needed in relationships.

Historically, Elul is the time period during which Moses returned to Mount Sinai to plead for forgiveness for the sin of the Golden Calf. Consequently, Elul is the month for us to work on forgiveness of ourselves and of others, allowing us to open to the higher worlds and receive new revelation. As we forgive others, so we open up to divine forgiveness. Much has been written about the benefits and importance of forgiveness. As difficult and stubborn as we can be, letting go of our hurts and anger is often the best thing we can do for ourselves. Though forgiveness is a spiritual practice for the whole year, it is a major theme for this month. As we approach the upcoming new year, forgiveness provides an opportunity to let go of the past and its limitations in order to enable us to open to the new year as fully as possible.

The spiritual awakening of Elul was augmented during the year of the writing of this book on September 11, 2001, the twenty-third of Elul, when the World Trade Center was destroyed by terrorism. In this unique event, over three thousand people from all nations, all ages, all religions, died together. This horrific event was a shofar blast, a divine wake-up call, in line with the energy of this month of Elul. We woke up as a nation. People turned to God in a more immediate, authentic, and direct way. There were prayer services throughout New York City and national prayer vigils. This event facilitated a dramatic and authentic *teshuvah* experience for many people, which is characteristic of this month.

Out of such horrific events, people transform themselves in ways that they might not do when life is taken for granted. In light of this tragedy, there has been greater spiritual clarity about what is really important in life ever since. It is not the money one has, but the love. Our priorities shifted. We cared about people, not about business. We realized how precious and holy a human life is and how connected we really are to each other. We truly felt each other's pain. We cried together and felt a new degree of intimacy with people. America grieved and unified in a way it hadn't done in a long time. Particularly in New York City, people have become instantly connected to each other. Strangers even make eye contact on the street. There is a generosity of spirit and caring and opening of the heart that is extraordinary. There is a commitment and dedication to make this world a better place, and be the people God wants us to be. All of this is characteristic of the transformational energy of Elul. September 11 was a powerful *teshuvah* experience. One hopes we will maintain the awareness of the spiritual opening we received on September 11. Some people want to return to a September 10 world, but it is impossible to go back.

If something horrific like this was going to happen, this was the month for it. It was even predicted in the *Zohar,* the principal ancient book of Jewish mysticism. In the chapter of Balak it is said that three buildings in a major country would be destroyed on the twenty-third of Elul and that this event would begin the prophesied process of redemption. Many people in the Jewish community feel that we have now truly entered into this period.

General Guidelines and Goals

These guidelines and goals enable us to direct our energies in the ways that are optimal for our growth and transformation in accordance with the energy of this month. It is recommended that you read and meditate upon them often in the course of the month. Reflect on their applicability to you, and allow them to direct and inspire you often this month.

1. COMPLETE UNFINISHED BUSINESS AND PLAN FOR THE FUTURE.

Take time to review the last year. What were the major themes? What do you still need to complete before the year is over? What was last year about? Take time to record any insights from these reflections.

Personal transformation and growth can begin only from where we are. Take time to review where you are. Be as honest and objective as you can be in the following reflections. Write a brief description and evaluation of your current status for each one.

Reflect on your physical well-being—your health, diet, living situation, and livelihood. Are you satisfied, or would you like some improvement?

Reflect on your emotional well-being—your relationships with family, friends, colleagues, and community. How would you define your general disposition? Are you satisfied or are you open to expansion?

Reflect on your spiritual well-being—your inner prayer life and your connection to God and Judaism. Are you satisfied or open to enhancement?

Accepting ourselves and acknowledging the areas in our life that need rectification, improvement, and expansion is the foundation for growth. In preparing for the new year, reflect on what you would like to let go of and what you would like to continue, expand and bring into the upcoming new year. Remember, if nothing changes, nothing changes. If we do what we have done in the past, most likely we will get what we always got. Most of us want more than what we have, yet we do not know how to really change. Begin to formulate a plan to rectify the areas in your life that are not in accordance with what you really want.

2. DO THE WORK OF *TESHUVAH*.

When we do *teshuvah,* we acknowledge the mistakes we have made and the actions we have taken that are not in accordance with how we want to be in the world. This is not an easy process, but it is necessary if we are to grow and become the people we truly want to be. The *teshuvah* process asks us to assume responsibility for our actions, to feel regret for the mistakes we have made, and pledge to do differently in the future. And, finally, we make penance for any suffering we have caused. Here are some guidelines to assist you in this reevaluation process.

Identify the particular actions, behavior patterns, personality tendencies that you would like to change. Without making a vow, state how you plan to change your behavior in one or two ways. What compensation are you willing to offer for the pain and suffering you caused yourself, others, and God?

3. FORGIVE GOD, YOURSELF, YOUR FAMILY, FRIENDS, EMPLOYER, EMPLOYEES, AND SO ON FOR THE PROBLEMS AND DIFFICULTIES YOU HAVE FACED IN THIS LAST YEAR.

Forgiveness is an ongoing process. It is not always easy, because the ego likes to be right, especially if we feel we have been wronged. Though forgiveness is a great gift we can give to another, it is primarily an act of compassion toward ourselves. Anger and resentment keep us bound to limiting ideas of who we are—we feel like a victim, we feel stuck, and so on. Forgiveness and compassion purify, heal, and liberate us—we feel free and whole.

Make an effort in this month to practice forgiveness and compassion. Forgiveness does not mean that we condone negative behavior, nor do we deny our angry or hurt feelings. However, forgiveness asks us to see beyond the limits of our personality or that of the person who hurt us and open our heart to love. Though it is an act of grace, forgiveness is a process and may take some time. It is easier to forgive others and even ourselves when we are willing to take responsibility for the negativity we experienced. We are not victims. In the act of forgiveness, we substitute compassion for blame, and we trust ourselves and God that we have grown and will continue to grow from the pain or challenge we have experienced. Forgiveness is complete when we gain insight into how the challenges and difficulties we have faced in this last year support our growth.

During this month, reflect on the relationships in which you may harbor continuing resentment or anger. Reflect on relationships with people whom you may have caused pain and who may harbor anger toward you. Reflect on the ways you have been judgmental or unforgiving with yourself. Use the meditation provided in this chapter to work on forgiveness in preparation for approaching people directly.

4. REPLACE THE INNER CRITIC WITH THE INNER CARETAKER.

As a therapist and teacher of Jewish meditation, I am very aware that many people suffer from feelings of inadequacy, low self-esteem, and unworthiness. It is very hard, if not impossible, to change if we feel negative about ourselves. When we think about changing ourselves, we encounter our own resistance and often doubt that we can ever change.

Many people may have heard negative messages about themselves as children, messages that have become a part of how they experience themselves today as adults. Though people may know intellectually that these ideas have no basis in truth, they do not know it emotionally. As a result, they continue to feel deep inside that they are not good enough, not smart enough, not entitled to have the feelings that they do—all the things they were told as children—even though they may be externally very successful in their lives. Though not psychotic, they have ongoing internal conversations in which they criticize themselves and others. They continue to judge themselves harshly as adults and feel a lot of shame about things that have happened in their life. When we think about making changes in our lives, these negative voices may actually become stronger.

Take note of the inner critic, that negative voice within you that judges and criticizes you and others. Don't get into an extended battle with that part of yourself. Simply make an effort to substitute a loving, caring, nurturing voice in its place. Tell yourself how beautiful, wonderful, and lovable you really are. Accentuate the loving voice within you until it becomes integrated and prominent. Affirm yourself and others. Look to see the light rather than the darkness. Remember, the glass is half full rather than half empty.

5. MEDITATE, AND IDENTIFY WITH THE WITNESS, THE OBSERVING PART OF YOURSELF.

Completing one year and preparing for the next year is a time of major transformation. In times of change, it is helpful if we anchor our awareness in the part of us that is constant and does not change. As we meditate, we access the witness part of ourselves. This witness consciousness is greater than our minds. From this place within us, we have objectivity and detachment. We realize that we are not our bodies, we are not our emotions, and we are not our thoughts. We are this pure divine soul. We are this listening awareness, this observing consciousness.

Many meditation techniques assist us in accessing this part of ourselves, and all meditation techniques do this to varying degrees. Meditate on a daily basis. Meditations can be brief; even five to fifteen minutes will make an important difference.

6. DEEPEN YOUR RELATIONSHIP WITH GOD.

Elul is the optimal time to develop intimacy with the Divine. Give yourself time to develop a personal relationship with God. In addition to formalized prayer and meditation, take time to talk directly to God in your own words. Share your hopes, dreams, fears, and pain. Ask for God's help, strength, and guidance. Ask God to help you change in the ways you want.

If it is hard for you to talk to God in this way, ask for God's help. Plead and beg if necessary. A relationship with God is the most important relationship in your life. Even if you are not sure whether you believe in a personal God who hears the needs of individuals or even if such a Being as God exists, pretend that you do and speak to God about your resistance or doubt. Take time to speak and time to listen to any changes that occur within you as you speak.

Astrological Sign: Virgo

The qualities of the sign of Virgo reveal much about the energy of this month. First, the sign is represented by the virgin. The virgin symbolizes purity and modesty. The virgin represents the part of us that has remained pure, untainted, and unchanged by the vicissitudes of life. It is this deep part within us, the pure holy soul, that calls for our attention this month.

The virgin indicates that feminine energy is dominant in this month. Feminine energy according to kabbalah is grounded, detail-oriented, and more practical than masculine energy. Virgo is an earth sign, which further suggests that the focus this month is practical. Indeed, this is the month of the healing of action.

Like Gemini (Sivan), Virgo is ruled by the planet Mercury. Mercury, the mythological messenger of the gods, represents communication as well as reasoning and the analytical powers of the mind. People born under this sign are known for these qualities, as is the energy of this month.

Quite different from the exuberance and emotional intensity of Av's Leo, the energy of Virgo is introspective and disciplined. While people born in the previous month might be flamboyant and passionate and desire to be the center of attention, people born in Virgo tend to be conservative by nature, analytical, emotionally restrained, and detail-oriented.

With a gift for systematic organization, Virgos love a sense of order. I was married briefly to a Virgo. Not only was his desk totally neat and organized, he knew what and where every piece of paper in his desk was. Virgos tend to be observers rather than leaders; they like to work behind the scenes. They are great problem solvers. They are more emotionally detached than people of other signs. They stand back in life, observing, scrutinizing, and analyzing in order to better understand the underlying dynamics of the life situations they are in. When they do finally act, they do so purposefully.

In their search for purity and order, on the negative side, Virgos tend to be judgmental, self-critical, and critical of others. They more easily see what is not in place rather than what is. Skeptical that others can ever meet their high standards, they tend to be aloof. Afraid that they might not be able to meet their own high standards, they tend to avoid taking chances for fear that they will make a mistake and be judged by others the way they tend to judge themselves.

According to astrology, the Virgo energy of the month at its best supports introspection, analysis, and objectivity and, at its worst, judgmentalism and aloofness.

Hebrew Letter: Yud

The Hebrew letter for Elul is the yud. The smallest letter in the Hebrew alphabet, the yud is simply a point. The yud is part of all letters and represents the essential life energy in the letter.

According to kabbalah, creation began with a yud, which represents the original point of entry of the infinite into the finite. As the smallest letter in the alphabet, the yud represents the self-nullification of the ego necessary for coming close to God. The yud is the essential point. The yud represents the soul, in its most pristine state, at the level of its union with the Divine.

The yud is the first letter of the Divine name, YHVH, and in this place the yud represents the *sephira,* the quality of Divine Thought *(chochma).* The yud is the first letter in the name Israel (Yisrael) and is also the first letter in the word "Jew" (Yehudit). It is the first letter in the names of many of the biblical prophets, such as Joshua (Yehousha), Jeremiah (Yirmiyahu), Isaiah (Yeshayah), and Joel (Yoel). Many holy words, names, and things begin with this letter.

The numerical value of the yud is ten. Ten is accepted as the basis for the universal number system. Ten represents plurality, but it contains within itself the initial and essential unity. It is no coincidence that we have ten fingers, ten toes, ten *sephirot,* ten commandments, and ten people as a requirement for a prayer *minyan* (quorum).

Meditating on the yud this month supports the inner turning to the most essential inner point within us. Place the yud on your inner screen, meditate upon it, merge with it, and let it teach you the secrets of the power of becoming small.

Hebrew Tribe: Gad

When Leah saw that her sister, Rachel, had given her maidservant to Jacob to bear a child with and she herself had not conceived a child in a while, she gave her maidservant Zilpah to Jacob. Leah named the first son of this union Gad. Gad means "good fortune" (Gen. 30:11). This name is a sign of the good energy of this month.

When the Jewish people were entering the land of Israel, the tribe of Gad requested the land not in Israel, but east of the Jordan. They expressed their willingness to join in the fight with the other tribes for the land of Israel and only afterward would they then return to the land they preferred. Moses complied with their request and blessed them with extraordinary strength and good fortune. During the conquest of the land of Israel, they even marched in front of the other tribes. Because of their generosity and courage, their territory was larger than the territory of any of the other tribes. Living on the border, they remained continually protective of Israel.

Commentators on the Torah such as Rashi have also said that Gad chose the land on the east side of the Jordan because they wanted to remain close to Moses, who would not be entering the land. They guarded the burial site of Moses and they guarded the land of Israel.

Gad is the perfect tribe to represent the energy of this month in many ways. Gad, the tribe that served and protected the borders of the land, represents the month that is on the border of one year and the next. We need to tap into the strength of Gad to review the last year and prepare for the coming year. Gad is the energy that defines boundaries, and boundaries are important. Many problems in life occur because people have diffused personal boundaries. They do not know where they end and where others begin. They do not distinguish the past from the present or future. During this month of Elul, we are better able to make these distinctions.

When boundaries are clear, we can assume responsibility for ourselves and make choices about extending ourselves to others. As Gad did with the other tribes of Israel, Gad is the energy that both defines boundaries and is willing to extend beyond them when necessary. This Gad kind of knowing so essential this month enables us to know our own boundaries between self and others, as well as make distinctions between the past and the future.

The prophet Elijah came from the tribe of Gad. Interestingly, the oral tradition says that Pinchas, who slew Zimri, the prince of the tribe of Shimon, along with Cosbi, reincarnates as the prophet Elijah. It is predicted that Elijah will blow the shofar and bring the people back to the land of Israel. It is this returning to the land, to the essence of oneself that the shofar awakens within us.

Divine Name Permutation: HHVY

The permutation of the Divine Name for this month is HHVY. From the placement of the hays (H's) in the first and second positions, we see expansiveness in the higher worlds of Atzilut and Beriyah. These worlds are spiritual, not physical, and the letters in these worlds shape the flow of Light above creation. The hay is a feminine letter, so we see once again the prominence of the feminine in this month. With the two hays in the first and second positions, we need to turn inside and upward.

The position of the last letter in this permutation, which corresponds to our physical world, known as Assiyah, is occupied by the yud (Y). As we learned earlier, the yud is the smallest letter in the Hebrew alphabet, just a dot. Even to sound the letter yud, the mouth has to close almost entirely so only a minuscule amount of air is released. The yud in this position indicates that at this time spiritual light is dim and hidden in the physical world. We have to nullify ourselves, reach deep inside ourselves and beyond ourselves to draw down the tremendous spiritual light that is so available in the higher dimensions. The vav (V) in the position of the world of Yetzerah is the only letter that is in its optimal and usual placement. This placement corresponds to the heart and informs us that the heart is the direct channel through which we draw down the light.

The permutation demonstrates that the energy of this month is reflective, rather than active. Taking time to go inside yourself so as to contact the higher levels of your being will be most productive at this time.

Torah Portions

The first Torah portion of this month (Deut. 18:1–20:20) begins with the *shoftim*, which means "judges." Moses is instructing people to appoint judges who will judge righteously and objectively. So begins the process of judging oneself of Elul. We need to access the part of ourselves that can be objective and can review, reflect, and judge ourselves in this past year.

The next Torah portion, Ki Setzei (Deut. 21–26), begins with "When you will go out to war against your enemies, God will deliver them into your hand and you see among the captives a woman who is beautiful in form and you desire her, you may take her for a wife" (Deut. 21:10–11). Though these are instructions for war, they are interpreted by Jewish mysticism as instruction for the inner battle that occurs in this month. The enemies are internal, and with God's help you will access the soul, which is the beautiful woman. There is a battle that we each must wage at this time and the Torah gives us guidance in how to be victorious. We are told that we can take this woman, but "shave her head, remove the garment of captivity from her" (Deut. 21: 12–13). Basically, strip yourself of all the external garments of self, so you see the true intrinsic goodness of the divine soul.

The next Torah portion, Ki Tavo, begins, "When you enter the land, you shall take the first fruits . . . and go to a place where God will choose to make His name dwell" (Deut. 26:1–2). The declaration mandated in the verses that follow these helps one purify the soul and connect with one's past. The willingness to offer one's first fruits strengthens one's devotion and connection to God. The chapter lists the blessings we will receive for aligning with Divine Will and the curses for not doing so. This reiterates a basic concept within Judaism, that of free will. We choose our actions and must reap the consequences of them.

Holiday

Selichot

HISTORY   Selichot literally means "forgiveness" and refers to special prayers said during Elul. The daily recitation of these prayers along with the sounding of the shofar during this month is rooted in the Torah. The Torah informs us that it was on the new moon of Elul that Moses returned to Sinai to ask for forgiveness for the sin of the Golden Calf. Moses remained on Mount Sinai for forty days and returned with new tablets on Yom Kippur. This forty-day period between the beginning of Elul and Yom Kippur has been historically designated for repentance and forgiveness.

During ancient times, the shofar was sounded each day to remind the people that Moses was pleading for God's forgiveness for their sins as well as to facilitate the process of *teshuvah* within the people themselves. The sounding of the shofar reminded them of their sin of idolatry and awakened them to the possibility that they could find God within themselves.

OBSERVANCE   Today, in synagogues throughout the world, special prayers of repentance and forgiveness along with the sounding of the shofar occur daily to commemorate this biblical forty-day period. The shofar blowing is the wake-up call for the soul. Many people recall the shofar blasts as they are blown on Rosh Hashanah and Yom Kippur. But if you go to synagogue in the morning in Elul you will hear these sounds every weekday.

There are four different sounds by the shofar blasts. Some sounds are long and steady and pierce the depths of the heart and soul. Other sounds are short and broken and open us to the brokenness of our hearts and souls. Hearing the shofar blasts we are automatically turned inward, and we hear the crying of our own souls. If we go deep inside and truly open our hearts, we may even weep. This is a wonderful sign of the *teshuvah* and purification process possible this month.

On the Saturday night approximately a week before Rosh Hashanah is a special midnight service entitled Selichot, when prayers of penitence are recited along with the Thirteen Attributes of Divine Compassion. An invocation, this powerful verse of the

Thirteen Attributes may be translated in English: "Adonai, Adonai, God who is merciful, and gracious, long-suffering, abundant in loving-kindness and truth, guarding loving-kindness to the thousandth generation, forgiving transgression, iniquity, and misdeeds, and cleansing, not holding guilt" (Exod. 34:6). This verse is repeated many times on the holiday of Yom Kippur.

Many of these prayers were composed before the seventh century. Although, historically these prayers were said during the days between Rosh Hashanah and Yom Kippur, in the eleventh century this practice was extended to the entire month of Elul. According to kabbalah, the gates of compassion open at midnight. We are told that the recitation of the attributes as received by Moses will solicit God's forgiveness.

Meditation

Since forgiveness is a major theme for this month, here is a meditation to support you in this process. It is important to know that forgiveness is a process of letting go. It takes time, patience, and compassion.

Take a few breaths, relaxing the body and mind, and call to your inner screen and to your heart the image of someone who has hurt you, someone toward whom you continue to hold feelings of anger and resentment. Do this with each person toward whom you harbor negative feelings. This meditation may prepare you to better respond to a possible request for forgiveness from someone who has hurt you.

Silently say in your heart, "I forgive you. I forgive you for whatever pain you caused me either intentionally or unintentionally. I forgive you." Tell this person how you were hurt, and how you now want to forgive him or her.

Ask God to help you have love and compassion for the person. Tell God you do not want to be stuck in your anger and hurt. Reflect on the pain this person must have felt inside when mistreating you. Consider how you may have contributed to the pain you experienced. Repeat several times: "I forgive you." Allow yourself to be with any feelings that occur within you.

Begin to let go of the pain and resentment. Breathe it out, and let your heart open. Ask God to open you heart and fill it with God's love. Imagine that God is pleased with you. Open to feel God's love and compassion between you and this person. Open to the possibility that this person was a messenger from God bringing a teaching you needed.

Practical Recommendations

1. DO A SPIRITUAL ACCOUNTING FOR THE PAST YEAR.

As if you were watching a movie of your life, allow yourself to review, reflect, and reexperience the highlights of the year. Outline the major events, accomplishments, and challenges of the past year on a piece of paper or in your journal under the headings Fall (Tishrei, Cheshwan, Kislev), Winter (Tevet, Shevat, Adar), Spring (Nissan, Iyar, Sivan), and Summer (Tammuz, Av, Elul). Record the feeling tone and the themes for each portion of the year. Consider what remains unfinished in your relationships or projects. Reflect upon the way you shared in the joys and sorrows of members of your family and community. What relationships strengthened in this last year? What relationships were diminished or challenged?

2. MAKE FORGIVENESS A PART OF YOUR DAILY SPIRITUAL PRACTICE.

Identify the people toward whom you hold continuing resentment and negativity. Begin the process of forgiving. It may be important for you to tell the individuals that you continue to have angry feelings about something they have done. This gives them the opportunity to apologize and make amends. It is much easier to let go of your anger and resentment and forgive someone who wants to be forgiven.

With certain persons you may have already done this many times, and it was not helpful. They do not feel regret for what they have done and do not want to be forgiven. They may claim that you are overly sensitive. It is not necessary to continue to make yourself vulnerable to these people, but it is important that you let go of the hold that your anger has in your life.

In your effort to forgive people, the spiritual practice of imagining yourself on your deathbed may be helpful. From this perspective, your anger and resentment toward people seem petty and you can let them go. You feel greater appreciation and compassion for people. You know that you want to be free to make this transition.

Another variation is to imagine people you resent on their deathbed. What would you say to them? We never know when death will occur, our own or someone else's, so we want to say what is really important and essential to each other when we can. Imagine what you would say to your mother, your father, your husband, your siblings, your friends at this time. Take time to express your deep feeling to people in your life, even those for whom you harbor no ill feelings.

3. SAY A DAILY PRAYER OF FORGIVENESS.

Forgiving others is so important that there is a prayer to be said every night before sleep. It often takes a lot of prayer to be able to forgive another who has hurt you deeply. You might find it helpful to recite this prayer every day during this month. "Master of the universe, I hereby forgive anyone who angered or antagonized me or who sinned against me, whether against my body, my property, my honor or against anything of mine, whether he did so accidentally, willfully, carelessly, or purposefully, whether through speech, deed, thought, or notion, whether in this transmigration or another transmigration, I forgive. May no man be punished because of me. May it be your will my God, God of my forefathers, that I may sin no more." In this prayer, we declare our willingness to forgive everyone. We forgive anyone who has antagonized or done harm to us or our property either intentionally or accidentally. Reciting this prayer before sleep may help you to forgive the people who have hurt you.

4. SEND NEW YEAR GREETING CARDS TO PEOPLE WITH A LITTLE PERSONAL NOTE AND BLESSING.

This simple gesture becomes an opportunity to heal and strengthen your relationships with others. Take time to call people you are connected to and have not been in touch with. Express your appreciation for what they have meant to you in your life.

5. BLESS PEOPLE WITH A HAPPY AND HEALTHY NEW YEAR.

It is customary to bless everyone you encounter with a happy and healthy new year. Blessing others allows you to become a channel of divine blessing. As we bless, so are we blessed. Bless people you love and people you do not yet know you love. You can easily give a quick blessing in almost any conversation or you can do an extended blessing meditation.

Visualize someone on your inner screen or see this person standing before you. Consider what this person wants and needs and open to bless him or her in ways beyond what the individual would request. Utter a blessing in your mind, then speak the words. You may want to begin with "May you be blessed . . ." or "May God bless you . . ." or "You are blessed with . . ." and allow the outpouring of your heart to be expressed. If the person you are blessing is not in front of you, visualize that he or she accepts the blessing and say "Amen" for the blessing you have just given. The saying of "Amen" seals the blessing.

6. SAY PSALMS.

The recitation of Psalms (Tehillim) is said to have the power to cleanse and purify the soul. There are several different kinds of books of Psalms that are universally numbered. For thousands of years, Jews and Christians have turned to the psalms for comfort and strength. It is particularly beneficial practice during this month of Elul.

As you say the psalm, seek to find yourself in the psalm and feel its relevance and application to your life. If possible, say the psalm in Hebrew, even if your Hebrew is not very good, but it is fine also to say the psalms in English. If you are feeling sad, say Psalms 3, 6, 10, 13, 22, 31, and 51. Psalm 23 is a basic and popular one and always relevant. It is actually said every Shabbat.

It is a traditional practice to repeat Psalm 27 daily during this month. Some verses from this wonderful psalm follow. Repeat these verses many times, as a mantra, and see how your consciousness is lifted upward.

"God is my light and salvation; whom shall I fear. God is the strength of my life; of whom shall I be afraid?"

"One thing I ask of God, one thing I seek, that I may dwell in the house of God all the days of my life."

"God, hear my voice when I call, be gracious to me."

A Tale to Live By

We blow the shofar each day in Elul to open the gates of our hearts and souls. The following story about shofar blowing carries an important message for this month, a month about getting to the essence of what is really important.

The Maggid of Mezerith, the successor of the Baal Shem Tov, needed someone to blow the shofar for Rosh Hashanah. Many people wanted the honor of this *mitzvah,* so a time was set aside for auditioning. In preparation for the audition, the men went to the *mikvah,* studied kabbalah, fasted, gave charity.

The Maggid was present for the auditions and would select the person. Each man had an opportunity to blow the shofar and share with the Maggid what he was thinking about when he blew. Each blowing was more beautiful than the next. And when each man shared the complex and intricate kabbalistic intentions that were in his mind at the time, it was very impressive.

Then Moshe, the water carrier, blew the shofar. When asked what he was thinking about when he blew, he confessed, "I do not know kabbalah, so I do not have any lofty intention. I am ashamed to tell you, but when I blew the shofar, I was crying to God. I have four daughters who need to be married. I need a *shidduch* (marriage partner) for each of them, and money to pay for the dowry and wedding. I am a simple water carrier. Please, God, help me. I can't do this without You."

The Maggid selected Moshe, the water carrier, to blow the shofar in his congregation, declaring that the prayers of a sincere and broken heart open the gates of heaven. So remember, it is your cries, your sincere prayers, your tears that are precious to God. These tears purify you as well as the world.

Closing

The first commandment in the Torah is the sanctification of the moon. It is through this process that the Jewish calendar was developed with months formed according to the cycles of the moon. The Hebrew word for month is *chodesh,* which also means "newness." The Hebrew month begins with the new moon, and every moon cycle, every month, ushers in new energies, as we have learned in this book.

Like the moon, people also go through cycles. There are times in life when our light is shining and we are radiating who we are for the world to see, and there are times when we are tested and humbled, feeling that our light is diminished. Life is a spiral. *Kabbalah Month by Month* was written to assist you in growing and flowing through the cycles of life with faith and grace.

It is my sincere prayer that this book will be a good loving friend to you; empower you to go forward in your life, actualizing and expressing all your magnificence; and console and unconditionally love you through the challenging times.

It is always a great privilege to write a book. It is my antidote to loneliness. I sit down at my computer, open my heart, and let the words flow out. As our sages say, "Words from the heart enter the heart." When I write, I feel that I am making a deep personal connection to the readers of my books. We haven't met on the physical plane, but we are connected on the spiritual plane. I invite you to contact me personally, attend a meditation workshop, or join my virtual community, Beit Miriam, by contacting me at Ribner@msn.com or beitmiriam@yahoogroups.com. Blessings for a year of much blessing.

Bibliography

Fenton-Smith, Paul, *Astrology Revealed,* New York: Simon & Schuster, 2000.

Ginsburg, Rabbi Yitzchak, *The Alef Beit,* Northvale, N.J.: Jason Aronson, 1995.

Glazerson, Rabbi Matityahu, *Above the Zodiac,* Northvale, N.J.: Jason Aronson, 1997.

Greenberg, Rabbi Irving, *The Jewish Way,* Northvale, N.J.: Jason Aronson, 1998.

Kaplan, Rabbi Aryeh, *The Living Torah,* New York: Maznaim, 1981.

Kaplan, Rabbi Aryeh (ed.), *Sefer Yetzirah,* York Beach, Me.: Red Wheel/Weiser, 1997.

Kitov, Rabbi Eliyahu, *The Book of Our Heritage,* New York: Feldheim Publishers, 1997.

Nadborny, Nechama Sarah, *Twelve Dimensions of Israel,* Ya'alet Chein Publishers.

Ribner, Melinda, *Everyday Kabbalah,* Seacaucus, N.J.: Citadel Press, 1998.

Ribner, Melinda, *New Age Judaism,* Deerfield Beach, Fla.: Simcha Press, HCI Inc., 2000.

Scherman, Nosson (ed.), *Tanach: The Torah/Prophets/Writings* (The Stone Edition). Brooklyn, N.Y.: Mesorah Publications, 1996.

Soffer, Shirley, *Astrology Sourcebook,* New York: McGraw Hill, 1998.

The Author

Mindy (Melinda) Ribner, C.S.W., is the founder and director of the Jewish Meditation Circle and Beit Miriam in New York City. She has taught Jewish meditation for more than eighteen years at synagogues of all affiliations, national conferences of Jewish learning, and respected New Age centers. Mindy received a nonrabbinical ordination to teach Jewish meditation from Reb Shlomo Carlebach. She is also a certified social worker and a psychotherapist in private practice, where she uses meditation as part of treatment. She is the author of *Everyday Kabbalah: A Practical Guide for Jewish Meditation, Healing, and Personal Growth; New Age Judaism: Ancient Wisdom for the Modern World;* and *A Gift of a New Beginning.* To contact Mindy for speaking engagements, meditation workshops, counseling, and tapes, call 212–799–1335 or e-mail Ribner@msn.com.